FEEDBACK!

Sales Advice from the *Buyer's* Desk.

Observations, Insight & Buyer-Endorsed Sales Techniques

Christopher Locke, C.P.S.M.
Corporate Global Buyer

This unique publication is designed to provide candid and authoritative information regarding the sales process as seen from the perspective of the Corporate Buyer. It is provided with the understanding that the author and/or publisher are not rendering legal, accounting or other professional services. If you require legal advice on the sales process or other assistance, please seek the services of an associated professional. *(Based on A Declaration of Principles jointly adopted by a Committee of the American Bar Association and a Committee of Publishers.)*

PLEASE NOTE: Any views, advice and/or opinions presented in this book are solely those of the author and do not necessarily represent those of any current or previous employer of the author.

To my Parents for their strong work ethic.

To James W. Schultz, my first business role model.

And to my Wife, Margaret, for her love and support.
(See, I told you I was working on it!)

On August 29, 2005, then Chrysler Group President and CEO, Thomas LaSorda, spoke to an automotive industry audience in Detroit about overcoming negative economic issues, redefining the OEM-supplier relationship model and the approach to build long-term relationships with key suppliers. During the speech, Mr. LaSorta explained that if Chrysler Group and its suppliers were going to work closer with each other, then suppliers needed to understand how an OEM thinks. He said:

"Some suppliers could greatly improve their sales approach by understanding how we think – what our Procurement and Supply organization needs to hear."

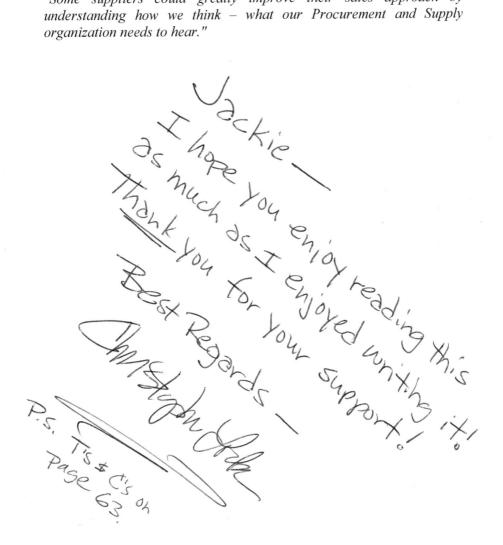

Jackie –
I hope you enjoy reading this
as much as I enjoyed writing it!
Thank you for your support!
Best Regards –
Christopher Hall

P.s.
T's & C's oh
Page 63.

C O N T E N T S

INTRODUCTION

FEEDBACK!
Sales Advice from the *Buyer's* Desk.

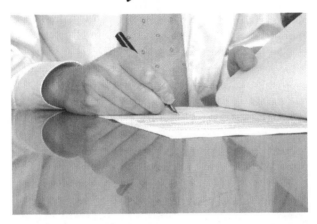

You are a Sales Professional. You are responsible for developing and implementing strategies with the intent of selling the products and services your prospect needs. No doubt you've attended numerous sales seminars and have read various books written by seasoned experts edifying the *Sales* side of the business. You've also learned from your colleagues and from sales managers how to conduct business with Corporate Buyers and 'close the deal'. *And all of that is good.*

I am a Corporate Buyer. During my gratifying career in global procurement I've purchased billions of dollars-worth of diverse products and services. Everything from office supplies worth a few dollars to complex industrial assembly systems worth tens of millions. And during that time I've worked with thousands of *green* and *seasoned* Sales Professionals through the cradle-to-grave process of buying and selling.

Sitting behind the Buyer's desk puts me in a very unique position to observe and comment on the sales strategies used by the supply base. After all, these very strategies are used on me eight hours a day, five days a week. *Think about that.* **I am the *recipient* of sales strategies!** I'm the litmus test of what you've learned to do and say to make the sale. And while I don't claim to be a *Sales* expert . . . *I am a 'Buying' expert!*

So who better to provide *candid, constructive feedback* on the strategies being used by today's Sales Professionals and their level of effectiveness on Corporate Buyers? Who better to confirm what *really* works in securing an order and what falls short?

That's exactly what this book is about. This is not a basic 'how-to' book about selling. If that's what you're looking for, then put this one back on the shelf and continue your search. *This book is about providing FEEDBACK!* Feedback on the very strategies that sales experts are telling you to use on Buyers like me. Feedback on what Sales Professionals do and say to those they're attempting to sell to. Feedback on the actual business practices Corporate Buyers prefer, as well as those they secretly despise . . . *but aren't telling you.* And Feedback on the sales approaches we Buyers would use if *WE* were in Sales . . . things most Sales Professionals don't do, *but should!*

But don't just take my word for it. Because since the year 2000 I've communicated with hundreds of Buyers and End-Users of diverse products and services from across the globe. I've intentionally documented their insight and compared notes based on their preferences and concerns for what Sales Professionals are doing or failing to do. And it doesn't matter if you're selling office supplies worth a few dollars, industrial assembly systems worth tens of millions, or something in between. This is *firsthand customer feedback* that has not been readily available to the supply base until now. *And isn't it about time?*

So close the door, pull up a chair and let's talk. Let's talk about the everyday issues facing Buyers and Sellers. Let's talk about *real-world* buying and selling scenarios. Let's give you an insight into the confidential world of Global Purchasing. Let's discuss the roles, responsibilities and preferences of Corporate Buyers. Let's review cold-call approaches, sales meetings, the quoting process, effective communication, successful negotiating, standing out from your competition, and developing a business relationship. Let's talk about what 80% of Buyers prefer but less than 20% of Sales Reps are doing. And while we're at it, allow me to offer sales advice - *not* from the perspective of a professional Seller, *but from the perspective of a professional Buyer!* Things you wouldn't have thought of unless you had spent time sitting behind my desk as a *recipient* of sales strategies.

So why am I willing to offer this feedback? First, because I *truly* believe that sales is a noble and essential profession. All of our lives we are continuously surrounded by the *influence* of successful Sales Professionals. Everything we see, hear, touch and experience is a direct or indirect result of the sales process. From the roof over our head to the concrete below our feet, and everything in between. It's that *influence* that makes sales a valuable profession; an influence that touches and affects all of us in our private and professional lives.

Of course, I do have an ulterior motive for providing this feedback. If Sales Professionals can better understand who we are in Corporate Purchasing, what makes us tick and how we prefer to conduct business, it will make our professional lives that much easier.

Whether you're a Business Owner, a Sales Executive/Manager or a Representative, I know that Sales is not an easy profession. It's not an easy career no matter how much you love it. I know because I witness it firsthand! So it's my sincere hope that this *'Sales Advice from the Buyer's Desk'* will improve your opportunities with Corporate Purchasing by changing the way you think, act and approach business. *And we'll do that by putting you behind the desk of those who buy from you.*

One last thing. The pragmatic feedback in this book is presented in a somewhat chronological order. It starts with the world of Corporate Purchasing and is followed by the typical progression of the sales process; prospecting, cold-calling, sales meetings, quoting, negotiating, communicating and developing a business relationship. Following each topic is a bottom line suggestion titled **FROM THE BUYER'S DESK**.

In most cases this is followed by the responses of the Buyers and End-Users mentioned earlier. Each of them were asked about their preference in regards to the topics and advice presented. Their collective responses are represented by **BUYER'S WHO PREFER THIS**.

They were then asked what proportion of the Sales Professionals they encounter are actually using the strategies they prefer. Their collective responses are represented by **SALES REPS WHO DO THIS**.

Both collective responses are in the form of *percentages*. This simple but revealing format will allow you to better understand how Buyers prefer to conduct business, and how many Sales Reps are actually doing the things Buyers prefer. In most cases it verifies the old axiom: *Only 20% of Sales Professionals are doing the things that 80% of Buyers prefer.*

CHRISTOPHER LOCKE, C.P.S.M.
Corporate Global Buyer

SECTION 1

The World of Corporate Purchasing

- First and Foremost, Why Are Buyers So Damn Rude?
- What a Buyer Expects
- Gaining Access to the Buyer
- Connect With Buyers on LinkedIn
- Gaining and Maintaining a Buyer's Trust
- What Buyers Fear Most
- Six Things Buyers Don't Want You to Know
- The Supplier-Selection Process
- Think Like a Buyer
- Talk the Language of Purchasing

"First and Foremost, Why Are Buyers So Damn Rude?"

Let me guess. As a Sales Professional it's your humble opinion that Buyers are rude, grouchy, obnoxious people who are difficult to contact, demand unreasonable requests and enjoy making your sales career miserable. **Of course, we Buyers don't see ourselves in that light.** We think we're just doing our job with the time and resources we have. But sitting on *your* side of the desk, it's understandable how we Buyers can be perceived as *'the dark side'* of the sales process. And before we get into the reasons why Buyers seem to act with a *'less-then positive'* approach, let's first lay the foundation of their actions by examining an important truth about those in Purchasing.

If there's one truth about Buyers, one bit of information you need to incorporate into your sales strategy, it is this: By the very nature of their job, *Buyers are busy people who don't have time to waste.* Well big deal. Who isn't busy, right? Sales professionals, business owners, retail specialists, engineers, managers, accountants, administrators; there aren't many people in today's business environment sitting around with nothing to do. In the last few years, deficient economic conditions have led to corporate downsizing. Which means that those of us left must make up for the losses and somehow maintain, if not increase, sales and productivity. And no matter how good your time management skills are, there simply aren't enough hours in the day to accomplish everything that needs to be done. Now that we understand why *you* are so busy, the question begs, *"Why are BUYERS so busy?"*

The best way to explain why Buyers are busy people is to have you picture the Purchasing Department as the **Hub of a Wheel.** In order for the wheel to turn, the spokes resting on and connected to that hub are relying on it to do its job. So if the Buyer is the hub of the wheel, *who are the spokes?* Well, how about the dozens if not hundreds of Sales

Professionals the Buyer deals with on any given project. They're all asking for the Buyer's time to sell product, resolve issues and maintain a business relationship. Other spokes on the wheel are your accounts receivable department as well as other internal groups within your company. Then there are the client's own internal departments including finance, quality, corporate legal, management, engineering, logistics, manufacturing, material planners and accounts payable. If the Buyer you're dealing with has *'cradle-to-grave'* supply-chain responsibilities, then he will seem to have his hands into *everything* simply because he has relationships with so many! Numerous spokes, but only one hub.

Here's another way to think of it. Concerning the *control of costs*, Purchasing is the most significant department in any organization. That's because on average, two-thirds of the cost-of-goods sold are purchased items. Two-thirds of the product my company sells to its clients are directly or indirectly made up of the products and services I buy from suppliers. Now sometimes it's true that overhead, design and manufacturing provides the most significant impact on costs. But that's only true if those organizations are not run correctly.

Due to the fact that most corporate internal departments are so heavily reliant on the costs, quality and delivery of their supplier's products, the role of the Purchasing Department is exceptionally vital to their success. They know by the very nature of their job that Corporate Buyers hold the *financial hammer* over the head of suppliers. Buyers can make supplier's jump when the End-User can't. That's why most internal departments are in contact with Purchasing on a near-daily basis.

Okay, this isn't a pity party on my part, it's simply the facts. Because of their financial and legal responsibilities to the company, everyone wants and needs time from the Buyer. So including the endless suppliers they deal with on any given project, the Buyer's time is extremely limited. Keep that in mind. Because it's important to understand that how you conduct business in the limited time you have with Buyers will ultimately affect your professional relationship with them.

Now there's an old saying in Purchasing that goes, *"If you want a P.O., don't P.O. the Buyer!"* (Get it?) As stated earlier, the perception of most Sales Professionals is that Buyers are obnoxious people who like nothing better then to yell at suppliers and make their lives miserable. *So why do Buyers get so upset?* Easy. Buyers get the most upset when they're prevented from completing their *core responsibilities.* Hey, who wouldn't? If core responsibilities aren't met, they hear about it from their management and that's not good for anyone. *So what are a Buyer's core responsibilities?* Although industries and procurement departments can vary, Buyers are usually responsible for the following tasks:

- Placing purchase orders and creating commercial contracts. This is obviously the Buyer's number one core responsibility.
- Requesting quotes from Sales Professionals and completing comparisons of supplier quote packages.
- Negotiating price, delivery and contractual terms and conditions.
- Completing management-mandated assignments and KPI's, some of which may have nothing to do with anything suppliers are involved with.
- Completing mandated corporate goals such as cost savings, supplier reduction, training and other tasks that financially and legally protect the company.
- Resolving commercial issues both internally and within the supply base.

So understanding a Buyer's core responsibilities, what types of things might Sales Professionals do that prevent Buyers from completing their tasks, thereby turning them into the *benevolent* people we all know and love? *How about:*

- Long, non-value-added meetings.
- Constant interruptions; a lack of respect for the Buyer's time.
- Lack of sufficient communication skills.
- Incomplete or incorrect quotes that need to be sent back to the supplier for corrections.
- Supplier issues regarding late delivery, product failure or inadequate service.

So what can Sales Professionals do to assist Buyers in completing their tasks and stand out from their competition? *How about:*

- Short, constructive meetings.
- Minimal interruptions; showing respect for the Buyer's time.
- Professional and responsive communication skills.
- Complete client-mandated quotes.
- Responsible, attentive and proactive actions.

What most Sales Professionals fail to remember is that the majority of the Buyers they deal with are responsible for more than just one project or one type of commodity. I'm personally working on a project with dozens of commodities, each represented by numerous suppliers who are not necessarily in competition with each other. For every telephone call, e-mail, voicemail and meeting a Sales Rep wants to make, there are at least a dozen more Sales Reps calling, e-mailing and expecting part of my day. At the same time I'm handling internal requests from management, engineering, finance, accounts payable and the End-Users of your products and services. (Remember: the Hub of the Wheel.) This obviously limits the amount of time I have to complete my responsibilities. *Most important, it limits the amount of time I have to spend with any given Sales Rep on a daily or weekly basis.*

So the next time you call a Buyer, imagine there are a dozen more Sales Reps waiting to call that same person after you hang up. That should motivate you to conduct business quickly but thoroughly. It should also make you understand that if you send an e-mail or leave a voicemail with the Buyer, you may never get a response.

The next time you have a meeting with a Buyer, imagine there are a dozen more Sales Reps wanting to meet with that same person. That should motivate you to ensure your meeting is short but constructive.

If you have ever dealt with a Buyer who was rude, stressed out or short-tempered, you need to understand that it may not have been *your* specific phone call, e-mail, interruption or problem that upset him. *It's the constant multitude of phone calls, e-mails, interruptions and problems that upset Buyers!* Yours may have simply been the straw that broke the camel's back. What upset the Buyer during your own interaction with him could have been a lingering emotion from the last issue he dealt with. *So don't take it personally, we're only human!*

Trust me, I'm not expecting sympathy from the Sales side of the desk. But the statement, *"Buyers are busy people who don't have time to waste"* is probably the most important reality that you as a Sales Professional should take under consideration. If you can understand that reality, incorporate it into your sales strategies and consider it every time you conduct business with the Buyer, *you will already be ahead of 80% of your competition!* Because 80% of the supply base *does not* conduct business with that thought in mind. Eighty-percent of the supply base conducts business as if THEY are the only supplier, as if THEIRS is the only product for sale, as if THEY are the only ones who need time with the Buyer. *From the Buyer's perspective, it's in your best interest to be part of that 20%.*

FROM THE BUYER'S DESK: Show respect for the Buyer's time, and they'll be more receptive to consider your products and needs.

BUYERS WHO PREFER THIS: 92%
SALES REPS WHO DO THIS: 23%

"What a Buyer Expects."

A few months ago I had a nice dinner at a great beachside restaurant. Nothing fancy, just the typical seafood, beer and burgers. I had no high expectations of the food or the service. After all, there weren't many restaurants on the beach. People would spend their money regardless because they wanted a meal near the water. It turned out the food was actually pretty good though a little bit pricy. *But the service was outstanding!* I have been wined and dined at many fine establishments in my life. (*Are you kidding? I am a Corporate Buyer after all!*) So I do expect good service. But it's not likely to happen at a place like this and again was certainly not expected. *Maybe that's what made the service I received even more exceptional.*

Now, I'm embarrassed to say I don't remember the name of the waitress, but from the very beginning she was friendly, personable and down to earth. At no time did she rush or try to pressure me into ordering something I didn't want. She asked what type of cuisine I preferred, then told me what other customers raved about. She didn't hasten my selection and took my order only when I was ready. *She even read it back to me to ensure she had understood what I asked for.*

While my meal was being prepared she stopped by periodically to fill my water glass and to let me know the progress of my meal. And when she set the plate on the table in front of me the food was still piping hot. That's because she managed her time well between being on the floor and checking for her customer's orders. After a few bites she stopped by to make sure it was prepared to my liking. And even though she had already delivered the food, she continued to check on me to make certain everything was to my satisfaction.

She wasn't overbearing about it but seemed to know the right time to stop by. At the end of the meal she made a recommendation on dessert which I ordered. And when the bill came she didn't make me feel rushed to pay it in order to make the table available for another customer. I eventually left but not before leaving a *very* generous tip.

I have no idea if the other wait staff at that establishment was as exceptional as my server, and I don't know if management was the driving force behind the service I received. But the fact that my experience was great, I will make every effort to go back again.

By now you probably know where I'm leading with this. Here was a business without many competitors and no incentive to perform like there were. And yet their representative treated me like I was her only customer of the day. She made me feel special and comfortable. She looked out for my best interest. She delivered on time what the company promised and she followed up after the sale even though her commission was already guaranteed.

It's sad that good service in our private life is so rare. In fact it's so rare and so sporadic that when it does happen it gets our immediate attention. We CRAVE good service because we want it and miss it. *And we'll go back to the same place searching for it again.*

As a consumer of products and services in your own private life, you want *the best product for the best value that best fits your needs.* Above all you want *satisfaction.* And if you don't get satisfaction you want someone to take care if it immediately and without hassle. **And that, ladies and gentlemen, is Corporate Buying in a nutshell!** That is what Buyer's expect from the suppliers and Sales Professionals they place orders to. *Are we asking for too much?* I don't think so. After all, isn't that what you expect in your own private life from the companies and representatives you deal with? Of course it is. *And do you know why you expect it?* **It's because YOU are a Buyer!**

Now, you may not be a Buyer for a Fortune 100 company, but you are nonetheless *a Buyer.* You buy food, clothes, cars and a house. You buy electronic equipment, home services, furniture and power tools. And in doing so there aren't many differences as to how *you* think and act as a domestic buyer, and how *Corporate Buyers* think and act. The same basic things that upset and entice you when buying products and services in your personal life, also upset and entice Corporate Buyers!

So what UPSETS you as a domestic buyer? Have you ever had a bad experience buying a big ticket item? If so, think about that experience and think about the things that annoyed you going through the buying process. *How about:* Salespeople who tried to sell you something you didn't need. Tried to sell you options you didn't want.

Acted in an unprofessional manner. Did not pay enough attention to you. Were unprepared and not sure what to do. Over-promised and under-delivered. Were insincere and concealed information. Were too persistent or aggressive. Did too much talking and not enough listening. Failed to do any post-sales follow up.

So now, what ENTICES you as a domestic buyer? Have you ever had a great experience buying a product or service? Think about that experience and what excited you as a consumer that made you want to go back to that same company. *How about:* Salespeople who looked out for your best interest. Didn't try to sell you on options you didn't want. Acted in a professional manner. Paid attention to you and your needs. Were prepared to work with you. Delivered what they promised. Were trusting and sincere. Did not pressure you into anything and yet was able to educate you on your choices. Listened to you and responded to your needs. Followed up after the sale.

So you really don't need to imagine what Corporate Buyers expect with the products they buy, with the companies they place orders to or with the Sales Professionals they conduct business with. It's no big secret. *Because you expect the same things numerous times a week in your own private life.* That's what you expect, and that's what I expect. *Welcome to the Buyer's side of the desk!*

FROM THE BUYER'S DESK: Think like a Buyer by conducting business based on your own personal expectations as a consumer.

BUYERS WHO PREFER THIS: 87%
SALES REPS WHO DO THIS: 23%

"Gaining Access to the Buyer."

In regards to some of the companies you'd like to do business with or those you've already quoted to without success, the Buyers can be somewhat, if not totally, *off limits*. You can't call them, you can't meet with them and you can't get them to respond to you. It's frustrating, I know. But what you need to understand is that even though you may not have *direct* access to the Buyers, it's very possible they still deal with you in a very direct way. (1) They still receive, review and compare your quote packages. (2) They are still involved in the supplier selection process. (3) They still hear about how your products and services are working in the field, either from their own End-Users or from other Buyers in the industry. *(That's right – we actually talk to each other!)* So even though you may not have direct access to a specific Buyer, he is still directly influenced by you as a supplier based on how you conduct business in those areas. *In this case, out of sight is not out of mind.*

So what do you do if you don't have access to the Buyer? What do you do if you can't get a Buyer to respond to you? The answer is a simple one: **NETWORK!** In other words, *find someone they WILL respond to!* Find and network with someone who already has the Buyer's attention. Most likely that person will be a potential 'End-User' of your products and services who works at the Buyer's company.

The **End-Users**, depending on what type of industry you sell to, could include engineering, manufacturing, retail specialists and production personnel. In other words, the eventual 'end-users' or 'end-receivers' of your products and services within the client company. From this point on, these groups will simply be referred to as the 'End-User'. This term will encompass all of the groups, other than Purchasing, who are directly or indirectly affected by how your products and services perform, and those who can influence your future business opportunities.

It's important to note that End-Users may work in the same company as the Buyer, or they may be a client of the Buyer's employer. The End-User could also be someone who has an indirect business association with the Buyer but is still affected by your company's capabilities.

If the End-User works at the same company as the Buyer, they usually hold the budgetary purse strings from which Purchasing awards orders against. In most companies, Buyers do not have project money of their own to spend. They spend other department's money from various project budgets and cost centers. *Think about that!* And since it's usually the End-User's budget, that End-User has the Buyer's immediate attention. That same End-User is probably involved in the decision-making process; that is, which suppliers will be allowed to quote and which supplier will end up with the order. In fact you may be interested to know that the majority of Sales Professionals I've met and eventually conducted business with was *not* through cold-calling. *It was through an introduction by an End-User.* For the Sales Rep, the End-User can become the *'Trojan Horse'* in getting access to Purchasing.

The key to this technique is to first get the End-User interested in your products and services based on what it will do for them. The End-User will then need to convince the Buyer to meet with you and allow you to quote in order to see what your company can technically and commercially provide. It's up to you as a Sales Professional to provide the End-User with the information and justification they'll need to convince the Buyer to meet with you. *So sit down right now and make a list of potential End-Users you have access to who could get you connected to any given Buyer.* Remember, they may be one, two or even more connections away from Purchasing.

Of course there are other people besides the End-Users who could get you access to the Buyer. For instance, other Buyers in the same department you're currently working with. It could also be your own business associates who already have access to the Buyer. These business associates may work for your company or they may work for one of your own sub-suppliers. It could even be someone who works for one of your own clients. *The fact is, Buyers appreciate supplier references from other Buyers working in the same industry.* So add the names of the people who fall under those categories to your list.

Again, the main key to gaining access to a Buyer is **NETWORKING!** Networking is both underrated and underused. Networking is a combination of social skills, business skills and sales skills. And if it's done consistently and correctly it will eliminate the need to cold-call Buyers. Let me repeat that: *Continuous and successful networking can eliminate the need to cold-call Buyers!*

Every Sales Professional should constantly keep their eyes and ears open for any opportunity to network. Ask yourself this pensive question: *How many business colleagues do you make cold-calling companies?* **ZERO.** *But how many business colleagues can you make networking?* **DOZENS!** All things being equal, people would rather conduct business with their colleagues then with a complete unknown. This is true whether they've known the person for a long time or if they belong to the same group or organization. In fact, all things *not* being so equal, people would *still* rather conduct business with someone they know. Think about every job you've had and how many of them were secured based on networking vs. a cold-call approach. Personally I've worked for eight different companies in my career and for every one of them I've known someone who was able to help get my foot in the door. *Just submitting a cold-call resume to their HR Department never worked.*

From The Buyer's Desk I can share with you another good technique to meet Buyers. On one or more occasion in a typical year, Buyers will attend a trade show or industry event. Sometimes it's mandated by the Buyer's department to attend. Sometimes the Buyer requests the chance to go on their own. And when Buyers attend trade shows, remember that their name, company and occupation is usually right there in plain sight on their name badge. While attending a trade show last year I actually had a Sales Professional spot the words 'SENIOR BUYER' on my name badge from across the hallway. *He was immediately drawn to me like a moth to a flame!* Funny but impressive.

You also need to think about the types of events Buyers might attend based on their responsibilities. For instance, if the Buyer's company has minority-sourcing goals, the Buyer will most likely be requested to attend a minority trade show or event of some sort. When I was a Global Lead Buyer at DaimlerChrysler Corporation, minority sourcing was an important and major goal of the Procurement Department. Part of my yearly review depended on how well I was able to source to minority companies, and how well I got my Tier 1 suppliers to use minority-based products and services. So every year our group attended the Michigan Minority Business Development Council (MMBDC) Awards Dinner. Attending that event were *hundreds of Buyers* from GM, Ford, Chrysler and other major companies. Anyone could attend as long as they bought a ticket. ***Yet I rarely ever saw a Sales Professional there!*** That's because most did not think about the quantity and quality of Buyers who would be attending. And there were hundreds of us Buyers walking around mingling with people, wearing those name badges with our information on it. *Unfortunately, very few Sales Professionals ever took advantage of that event to network!* I never could figure that out.

So here is my challenge to you from 'The Buyer's Desk': Between today and a month from now attend at least two networking functions. It could be an industry, cultural or charity event . . . a club or a trade show; *some place where Buyers might be in attendance.* Conducting event research on your prospect's website could provide you with the names and locations of events you're allowed to attend. Do your research and take advantage of the opportunities these types of events can provide.

Of course there are other ways to get in front of the Buyer. They're not as sincere or ingenuous as the ideas already listed. But they've been shown to be effective. After all, your first priority is to get your foot in the door and in front of the Buyer so you can work your smooth-talking magic on him! So here are a few ideas that deal more with *human nature* than thinking like a Buyer. Because they all involve the one thing humans love to give *(their opinion)* and the one thing humans love to receive *(a stroked ego)*:

- Tell the Buyer you have a relative who is interested in their line of profession and you were wondering if he could spare a few minutes to discuss his role and responsibilities and provide some professional advice.
- Ask the Buyer if he could spare a few minutes to give his professional opinion as to what direction he believes the industry is heading and how it's affecting Purchasing.
- Tell the Buyer you have a relative who is working on a Masters thesis on the business relationship between buyers and sellers and you were wondering if he could spare a few minutes to give his professional opinion.
- *(Here's my personal favorite!)* Tell the Buyer you just read a book called *"FEEDBACK! Sales Advice from the Buyer's Desk"* and you were wondering if he could spare a few minutes to give his professional opinion on some points the book made.

Instead of asking for a few minutes of their time, see if they can break for lunch or meet after work . . . but only if their corporate ethics allows it. This will give you more time to develop a business relationship and remove the distractions of the office environment so you can prudently steer the conversation to your company's products and services.

FROM THE BUYER'S DESK: Think of creative ways to get in front of the Buyer. Network with those who already have access to them.

"Connect With Buyers on LinkedIn"

As stated earlier in the book, *the process of networking is underrated.* **Networking** is a powerful combination of social skills, business skills and sales skills. And if it's done correctly and consistently it will eliminate the need to cold-call. Every Sales Professional should keep their ears and eyes open for opportunities to network with Buyers, or at least to network with those who are connected to Buyers. So now that we agree on the power of successful networking, *welcome to the 21st Century!* Because networking has never been easier and its potential rewards attained quicker thanks to a practical website I highly recommend called **LinkedIn.com** (www.LinkedIn.com).

'LinkedIn' allows you to not only tell the world who you are and what you're capable of, it allows you to research and connect with companies and individuals who, prior to the Internet, were unattainable, . . . *including Corporate Buyers.*

So the purpose of this Section is to provide tips for using LinkedIn to connect with Buyers and, most important, at no cost to you! By the way, I do not work for LinkedIn and I do not know anyone who does. I do not receive anything from LinkedIn, monetary or otherwise, nor have they ever asked me to endorse their site. This is merely a professional recommendation and not a sales pitch.

First, you need to know that LinkedIn can connect you to specific Buyers you're interested in doing business with based on their procurement responsibilities and who they work for. *Please note this is not an instruction booklet as to how to get started on LinkedIn.* You'll have to figure that out yourself. I can tell you that it's simple and best of all, it's free! I do have just one tip regarding your own LinkedIn profile: use other people's profiles as examples as to how you would like yours to look. And once you're up and running on LinkedIn, here are some tips to help you connect with Buyers.

STEP 1: Join some Groups on LinkedIn. There is a function on LinkedIn to join Groups. This includes college alumni, industry groups, special interest organizations, etc. Join as many as possible that are relevant to you because it will increase your chances of having something in common with someone you want to connect with. There are thousands of Groups to join and you can conduct a search for ones that are most applicable to you and the Buyer. In joining a Group you may be asked to explain why you want to join in order to be accepted. Most Groups will allow you to join immediately and without hassle. The tip here is to look up the Buyer you're interested in on LinkedIn, find out what Groups he belongs to, and join at least one of them based on your own background. ***There's your icebreaker!***

STEP 2: You need to know that every time you connect with someone on LinkedIn, you're also one step away from connecting to their connections. This creates the potential for hundreds of opportunities with other Buyers and End-Users. But it also works the other way. *Connect with someone who may be connected to the Buyer you want to meet.* There's an area called 'People You May Know'. Click on the link and it will show you a list of potential contacts.

LinkedIn will pull up a list of people based on the companies you've worked for as well as your own profile information and keywords. Or you can simply type the person's name in the 'Search Box' at the top of the page; there's a pull down menu next to it. Let's say you know for certain that someone named 'John Welsh' personally knows the Buyer you want to connect with. Click on John's name to pull up his Profile. Then click on the link on the right side that says **Add John to your network**. Don't click on **InMail**. If you're not already connected with the person you will NOT be able to send an InMail. However, you can pay LinkedIn to use the InMail function if you wish.

When you click **Add John to your network** another page will come up that says, **Invite John to connect on LinkedIn.** You can do that based on how you know them: as a **Colleague, Classmate, Group, We've done business together, Friend, Other**, or **I don't know John.** Don't ever select **Friend** if you're not one. And don't select **I don't know John** because it will ask for his personal e-mail address. So if you really don't know the person, that function won't work. This is the reason why you need to connect with as many people as possible and join as many LinkedIn Groups as possible so you have some functional way to connect. It also increases your chances of having something in common with the person to use as a conversation icebreaker.

The next thing to do is to ask the person to connect with you. Let's say your name is Cathy Wood and you want to connect with a Buyer named Jim Hutton. Don't just send them LinkedIn's pre-written note: **I'd like to add you to my professional network on LinkedIn. – Cathy Wood.** I've had many people send me an invite to connect using that generic, pre-written introduction. But I refuse to connect to anyone who doesn't show a little creativity and ingenuity. You need to *entice* me; give me a *reason* for wanting to connect with you. You could say:

"Hello Jim. I read your profile and would appreciate your thoughts regarding the industry you work in. I'd like to add you to my professional network. Thank you. – Cathy Wood."

If you have an icebreaker such as a School or Group you're both connected to you can say:

"Hello Jim. I see we both went to Central University. I'd like to connect and discuss how your education has helped in your career. Thanks. – Cathy Wood."

Or,

"Hello Jim. I see we both belong to the Parklane Business Group. I'd like to connect to ask your expert advice on specific industry issues. Thanks. – Cathy Wood."

A great feature about LinkedIn is that even if you're not connected to someone specific, you can still review that person's profile at any time to see what Groups they belong to. And if you're not already connected to one or more of the same Groups, it's easy to join them on LinkedIn. *The important thing to remember is to provide a good reason for the person to want to connect with you.* Give them an incentive. Brown-nosing helps. By the way, the initial message you send them is limited in the amount of text you can use, so use the space wisely. LinkedIn will tell you if you went over in text usage.

Here's another tip regarding the list containing **People You May Know**: It will automatically tell you how many people you're away from connecting to someone. If you're one person away from the Buyer, you can ask your connection for assistance. Write a short message to the person asking for their help, knowing that your message may be forwarded to the Buyer. Those types of messages can be any length but it should be to the point and provide a reason for them to help you.

There's another great function you can use if you don't know the name of a Buyer who works at a company you'd like to do business with. There's a 'Search' function to find people who are already registered with the site and who work at specific companies. To find them, go to your **Home Page**. At the top of the Home Page is a Search Box with a drop down menu. Set the drop down to **People**, then type in the name of the *company* you're interested in doing business with. A list of the people who work at that company who are registered on LinkedIn will appear on the Page. Not only their names but their job title, background, responsibilities, schooling and LinkedIn Groups they're associated with. Click on the person you want to be connected to and it will show how many connections you're away from them.

Not only will LinkedIn show some of the people who currently work at any given company, it will also show you past employees who worked there. *Don't discount people who no longer work at the company!* They may be able to provide useful information that could work to your advantage. Searching for companies in the Search field is perhaps the best function on LinkedIn! That's because it allows you to find and connect with people who work at companies you'd like to do business with . . . *including their Buyers and End-Users.*

Again, this valuable function will provide you with their names, job titles, responsibilities, background, and sometimes even their e-mail address and phone number. This method will allow you to view their Profile so you can find an *icebreaker* to use in order to connect with them. It will also show if you're already connected to someone that the Buyer is also connected to. The "1st", "2nd", "3rd" indicators next to their name will provide that information and how many connections you're away from that person.

If you find a Buyer you want to connect with, click on their name to look at their **Profile**. Then use a personal icebreaker to get them to want to connect with you. If you don't have an immediate icebreaker, review their Profile for something you can use; perhaps a company they used to work for or some interest they have. Again, since the best way to connect with someone is through an icebreaker, find out what Groups they belong to and join one or more of them before attempting to connect. Read that line again because it's extremely important! Once you belong to a Group then you're ready to send them a Message:

"Hello Muriel. I see we both belong to the Central Services Group. I'd like to connect to ask your expert advice on specific industry issues. Thanks. – George Kellogg."

Once they agree to the connection, you can send them a message of any text length. But NEVER immediately ask them for a sales meeting through LinkedIn. Don't put pressure on them or they may not respond. Instead, you could say something like:

"Hello Muriel. Thanks for connecting. Again, I saw that we both belong to the Pullman Services Group. I'd like to ask for your expert insight as to where you think the service industry is headed, especially in regards to home services."

Start an **'industry' relationship** with them before you attempt to start a **'business' relationship.** In not directly asking for a sales meeting, you're not putting any pressure on them. At the same time, you're acknowledging their expertise in the field and asking for their opinion, *which everyone loves to give.* If your request is sincere and to the point, most people will respond. From there you can start building your professional relationship. Also keep in mind that once you're connected to them, you can see who *they're* connected to and be one step away from even more opportunities.

One more tip regarding searching for Buyers at specific companies: Since some companies are widespread, even global, connecting with someone in California or Thailand may not work when you live in Ohio. So after you enter the company name in the Search Box, go to the **'Filter by'** function on the left-hand side and click on or type in the State, city or local area of people you want to connect with. Then, hit your keyboard **Enter** button and it will pull up people who work in that specific area for that specific company.

FROM THE BUYER'S DESK: Network with Buyers and those who have access to Buyers through LinkedIn.com.

"Gaining and Maintaining a Buyer's Trust."

In the current business environment it's not easy to attain, much less maintain, the status of *'Preferred Supplier'*. Sometimes it takes years of personal contact, an unremitting business relationship, and a continuous and successful utilization of your products and services. From the Buyer's perspective, the best way to become and stay a Preferred Supplier is to understand and live by this fact: **A Buyer's behavior is influenced by the relationship they experience with the Seller, in particular through TRUST.** Now in using the word *trust*, I'm not simply implying whether or not a Sales Professional is honest or truthful. From the Buyer's perspective, trust comes from a mix of three things: **Credibility, Reliability** and **Familiarity**.

Credibility: Do you do the things you *say* you're going to do when you say you're going to do them? Are you known as someone who is trust worthy and considered an expert in their field?

Reliability: Can the Buyer rely on you completing tasks on time, or can he expect you'll be late with product, service and communication based on previous performances?

Familiarity: How long as the Buyer known you? How *well* does he know you? How well versed is he in your products and services?

From my side of the desk, trust comes from both words *and* actions. Can the Buyer trust you'll act in a professional manner? Can the Buyer trust you'll provide the best possible value that best fits his needs? Can the Buyer trust you'll deliver your products on time? Can the Buyer trust your products will work? Can the Buyer trust your service team will show up when you schedule them? Can the Buyer trust you'll call or send an e-mail when you say you will? Can the Buyer trust your project management team will be proactive? Or can the Buyer trust that you'll not follow through on *any* of these scenarios?

A Sales Professional can increase a Buyer's trust if they consistently adhere to three essential business values: (1) **Long-term Perspective,** (2) **Customer Focus,** and (3) **a Habit of Collaboration.** Let's cover each one of these values by seeing them from the Buyer's perspective.

(1) LONG-TERM PERSPECTIVE. Are you conducting business from your perspective only, or the Client's as well? Are you working on a project as if it's the only order you'll receive, or with the intention of securing future orders? Are you causing problems for the client, trying to nickel-and-dime the order, complaining about the other players, refusing to send service, refusing to be proactive with issues whether it's your fault or not? *Or do you want the client to experience complete satisfaction no matter what it takes because you know it will pave the path for future business?*

EXAMPLE: I once had a supplier contact me weeks after they had received a purchase order. They demanded that the order be amended with their own terms and conditions over mine. Negotiating terms and conditions during the quoting process is expected, but not weeks after the order has been awarded and received. In addition, the supplier already invoiced against the order. Legally that supplier had already accepted the contractual terms based on the amount of time that had gone by as well as the invoiced-funds requested.

I informed them what they were doing was both unprofessional and unethical. Their management insisted we accept their terms or they would pull the order. Not being in a position to find another supplier in time to meet project milestones, I reluctantly accepted their terms. *So you tell me, what are the odds they will EVER receive another order from me again?* How seriously did they destroy any *TRUST* I had with them? The ludicrous thing about this true story is that we're not talking about hundreds of thousands of dollars or a high risk project on their end. Yet they decided it was more important to force their terms down my throat after legally accepting the order than to think of their own long-term perspective with my company. *Unbelievable.*

(2) CUSTOMER FOCUS. Are you *assuming* you know how the Client wants to conduct business or are you systematically asking at each stage of the process if you're complying with their preferences? Are you making decisions based on the last project you completed, or are you focusing on the current project requirements? Do your words and actions show the Buyer that you're only interested in your *own* personal gain or are you demonstrating an interest to help the Buyer meet his goals and objectives as well?

EXAMPLE: It was late afternoon and I had been requested to provide documentation to my Director by the following morning. The documentation required one of my suppliers to crunch numbers, research material capabilities and provide an itemized quote. I contacted the Sales Representative, described in detail what I needed, and asked if it was even possible to have it by the next morning. She assured me she understood what needed to be done and promised to send it to me in time. I got into work early the following morning, logged onto my computer and saw an e-mail from the Sales Rep with the information I had requested. Then I looked at the time she sent it. *It was 2:16 in the morning!* She made a commitment and she got the job done no matter what it took. I now know that when she says she'll do something by a specific day and time, I can *TRUST* she it will get it done! And that ladies and gentlemen is *customer focus!*

(3) A HABIT OF COLLABORATION. Are you playing the role of the Lone Ranger, focusing only on what your roles and responsibilities are, not making sure how it affects anyone else? Or are you progressing through teamwork, partnerships and cooperation with the rest of the affected parties? Are you being proactive?

EXAMPLE: During a critical project a supplier informed me they were unable to machine my components and deliver as promised. This was due to the fact that the consigned castings from another supplier arrived at their facility much later than scheduled. So with other machining business in-house to be completed for other clients, the supplier had to push my project back. It wasn't their fault the castings from my other supplier arrived late, and I couldn't blame them for rescheduling our parts. After a couple days of frantic phone calls with other machinists I was able to resource the business to another supplier. When I informed the original machining supplier about my decision to resource the parts they didn't complain about losing the business. In fact, they stepped up to the plate and, that afternoon, shipped the machine fixtures, drawings and sub-components to the new machine shop. They didn't try to talk me out of waiting until their machines would be available. Instead they understood that my project was in jeopardy of being late and acted in an unselfish, proactive manner to ensure my project was a success. And now with any future business, I *TRUST* they will act in my best interest and not just their own.

FROM THE BUYER'S DESK: Influence the Buyer's behavior by developing a relationship based on trust. Gaining trust is not easy. *Losing it is.*

"What Buyers Fear Most."

I recently had a Sales Professional ask me something I've never been asked before; something that really made me think about my goals, responsibilities and profession in general. The question he asked was: ***"What do Buyer's fear most?"***

That question caught me off guard. If I had been asked, *"What are the biggest mistakes Sales people make?"* or *"What do Sales people do that engage Buyers?"*, I would have immediately replied with a dozen rejoinders. But the question, *"What do Buyer's fear most?"* had me thinking. And I did not have an immediate answer. All I could do was ask him, *"Why?"* He responded, *"Well, if I knew what Buyers fear the most, I could assure them with words and documentation that they wouldn't have these anxieties with me or my company. Then I would do everything in my power to prove myself right."* Good response!

So as I left work that day I considered what I fear most as a Buyer. But in revisiting my thoughts it came to me that perhaps my fears were too personal. So I asked a few of my colleagues in Purchasing about their own fears as a Corporate Buyer. And when I tallied up their responses I found that the majority of them had five specific trepidations. *Here they are in no particular order:*

1. Buyers fear the thought of suppliers going out of business. Of course not every supplier, but those who provide product that would be extremely difficult, if not impossible, to replace. A pencil supplier goes out of business, no one cares. That's because there are countless companies who could ship pencils that same day. *But a supplier who manufactures a unique, complex component, product or service that's not easy to replace has a Buyer's attention.* The more exceptional the product and the more time it took to get it to the marketplace, the more the Buyer worries. The more requirements, testing and qualifying the product had to go through to be accepted by the End-User, the more the Buyer worries about that specific supplier closing its doors. Generally speaking, Buyers will act more civil and go out of their way to make key suppliers feel like a member of the team in order to continue receiving product. Invoices are more likely to be paid on time and payment terms seem to be more flexible for a supplier that the Buyer wants to keep around. In short, the more complex the product and the longer the lead time to receive it in-house, the more sleep the Buyer will lose worrying about it. So no matter how complex your product is, take the advice of the Sales Professional I mentioned earlier: *"If I knew what Buyers fear the most, I could assure them that they wouldn't have these anxieties with me or my company. Then I would do everything in my power to prove myself right."*

Assure the Buyer your company will be around for many years to come by sharing your corporate balance sheet. Share your expected sales revenues. Let them know how much business you have coming in that will keep your company from closing its doors, and the Buyer will be more receptive to buy from you. Unfortunately, few Sales Reps do that.

2. Buyers fear not meeting project budget requirements. When budgets aren't met, expected corporate profit isn't realized. When that happens management gets angry, heads roll and annual raises and/or bonuses aren't realized. We all know the outcome if budgets aren't met, whether it's at work or in our own private lives.

As stated earlier, concerning the *control of costs*, the Purchasing Department is the most significant area in a corporation. That's because generally speaking, two-thirds of the cost of goods sold are purchased items. This means that Buyers are financially responsible for protecting their company. *This is by far their number one priority!* Knowing that, you can understand why Purchasing will do almost anything to keep your prices down and the budget at expected targets. *As a Sales Professional, you need to assure the Buyer that your final price IS the best you can offer.* Prove it by sharing with him your cost and pricing data. Prove it by assuring him you've already gone back to your *own* sub-suppliers and have negotiated the best possible deal. And if your price exceeds the client's budget, work with the Buyer in finding solutions to reduce or avoid costs. Point out areas where engineering, product expectations, specifications and commercial requirements are causing your prices to skyrocket. *That will get the Buyer's attention.*

3. Buyers fear product arriving too late. Buyers hate the concept of *Just-In-Time* deliveries! Just-in-Time, or *JIT*, is a production approach that attempts to improve return on investment by reducing in-process inventory and associated carrying costs. To do this, product arrives just when it is needed or just when it's to be consumed. Warehouse and inventory personnel *love* JIT because it reduces inventory costs. But Buyers hate and fear JIT because it relies on suppliers as well as internal departments doing nearly everything perfect for product to arrive on time. And if the product is late and holds up schedules, it's usually the Buyer who gets blamed. *Buyers would prefer to have a cushion.* Get the product in weeks in advance and let it sit on a shelf; that's the Buyer's mentality. So as a Sales Professional, let the Buyer know how your product can be completed within a reasonable amount of time, even before it's needed. Let them know how it could be readily available upon demand. Prove it by showing the Buyer your own production and delivery schedules. Then make certain you adhere to those schedules per the quality measures agreed to.

4. Buyers fear not meeting yearly corporate and management-mandated goals. It's a good idea to prudently ask the Buyer about his corporate and departmental mandated goals. Most likely the Purchasing department has yearly cost savings goals with specific strategies on how to achieve them. As a Sales Professional you may very well be directly associated with and affected by those goals. Not reaching departmental and corporate goals and assignments will most certainly affect the Buyer's performance evaluation, *not to mention a potential pay increase or bonus.* Ask the Buyer if he has any mandated goals or cost saving strategies for the year and how your company can help contribute.

In addition, many Purchasing Departments have internal and external programs the company supports. In most cases, the Buyer will have an active interest in these programs. *It's in your own best interest as a Sales Professional to be aware of and involved in applicable programs.* Make sure you can answer any question the Buyer may ask about your involvement. Not knowing about the client's programs if you're a first-time supplier is understandable. *Not showing involvement when you're an existing supplier is inexcusable!* It's important that someone at your company is responsible for these types of programs, including cost savings, minority sourcing, etc. Some programs may directly affect your ability to secure a purchase order. That's because reaching goals in these mandated programs can influence the Buyer's performance evaluation. If that's the case, you need to ask the Buyer about applicable programs and how to successfully participate in them.

5. Buyers fear not having enough time in the day to complete their tasks and duties. Due to their legal and financial responsibilities to the company, Buyers are busy people who don't have time to waste. *(Sound familiar?)* And no matter how good their time management skills are, there isn't enough time in the day to complete everything that needs to be accomplished. In many client companies, the Buyer's responsibilities dip into nearly every internal department within the company including legal, accounts payable, manufacturing, material planning, warehousing, logistics, quality and finance.

Everyone wants and needs time from the Buyer. So how you conduct business in the limited time you have with them will ultimately affect your business relationship. Assure the Buyer you understand their busy schedule and prove it through short, constructive meetings, through minimal interruptions, through professional communication skills, and through responsible, attentive and proactive behavior.

FROM THE BUYER'S DESK: Understand a Buyer's fears and reassure him of your commitment in relieving his trepidations based on buying products from your company.

"Six Things Buyers Don't Want You to Know."

Buyers are an enigmatic bunch. I'm sure that's not news to you. For some Buyers it's their nature to be secretive, aloof and demanding. For others it's a trait learned over time through corporate culture, departmental requirements and management expectations. We prefer to have control. We don't like to show our hand. We favor having the most leverage. That keeps the suppliers never really knowing where they stand. At least that's what we think it does. *In reality it can make your career in Sales a living hell!* Of course these statements are somewhat tongue-in-cheek. But whether a Buyer's peculiarity is in-born or absorbed through corporate osmosis, *Buyers prefer to keep certain processes, philosophy and objectives a secret.*

Of course, some information Buyers utilize certainly needs to remain confidential. This includes anything that would jeopardize the legal and financial protection of their company. But for purposes of ego, politics and negotiating there are some things we prefer you just didn't know. So if you promise not to tell anyone, I'll fill you in on a few secrets that Buyers would prefer to keep to themselves; some *Insight from the Buyer's Desk* that will help improve your business opportunities.

1. SWITCHING SUPPLIERS. So many Sales Professionals have said to me, *"I can save your company money. Why do you continue buying from my competitor?"* Some Buyers won't switch to a new supplier if it means only a minimal amount of savings. Depending on the time, effort and money it costs to add a new supplier, as well as the monetary 'break-even point', it simply may not be financially worth it. *Most companies are trying to downsize their supply base, not add to it!*

In fact, a good portion of procurement organizations have a yearly goal to reduce the supply base because it's been shown to save money. Think about that: *The Buyer has a goal to get rid of companies like you, though they may not admit it.* So if the savings you're providing are marginal at best, the Buyer may not bother to take the time or expense to switch to someone new.

Some clients require potential new suppliers to be visited, scrutinized and pre-qualified before being accepted. That means any given number of departments are involved, i.e. engineering, quality, finance and of course, purchasing. That tends to be expensive, especially if the supplier isn't local. So if the savings aren't significant enough to justify the time and expense of adding a new supplier, it simply won't happen.

Think about your own private life. Internet, cable and phone companies invite you to switch to their products and plans to save money. Insurance companies claim 15 minutes could save you 15% or more. *Do you every contact these companies?* Not usually. That's because most of us do not want to put in the time and effort if it means saving just a few bucks. We're also skeptical that any savings could be realized based on the one-time costs to join and the procurement or rent of new equipment. Well, it's the same with Corporate Buyers.

So ask yourself, what would these phone and insurance companies have to do to get you to even consider contacting them about switching? What would it take to meet with them and sign up? Somehow they would have to validate sufficient cost savings and product qualification based on what best fits your needs. Not an easy task because your cynicism is high and your time is limited.

Whatever it would take for a company to entice you to allocate time and resources to even consider their products and plans, those are the same measures you need to take in enticing and educating Corporate Buyers on your own products and services. What you'll have to prove to the Buyer is that *your* savings *ARE* significant, not just through the initial buy but through the process of **Total Cost of Ownership**. (See the Section titled *'Price vs. Value: Using TCO to Sell'*, pg. 171.)

2. ACCEPTABLE QUOTES. Some Buyer's won't tell you if your quote is technically and/or commercially acceptable. Some don't want to take the time to call suppliers to let them know there's an issue with the quote. They would prefer to mislead and let you think everything is fine. Now, I know that the time and cost putting quotes together isn't cheap. Personally I'd prefer if Buyers would let Sales Reps know when their quotes are inadequate.

Unfortunately, some Corporate Buyers just don't want to take the time to discuss what the issues are, especially if your competitor's quote is acceptable and their price is right. So when the Sales Professional asks, *"How is everything? Do you have any questions about my quote?"*, the Buyer may simply reply, *"No questions."* Then you wonder why you didn't get the order.

Finding out if your quote is acceptable isn't a matter of simply asking questions, but knowing which questions to ask. If you're trying to get a reply out of the Buyer about your chances of receiving the order, don't ask a question that will give a "yes" or "no" answer. Ask a question that compels the Buyer to reply with detailed information.

WHAT NOT TO ASK:

- *"Do you have any questions?"*
- *"Is everything okay?"*
- *"Do you see anything wrong with the quote?"*
- *"Do I have a good chance of receiving the order?"*

INSTEAD, ASK THIS:

- *"If there was something that was included or missed in a supplier's quote, would time allow you to contact them or would you be compelled to disqualify them?"*
- *"What items in our quote could prevent us from receiving the order?"*
- *"What specifically stands out in our quote that you like or that we could improve on?"*
- *"If we were the low-bid supplier for this job, what would technically prevent us from receiving it?"*

3. RISKY SUPPLIERS. Most Corporate Buyers who prefer *not* to switch to a new supplier are concerned that they are unproven, unqualified and untested in the field. Therefore it creates a risk in sourcing to them no matter what their prices are. Some Purchasing Departments have *problem suppliers* but continue to source to them because they're *aware* of the problems and feel they can live with them. Therefore the Buyer may prefer to live with their current supplier's issues rather than risking unknown problems with an unknown supplier. In your career as a Sales Professional I'm sure you've seen your competitors continue to get the business even though their track record of cost, quality and delivery is somewhat poor.

It's also important to know that sometimes the Buyer's Manager or Director will compel the Buyer to keep the deficient supplier on board, for reasons unknown to the Buyer. In that instance, you need to make the Buyer feel 'warm and fuzzy' about placing orders to your company. And don't forget to educate the End-Users as well. Let them know who your current clients are, especially if they're the prospect's competitors. Let them know about the projects you're working on that have made industry news. Provide a presentation that shows not only your products but your manufacturing systems that make those products work. If possible, have the Buyer and End-User visit your facility in person. Let them see for themselves your benchmark operations.

Another good approach is to show the Buyer products you currently provide to other clients that are above and beyond their need. Blow them away! I'll never forget visiting a supplier's facility that had the actual landing gear of a major commercial aircraft in their lobby. It was a product they offered to the aerospace industry. The product I needed from them wasn't even *close* to the complexity of this mechanism. And I remember thinking to myself, *"Wow, if they can build THIS, they should have no problem supplying the product I need!"*

4. SOURCING DECISIONS. At times, you can't even imagine why your competitor got the job and not you. There are a number of reasons why a Buyer may place an order to your competitor when it was clear you should have received it. As mentioned earlier, sometimes Buyers place orders to poor performing suppliers when they're compelled to do so by their Management. *And if that's the case, the Buyer may be too embarrassed to tell you the truth.*

Sometimes ego and politics stand in the way. The End-Users of products and services may also coerce the Buyer into placing the order to their favorite supplier. And the Buyer knows that if your product gets jammed down the throat of an End-User who clearly does not want you, *the odds are your product will not meet its expectations in the field.* At that point the End-User will look for any reason why they shouldn't use you again. *Chose your battles wisely!*

If you end up losing an order you know you should have received, don't complain. Instead, be proactive about it. Find out why you didn't get the order and how you can do a better job the next time. Maybe it wasn't *anything* you did or failed to do. Maybe it *was* a mistake that you didn't receive the order. Maybe it was due to ignorance or stupidity. It never hurts to ask for feedback: *"I believe my company would be a great asset to your firm. Can you offer any suggestions as to what we could do better with our next opportunity?"*

5. BACKGROUND. Though they may not want to admit it, a portion of Buyers do not have formal technical training in the products and services they procure. *Most Buyers come from an administrative or financial background.* That doesn't mean they don't know anything about the product. But odds are you know a hell of a lot more than they do. *(For your sake as a Sales Professional, I hope you do!)* Some Buyers simply don't have the time to completely understand what it is they're buying from a technical or capability standpoint. Others simply don't care and leave it to their engineering group. And the more complex the product, the less they may know.

The other reason why Buyers may not be as technically savvy about the products they buy is because they tend to move around in the company every couple years. They finally get to know the ins and outs of a specific commodity, then they're moved to a different commodity in order to 'broaden their experience'. If that's the case, offer some insight into your product in layman's terms and without being condescending. Act like *YOU* know they understand what you're talking about, but don't assume that they do. A sociable lesson in how the product is made, how it works and what it can do may be greatly appreciated by the Buyer and improve your opportunity to sell to him.

6. CALCULATION ERRORS. I know this one will totally shock you so I saved it for last. Ready? Here goes: **Buyers are not perfect!** There, I said it. Left a bad taste in my mouth but I got it out. *In fact, Buyers make mistakes more often than you think.* We Buyers deal with numbers all day long. Odds are we're going to screw up at some point. Odds are we'll add up costs incorrectly and not realize the true and total price from a supplier. If quotes are too confusing (as they often are), if itemized costs don't make sense, or if priced options aren't clearly separated from the base costs, the Buyer will eventually make a mathematical error. This is true whether we're talking about a few dollars or a few million. It's embarrassing when it happens and Buyers don't want you to know it. It's also possible that the total cost was simply fat fingered in their spreadsheet or on their calculator. *That's why it's always best to request time with the Buyer to go over every price and ensure what they've added up is what your total cost truly is.*

FROM THE BUYER'S DESK: Stay one step ahead of the Buyer by considering what he prefers you didn't know.

"The Supplier-Selection Process."

In your own private life, you most likely have specific criteria when deciding which companies are in the running for a product you're considering to purchase. Whether it's an appliance, a new car or a cell phone, specific manufacturers and retail stores automatically come to mind. Research is then completed on your end to determine *the best product for the best value that best fits your needs.*

So how do YOU determine which companies are on your short list and which one will end up with the sale? Do you talk to your friends and family and ask about their experiences? Do you conduct Internet research or buy publications that rate and compare available brands? Do you base it on prior experience with the company's products and services? Or do you simply shop by price? Whatever your criteria is, there's no guarantee that your selection will end up being the right one. Of course for the most part if you've done your homework you'll end up buying the right product that brings satisfaction. *But it doesn't always end up that way.* Sometimes, unforeseen scenarios and internal or external forces could steer you in the wrong direction causing you to knowingly or unknowingly choose the wrong company.

In the world of Corporate Purchasing, the supplier selection process isn't much different than your own domestic process. Buyers discuss supplier performances with their End-Users and internal departments. Buyers conduct Internet research and study their own internal databases. *And if a Buyer believes there's no differentiation between supplier products, he will most likely make his selection based on price.* But no matter which supplier a Buyer chooses, there's no guarantee the right decision will be made. Unexpected circumstances during the course of the project, or having management or internal department personnel twist the Buyer's arm can cause them to make the wrong decision. At the end of the day, Buyers also want the best product at the best value that best fits their needs. *But it doesn't always end up that way.*

In some companies, Purchasing is KING. That is, Purchasing is the absolute final decision-maker as to which suppliers will be allowed to quote and which one will be awarded the order. In that scenario, the engineer and/or End-User of the product may or may not provide the Buyer an evaluation describing which suppliers meet their own requirements. The Buyer may select the successful supplier based entirely on the commercial evaluations. This is especially true if suppliers have been *technically pre-qualified.* Buyers may also be authorized by Management to actively purchase products or services within certain cost limitations on their own to fill a corporate need.

In other companies, including those I've worked for, supplier selection is a shared decision between the Buyer and other internal departments. In that scenario, these groups will meet to review the evaluations and jointly decide which suppliers will be invited to quote and which one will end up with the order. Sometimes these meetings can become heated depending on how fixed an individual is in sourcing to a specific supplier. Still, there are also companies in which the Buyer is simply an administrative puppet following the lead of others.

There are obvious positive and negative consequences with each of these scenarios. ***But the reality is there's no perfect process in selecting the right supplier.*** Just as in your own private life, Corporate Buyers can define supplier selection processes and hope they make the right decision. But there are times when today's right decision ends up being tomorrow's headache. A supplier goes out of business half way through the project. The supplier overestimated its technical capabilities and can't meet project specifications. A sub-supplier is late in delivering essential materials. Other times the supplier may have done a great job on previous orders, but for whatever reason they can't seem to get it together on the current project. Maybe it came to the submission of a poor design or inadequate program management.

No matter what the unforeseen issues are, sometimes a sourcing decision ends up being wrong without any way for the Buyer or End-User to have known it ahead of time. Even the best of suppliers perform less-than-perfect at times. **The point I'm trying to make is that Buyers don't always make the right decisions, and may not always have the command to do so.**

Buyers are human. They are not perfect. *I know, shocking isn't it?* Buyers can make mistakes despite what they sincerely believe is the right decision. And in a perfect world there are processes that define the right supplier for the right job. But we don't live in a perfect business world.

And it's unfortunate that some Sales Professionals attempt to conduct business in the *vacuum* of a perfect world. They become incensed when they don't get the purchase order despite the fact they were the best supplier for the job. But we don't live in a fair and just society. We don't work in a fair and just business environment. And as a Sales Professional you can either accept this fact and attempt to *prudently* improve conditions, or you can distance yourself from Corporate Buyers and other decision-makers by complaining about how things *should* be.

In the real world, there are internal and external forces that directly or indirectly affect the supplier selection process. Those internal and external forces include politics, ignorance, stupidity, ego, supplier discrimination, the good ol' boy network, and the *"We've always done it this way"* mentality. Because of these forces, some orders have been lost to the wrong supplier for the wrong reason. *And due to these forces there are times when the Buyer's hands are tied during the supplier selection process.* For instance, a Production Manager fights for his favorite supplier to receive the order even though another supplier's quote is priced significantly lower. *In a 'Buyer vs. End-User Manager' wrestling match the higher grade-level usually wins,* depending on how far the Buyer's own Manager wants to take it.

So how do you digest the information given here and develop sales strategies to improve your opportunities? Here's some *Advice from the Buyer's Desk:*

STEP ONE: Find out how the client's supplier selection process is accomplished. Prudently ask which departments and which individuals in those departments are involved in selecting suppliers. That way you'll know who is directly involved in deciding which suppliers get to quote. Based on that information you'll find out who you need to get in front of that you haven't already met with. Ask the Buyer, *"Are you able to discuss the supplier selection process in a general sense? I can imagine there must be several departments involved."*

STEP TWO: Get in front of as many people or departments involved in the supplier selection process as possible. *Then sell to them based on what's important to their own individual needs.* As described later in this book, it's important to not use the same generic sales presentation on every department and every individual (See Section titled *"The #1 Sales Meeting Mistake"*, pg. 111). Your sales presentation should be tailor-made to every department and/or individual involved based on their own roles, responsibilities, yearly goals and project interests. As an example, don't spend your entire presentation on your *technical* capabilities when you're meeting with a Buyer who may only have *commercial* interests.

Of course, one of the best ways to be on the short list of preferred suppliers is to follow through with your own supplier-selection criteria you use in your own private life. How do you decide which companies are in the running for a product or service for your own home? Has the product worked in the past? Was the price fair and reasonable? Was it delivered to your home on time? Was it installed properly? Were their assembly directions confusing? Did it require maintenance during the warranty period and, if so, was service immediate and based on your availability? Would you recommend the product to others? *These are some of the same standards and principles Corporate Buyers look for when deciding who will be requested to quote and who will eventually receive the order.*

FROM THE BUYER'S DESK: Find out the supplier selection process within your prospect's departments and sell to each of the decision-makers based on their own specific roles, responsibilities, wants and needs.

"Think Like a Buyer."

I am a Corporate Buyer. I am responsible for the procurement of items and materials that compile the products my company makes, as well as the services that keeps my company running on a daily basis. **You are a Sales Professional.** You are responsible for developing strategies that provide me with the very materials and services my company needs to endure and grow. Sometimes your sales strategies work in securing purchase orders from me. Sometimes they don't. *And sometimes you end up with the order anyway, not really knowing if your strategies had anything to do with it.*

So how do you know if a specific sales approach actually worked or if some other factor compelled me to place the order to your company? How do you know if what you're doing is either enticing or upsetting me? How do you know what preferences I have in regards to communication, documentation, support and the development of a business relationship?

Due to the very nature of my position I am a reserved and cautious individual. **That's because as a Buyer, my main responsibility is to protect my company both *legally* and *financially*.** I feel it necessary to safeguard my company to the best of my ability. Part of that safeguard is to give you as little information regarding your chances as possible. Because the less information you have, the more leverage I have. So chances are I won't tell you about your competitors. I won't tell you whether or not your sales strategy actually worked in getting the order. I *will* tell you if your price is too high, but I'll never inform you if it's surprisingly low. I *will* tell you if your competitor has a lower price, but I won't tell you if your competitor can even provide what I'm asking for. *So in order to protect my company I must keep all of these things inside my head.*

That being said, the best way to sell anything to me is to attempt to get inside my head. What am I really thinking? What am I really planning? What compels me to place orders with specific suppliers? What ensures I'll never do business with any specific supplier again? As a Sales Professional, these are the types of things you need to know. **And the best way to *get* inside my head is to walk around in my shoes and sit behind my desk!** *Of course I don't mean this literally.* But try to see things from *MY* perspective and not just yours. Try to imagine *MY* goals and not just your own. Find out what I want and need to hear instead of what you can't wait to tell me, because those could be two completely different things. To do that you must understand what it is I do, what I am responsible for, what my goals are and why I make the decisions I make. And the first step in getting inside my head is to understand the world I live in; *the world of Corporate Purchasing.*

As stated several times in this book, concerning the *control of costs*, the Purchasing Department is the most significant area in a corporation. That's because generally speaking, two-thirds of the cost of goods sold are purchased items. Two-thirds of the product my company sells to its clients, I actually buy from companies like yours. Again, as a Buyer I am financially and legally responsible for protecting my company; financially by ensuring the best product value, and legally by developing sufficient RFQs, contracts, and master agreements that protect my company's interests. And in doing so it's my responsibility to know what suppliers are out there, what solutions they can provide and of what value that solution is to my employer.

SO THINK LIKE A BUYER. If you were a Buyer, how would you find out what suppliers are in the marketplace that could provide the products and services your company needs? *And as a Sales Professional, how can you keep the Buyers continuously informed as to who you are and what you can do for them?*

When you consider the Buyer's perspective, when you imagine what business is like from the Buyer's side of the desk, you gain valuable insight into how they think, act, react, feel, and see the business world. Sitting back for a moment and considering the Buyer's perspective also helps to change your own awareness of the business environment. It changes your assumptions, generalizations and beliefs that were created in your own mind due to the Sales world you live in. It changes the perceptions instilled by your co-workers and management.

Take time to brainstorm with your colleagues and consider what it might take for the Buyer to consider your company. What would it take to compel a Buyer to switch suppliers and place orders to you? What is it within their own responsibilities, goals, wants and needs that would compel them to consider you? *You never really understand a person until you consider things from their perspective.* Of course you may never agree with that perspective. But trying to understand it will improve your opportunities.

FROM THE BUYER'S DESK: Think like a Buyer. Think like the person you're trying to sell to. Consider their responsibilities, goals, wants and needs.

"Talk the Language of Purchasing."

If you are a *seasoned* Sales Professional you probably already know the everyday terminology and task descriptions associated with your client's Purchasing Department. But if you are still somewhat *green* under the Sales collar, the following procurement jargon and details will help you understand what Buyers deal with on a daily basis. Know these terms. Comprehend them. Because not only are they important to the Buyer, it's part of your job description as a Sales Professional to be able to *talk-the-talk* with them.

But whether you're a *green* or *seasoned* Professional, it's not only important to understand the Buyer's language, *it's equally important to know how each term applies to your ability to improve sales.* And while every Purchasing Department and Buyer differs in their lingo and tasks, the following list (in alphabetical order) gives a **Description** of everyday expressions and nomenclatures in the world of Purchasing. It next gives an **Explanation** as to how they play a role in your world of Sales. This is followed by **Sales Advice** on how to increase your business opportunities, as well as **Feedback** on how many Sales Professionals actually include them in their strategies.

COMMODITY STRATEGY

Description: A document created with the intent to plan, control, direct and manage the purchasing plan for a family of products.

Explanation: *Commodity Strategies* are created by Purchasing in order to plan and execute an approach in selecting a specific product line based on budgets, time-induced needs, global requirements and rated suppliers. If your company is not listed on any given Commodity Strategy for product you supply, the chances of being asked to quote or receiving an order are little to none.

Sales Advice: If at all possible, find out if your company is listed on the Buyer's Commodity Strategy as a preferred-supplier. If you are, inquire what rated concerns are listed either with the product itself or with your company. Cost, quality, delivery, technology and other related factors are covered in most Commodity Strategies. So if your company is listed in the document, prudently find out how it's being measured in those areas. *But if your company isn't even listed in the Buyer's Strategy you'll need to find out why.* Commodity Strategies also shed light on where the client is headed, both technically and commercially, and what areas they plan to focus on. If you actually had a copy of their Strategy in your hands you could easily define your own plan of action to meet their expectations. However, Commodity Strategies are usually highly confidential so it's possible the Buyer will not give you any information. But by asking the Buyer in a general sense where he thinks the commodity is headed, he may offer some insight into what his Commodity Strategy holds.

Feedback: During my career in Purchasing I've rarely had a Sales Professional ask me about a Commodity Strategy covering their products. I'm certain they know it exists and I would never share any confidential information it contains. But I'd be willing to review what my company expects in terms of price, technology, quality and delivery. *But I've rarely ever had anyone ask.*

COST OF GOODS SOLD (COGS)

Description: A term used for the total cost of a manufactured product, including but not limited to labor and material.

Explanation: Corporate Finance, as well as Purchasing, loves to roll every related dollar into a product so they clearly understand what's involved in its pricing. So *Cost of Goods Sold* is an important term to use and explain when it comes to educating the Buyer and the End-Users on the *value* of your product.

Sales Advice: The more the Buyer is educated on what's directly and indirectly involved in the development and manufacturing of your product, the more he'll be open to accepting the piece-price. Many times I thought Sales Professionals were smoking something funny when they offered the cost of their product . . . *until they explained exactly what went into its production.* And they explained it by sharing their *'cost and pricing data sheet'* developed by their own estimating department. It included the supplier's own cost for raw material, outside purchased components, in-house manufacturing, rework and scrap, transportation, quality tests, documentation, SG&A and profit. When I saw for myself what it actually cost them to produce the part, especially costs that were clearly out of their control, I was more willing to accept their initial price or at least negotiate to a reasonable level we could both live with.

Feedback: The vast majority of suppliers are not willing to offer such detailed information, especially their profit margin. And that's certainly understandable. But when attempting to negotiate, it's imperative you educate the Buyer on what it takes to provide your product or service, and what costs you're incurring that are out of your control.

DELIVERY SCHEDULE

Description: A timetable created by the Material Planning Department of a given client and sent to the supplier that defines quantities and required timing of specific goods and services. Sometimes the Buyer will send it to the supplier instead of the Planner.

Explanation: In some companies, *Delivery Schedules* accompany a Purchase Order or long term Scheduling Agreement in order to define when product is due and at what quantity. They are usually sent on a periodic basis to *remind* the supplier when product is due to ship.

Sales Advice: As a Sales Professional it's important for you to review the Delivery Schedule to determine if your company can comply with the client's requests. Some Delivery Schedules can be quite complicated and unreasonable. And if your company is unable to comply with product demand at the dates requested, you need to let the Buyer know ASAP and without hesitation. Allow the Buyer the chance to make contingency plans on his end if product will not be available per his company's demand. *Do not wait until the last minute to inform him the order will not be fulfilled according to schedule.* It's also a good idea to review the Delivery Schedule in case of an error on the client's part. If product is expected too soon or too late or if quantities don't make sense, make the Buyer aware of it. He'll be glad to know that someone is watching his back.

Feedback: It has been my experience that most delivery dates on supplier's quotes are not met. Sometimes it's my company's fault and sometimes it's the supplier's. But for something as important to the Buyer as on-time deliveries, very few Sales Professionals make me feel warm and fuzzy by informing me exactly *how* they plan to achieve it.

DEVIATION REQUEST

Description: A change in the defined tolerances, specifications and/or other technical requirements of any given product as requested by the supplier. Deviation Requests are usually created and approved by the client's design and/or quality department.

Explanation: When a supplier is unable to provide product per the client's request, a *Deviation Request* may be applied for either by the supplier of by someone within the client's internal departments. For instance, a Buyer sends a Request-for-Quote for a widget but the supplier is unable to provide the exact material it's made from. So a Deviation Request is sent to the client's design or quality department asking for a substitute material to be approved. Tolerances and other technical criteria can be areas for Deviation Requests.

Sales Advice: Earlier in the book we discussed how important it is for Sales Professionals to point out areas of potential cost savings to the Buyer. This is especially true when it comes to mandated specifications and requirements that are unnecessary or excessive. A Deviation Request is the perfect way to do it. Sometimes Deviation Requests are approved by the client, and sometimes they're not. But at least you're showing the Buyer you're looking out for his bottom line.

Feedback: I always try to ask Sales Professionals where we could save money based on potential Deviation Requests. *Unfortunately I've rarely been provided true cost-saving suggestions by a supplier.*

INCOTERMS

Description: A series of universally-accepted pre-defined commercial terms and codes primarily intended to clearly communicate the tasks, costs, risks and responsibilities associated with the transportation and delivery of goods, both domestic and international. *Incoterms* are also known as *Delivery Terms* or *Freight Terms*.

Explanation: Incoterms are usually first defined on the RFQ, and subsequently on the purchase order, contract or scheduling agreement. They provide the expected shipping methods and risks mandated by the client. The Buyer may have other shipping directions in the body of the order or in the boiler-plate terms and conditions, so it's important to read those as well. If you are not familiar with Incoterms, logon to:

www.miq.com/cms/INCOTERMS2013/index.html

Sales Advice: Every Sales Professional should have a basic knowledge of Incoterms. You should carry the full list of terms with you at all times. Sometimes a Buyer will have preferred Incoterms listed on their RFQ. If that's the case, make sure you quote per the terms indicated and *NOT* to your own company's preferred terms. Otherwise the Buyer can't complete an apples-to-apples comparison of quotes received. Many times I've indicated 'FCA' terms in the RFQ, which means my own company is responsible for the pickup, freight and insurance costs. And many times the supplier mistakenly *included* freight and insurance costs hidden in their quote, thereby needlessly increasing their total price higher than their competitors. So if Incoterms are *NOT* included in the Buyer's RFQ be sure to ask what delivery terms you need to quote to. Make sure everyone is quoting on the same playing field. It could mean the difference between receiving the order and not.

Feedback: A small number of suppliers I work with continue to ship product based on their own preferred terms and not what was specified on the purchase order. It ends up costing them money, especially if I clearly state that my company is financially responsible for freight. Suppliers also have a tendency to ship product using logistics companies other than those specifically preferred and indicated on the purchase order. *And I refuse to pay for their errors!*

LEAD TIME

Description: Generally, the time it takes between one action or milestone and another. As an example, the period of time between the date a purchase order is received buy the supplier, to the date the product or service is ready for delivery.

Explanation: A *Lead Time* indicates how well the Buyer can support his own company's needs and those of his company's clients. Since delivery is extremely important to the Buyer, it's imperative they know the lead time between milestones within their company and yours. Most lead times requested on an RFQ is from the day the purchase order is accepted by the supplier to the day the product is ready for shipment. But be aware that lead time definitions may be different from client to client and from Buyer to Buyer.

Sales Advice: Just like Incoterms, lead times can make or break a supplier's chance of receiving the order. If the lead time stated on the RFQ isn't clear or there isn't one at all, you need to have the Buyer clarify what "lead time" really means. Is it from the day the order is received to when product is ready for qualification? Or is it to the day product should arrive at the client's receiving dock? The difference could be days or even weeks. If the lead time isn't clear in the Buyer's RFQ or isn't clear in your quote back to the Buyer, it could make a world of difference, especially if the Buyer's schedule is tight. *Quoting faster lead times you can comply with could mean the difference between receiving the order and not.* Another important note is to ensure you actually *meet* the lead time indicated on your quote. If you quoted a four week lead time between order and shipment and it ends up being six weeks, the Buyer can now trust you **not** to meet schedules and may reconsider putting you on the next RFQ. So the next time a Buyer asks you for the lead time of a product or service, ask for the specifics . . . starting and ending with identifiable milestones and locations.

Feedback: Buyers and Sales Reps are both at fault for not clearly understanding and agreeing to what the lead time actually encompasses; what literally starts and ends a milestone. Improvement needs to be made by both parties. In addition, finding ways to improve lead time within your own company in providing quotes as well as the subsequent product, then informing the Buyer on your ability to improve lead times, will greatly enhance your opportunities.

LETTER-OF-INTENT (LOI)

Description: A preliminary contractual agreement customarily used in situations when the goods, quantities, price and delivery dates are unknown, or in situations where time is of the essence and work must begin immediately before the subsequent contract can be created and officially awarded to the supplier.

Explanation: When schedules are tight on the Buyer's end, he may ask you to accept a *Letter-of-Intent* to move forward. This is especially true if it will take too much time to get an order created, approved and in the hands of the supplier, thereby affecting the Buyer's project timing. The entire scenario is based on trust. The Buyer trusts you'll start immediately on the job to ensure a timely delivery. You trust the Buyer will follow up on the contents and pricing stated in the Letter with an actual purchase order within a reasonable amount of time. It's always best to ask what the timing will be between Letter-of-Intent and purchase order receipt.

Sales Advice: Some suppliers will accept a Letter-of-Intent to immediately move forward with a project. Others will not. If you are not certain if your company will accept an LOI to start work, ask your manager. Find out what signatures are required on the Letter and up to what maximum dollar amount your company is willing to accept an LOI. Then, provide that information to the Buyer. *Let the Buyer know under what circumstances your company is willing to move quickly on a project.* If you're willing to accept an LOI to immediately move forward to the Buyer's schedule, it could be an ideal opportunity to take business away from those who are not so willing. Some suppliers require an actual purchase order to start work or ship product. Period. No exceptions. But if time is of the essence and the Buyer is running out of it, knowing your company is willing to move with an LOI could create opportunities for you. That's valuable information the Buyer needs to hear during the initial sales meeting.

Feedback: Again, in my years in Corporate Purchasing, I've rarely had a Sales Rep or Business Owner inform me up front of their willingness to accept a Letter-of-Intent, especially during the initial sales meeting.

NON-RECURRING EXPENSES (NRE)

Description: Generally speaking, *Non-Recurring Expenses* are one-time costs or expenditure charged by the supplier that are directly or indirectly involved in the delivery of goods and services.

Explanation: Non-Recurring Expenses, or *NRE's*, are usually listed separately on the supplier's quote and are not part of the base unit product cost or piece-price. Tooling, design/engineering, start-up fees and quality processes are examples of non-recurring expenses.

Sales Advice: Buyer's need to understand up front what the NRE's are, as compared to the actual base price. Unfortunately, too many quotes are unclear and fail to properly separate *on-going* costs with *one-time* costs. When that happens, one-time costs can be easily and unknowingly rolled into the base or piece-price by the Buyer, thereby creating an erroneous quote comparison between you and your competitors. *Make sure your quote unmistakably labels which costs are NRE and which are not.*

Feedback: More than half of the quotes I receive are fairly clear in regards to NRE vs. base price. But most of the NRE costs are not itemized; that is, separated into what is actually making up those NRE costs such as raw material, overhead, project management, labor, design etc. Those who provide the Buyer an insight into what actually makes up their NRE's as well as their cost breakout stand a better chance of little-to-no negotiating compared to those who simply submit a sum total. *Educate and entice the Buyer!*

PAYMENT TERMS

Description: Payment terms are set, agreed-upon conditions in a contract and/or invoice that reflect the percentage and timing of payment(s) to be made by one party to the other.

Explanation: Typically, *payment terms* specify the period allowed for the Buyer to pay off the amount due. Payment terms may define cash in advance, cash on delivery, a deferred payment period of 30 days or more, or other similar provisions. For instance, *Net 30 Day payment terms* means the payment of the entire invoiced amount is to be made within 30 days of the invoice date.

Sales Advice: Knowing that Buyers are responsible for the financial protection of their company, payment terms are one of the most important areas of their responsibilities. The terms, timing and distribution of payment affects both the Buyer's and supplier's cash flow. Clients want to hang on to their money as long as possible, while suppliers want to get paid as soon as possible. Negotiating payment terms should end up fair and reasonable on both ends. And just like Incoterms, payment terms need to be fully understood by the Sales Rep.

If the Buyer's RFQ calls for *Net 30 Prox* but you quote something different, it throws off the Buyer's ability to complete an apples-to-apples quote comparison. So if the Buyer's stated terms are not the same as your company's preferred terms, *then you need to quote accordingly per the Buyer's request.* If the Buyer's payment terms mean you won't need to borrow money longer than what your terms call for, you may be able to lower the price of your quote. But don't forget to clearly show the price difference between your payment terms and the Buyers. *Educate the Buyer on how much lower your quote could be by issuing the order to your preferred terms.* It could be one of the reasons that compels the Buyer to place the order to you.

Feedback: Sales Professionals need to understand payment terms inside and out. *How much of the order is paid and when?* Unfortunately, as important as they are to the Purchasing Department and Supplier, it's been my experience they are not discussed in enough detail by either party. Most quoted terms are *NOT* to the terms of the RFQ nor the subsequent order. Then when payment isn't received per the quoted terms, phone calls are made by the supplier and tensions run high. Make certain you thoroughly discuss payment terms with the Buyer before the quote is accepted and the order is placed. Understand what the mandated payment terms mean to your company's cash flow. And include cost-savings opportunities for the Buyer in your quote by showing the price comparison between his terms and yours. *The vast majority of Sales Professionals I've dealt with do not.*

PREFERRED SUPPLIER

Description: A known and accepted supplier who has a proven track record of success in technology, quality, delivery, price, communication and service.

Explanation: What Is a Preferred Supplier? What is the criteria for selecting a supplier to be allowed to quote or receive a purchase order? Every client, every purchasing department, and every Buyer and End-User may have different criteria. The description above includes what Buyers look for in a supplier they prefer to conduct business with, but there are others. For the most part, a Preferred Supplier:

- Demonstrates an ability to comprehend and follow through with program specifications and requirements.
- Is certified to the current and applicable industry and quality requirements and registrations.
- Has a strong financial balance sheet and expected sales growth.

- Has sufficient sales representation and program management who can communicate and work with the client in an honest, professional and proactive manner.
- Is able to provide on-time product and service for the best value that best fits the needs of the client.
- Is able to provide a sufficient product or service warranty, or guarantee of satisfaction.

Sales Advice: As a Sales Professional, how many of these areas can you honestly say affected your ability to secure a purchase order? How could you have done a better job within these criteria, whether it was a shared responsibility or not. As a consumer in your own private life, you prefer to purchase products from a company that is well-recognized, has proven capabilities, appears to be financially strong, can provide a good product for a good price, and can back it up with a good warranty and service. *Remember, the same expectations you use to define a preferred supplier in your private life are also shared by Corporate Buyers.*

Feedback: I've been fortunate in my career to have worked with some outstanding suppliers and Sales Professionals. Each had their own strengths which identified them as a Preferred Supplier. *But very few have ever asked me what it actually takes to be considered a Preferred Supplier, both in my mind and my company's.*

PURCHASE REQUISITION (PR)

Description: A written or electronic request from internal corporate departments to Purchasing for the procurement of goods or services from a supplier.

Explanation: A *requisition* is an internal document that informs the Buyer a product or service is needed. Sometimes the Buyer is aware of the demand ahead of time and waits for the requisition to be created. And sometimes the requisition is the only form of internal communication that compels the Buyer to place an order. Depending on the company, requisitions can be created by a number of internal departments including sales, engineering, material planning, or the actual End-User of the needed product or service. The requisition normally contains the part or service number, description, expected delivery date, quantity and pricing. Some of these items are actually filled in by the Buyer at the time of placing the purchase order, including the name of the successful supplier. Some requisitions can have an unlimited amount of line items attached to it. Due to potential unethical outcomes, most Buyers do not and cannot create their own requisitions.

Sales Advice: Just as it's important to get in front of the Buyer and sell to them based on their wants and needs, it's equally important to get in front of the department or individual who will be creating the requisition! This is especially true if that department or individual is the eventual End-User of your products. That internal entity may have a say as to who is allowed to quote and who will receive the order. So it's in your best interest to prudently ask the Buyer about the requisition process and who specifically is involved.

Feedback: *Once again, in my years in Corporate Purchasing, I've rarely had anyone ask for that information.* In most cases the Sales Professional is only focusing on me and not on others who could directly or indirectly affect their opportunities.

PURCHASE ORDER (PO)
Description: A legally written or electronic contractual document prepared by the Buyer and awarded to the supplier to describe and bind both parties to the terms and conditions of a purchase.

Explanation: In most companies, *Purchase Orders* can be considered discrete spot buys since they are not usually created to reflect a long-term contract such as a *Scheduling or Master Agreement.* Placing purchase orders, along with their applicable commercial terms, is the number one responsibility of most Corporate Buyers.

Sales Advice: Sales Professionals should make certain they review the purchase order before accepting it. If product descriptions, payment or delivery terms, quantities, pricing or delivery dates are erroneous you need to let the Buyer know immediately. *Buyers make mistakes.* Don't count on the order being perfect when it's handed to you. And don't go back to the Buyer after it's been legally accepted complaining about terms and conditions that are not to your liking. Make sure the order is based on terms as agreed to by you and the Buyer.

Feedback: I've experienced suppliers who accepted an order and even invoiced against it, then refused to comply with specific terms and conditions of the order. Not only is this unprofessional and unethical, it's against contractual law. *If you are new to the Sales profession or could use a brush up, I highly recommend taking a course in contractual purchase orders.*

QUOTE COMPARISON, OR QUOTE SUMMARY
Description: The technical and/or commercial comparison of two or more supplier quotes for the exact same product or service.

Explanation: *Quote Comparisons* are created by the Corporate Buyer with the intent to verify and provide reasoning for the preferred supplier.

The summary is formatted for the input of key data taken from each supplier's quote. Data includes but is not limited to piece-price, payment terms, one-time costs, delivery and shipping terms, lead times and other commercial information. Technical and product capability data can also be included, depending on the company or purchasing department. Information pulled from each quote is then reviewed, calculated and compared. The final comparative data determines which supplier is commercially and/or technically preferred to receive the purchase order.

Sales Advice: If your quote is missing information or if data provided in the quote is not what was requested, it will cause the Buyer to do one of two things: (1) It will compel the Buyer to let you know what you missed so you can resubmit your quote, or (2) it will compel the Buyer to throw your quote in the trash. *Been there, done that.*

Feedback: Review your quote thoroughly before submitting it to the Buyer. Compare your data with the requirements provided by the client. Remember, it's not the Buyer's job to ensure your quote is accurate. . . *IT'S YOURS!*

REQUEST-FOR-INFORMATION (RFI)

Description: An informal request by Purchasing for one or more suppliers to provide a budgetary quote on goods or services based on specifications, quantities and other terms and conditions.

Explanation: A *Request-for-Information* is normally used by Buyers to help define the subsequent budget for a project. Not all project information may be known when the RFI is sent out. RFI's are usually used to obtain information and are not normally meant for the actual procurement of goods and services. A Purchase Order is generally not the result of an RFI.

Sales Advice: Because an RFI is meant to create budgets and not necessarily to order product, it's in your best interest to add some financial cushion in your RFI response pricing. For instance, if you offer a price of $100 for a product in the RFI but you end up pricing it at $125 in the subsequent RFQ, it will leave a bad taste in the Buyer's mouth. RFI's usually do not offer as much detailed information or requirements as an RFQ does. So if you don't include a reasonable financial buffer in your RFI pricing based on the unknown, the Buyer will expect the exact same price, if not a lower one, in the actual RFQ quote.

Feedback: For the most part, suppliers do a decent job of ensuring a financial cushion in their RFI's. But some suppliers refuse to even provide an RFI to the Buyer based on the time and expense of putting one together. *Unfortunately this only encourages the Buyer to not include them on future RFQ's.*

REQUEST-FOR-QUOTE (RFQ)

Description: A formal request by Purchasing for one or more suppliers to quote on goods or services for a funded, approved project based on defined specifications, quantities and other terms and conditions.

Explanation: A Request-for-Quote is normally used for the actual procurement of goods and services instead of budgetary uses like an RFI. In addition, RFQ's tend to contain much more detail and requirements than an RFI since it will be actually used for a funded project.

Sales Advice: There is an entire Section in this book dedicated to RFQ's and the quoting process. Not paying attention to the requests in the RFQ is one of the biggest reasons why Sales Professionals fail to get the order. Quotes are sometimes sent to the Buyer based on the suppliers-own requirements and perceptions, and not necessarily what the Buyer asked for. Quotes need to be compared to the wants and needs stated in the RFQ, then corrected if necessary before submitting it to the Buyer.

Feedback: Most quotes have something missing or include incorrect requirements. This is because the Sales Rep or their internal estimating department did not pay close enough attention to the RFQ. *At times the Sales Rep isn't even checking the quote before it's handed to the Buyer to ensure everything that was requested is included.* This is extremely frustrating on the Buyer's end.

RISK MANAGEMENT

Description: The identification, assessment and resolution of risks involving a supplier and their products.

Explanation: It's Purchasing's job to ensure suppliers are financially and technically capable of providing products and services. A supplier's inability to do so can greatly jeopardize the client's capacity to provide for its own customers, as well as maintain their daily business flow. *Risk Management* assessment areas normally include the suppliers financial status (D&B scores), the ability to meet specifications, or the capacity to provide requested quantities at desired timing. But risk can also include other factors such as potential environmental, government and political threats, a change in ownership or management, or a change in manufacturing locations.

Sales Advice: Research and define your own company's risks. Determine if they could be perceived by the client as a potential threat in conducting business. Discuss these risks, or lack thereof, with the Buyer especially during the initial sales meeting. Squelch any erroneous rumors about your company. Some of the Buyer's biggest fears are (1) a key supplier closing their doors, (2) a supplier not being able to make product, and (3) a supplier not being able to deliver on time.

Feedback: I've had very few Sales Professionals or Business Owners discuss how their company maintains a low risk, *or even those of their own supply base.* Reassure the Buyer in both words and documentation how your company is financially strong, able to provide what the Buyer needs, and able to do it in a timely manner. Reduce their perception of risk in your company, especially during the initial sales meeting. Unfortunately, the vast majority of Sales Professionals do not.

SINGLE-SOURCE

Description: Although several sources of the same goods or services exist, the order is deliberately given to a specific supplier over others in a competitive marketplace. Not to be confused with *Sole-Sourcing.*

Explanation: Reasons for *Single-Sourcing* include technical superiority or specific inabilities of the other suppliers. Buyer's don't usually care for single-sourcing because it means there aren't a sufficient number of suppliers capable of providing any given product or service. It's not that the product is proprietary. It's just the perception of the Buyer, justified or not, that there aren't enough qualified suppliers to provide it. This reduces sufficient competitive quoting and also creates a significant risk in the event the single-sourced supplier goes out of business.

Sales Advice: You're in good shape if the Buyer perceives your products to have limited competition, though you may never really find that out. *No Buyer in his right mind will tell you you're the only game in town.* If he does, *there goes his ability to negotiate.* If you really know your competition and their own capabilities, you should know how viable their quotes are. You should know how likely they can or cannot provide what you can. The Buyer may inform you they're requesting quotes from your competitors in order to keep your pricing down. In reality it may be based on their company's internal mandate to quote a limited amount of suppliers if a product is not deemed proprietary, even though no one else technically or commercially comes close to you.

Feedback: Most suppliers seem to quote a fair and reasonable price knowing they are practically the only game in town. *But some get arrogant and try to take advantage.* That only makes the Buyer work even harder to find capable global competition, even if it means changing the product design so it's no longer difficult for competitors to provide it. *So why encourage the Buyer to do that?*

SOLE-SOURCE

Description: Unlike Single-Sourcing, *Sole-Sourcing* goods and services to a specific supplier occurs when no other capable supplier exists or if the product, or facets of it, is proprietary to the supplier.

Explanation: Not to be confused with single-source, *sole-sourcing* only takes place when it's absolutely necessary. It's one thing to perceive a supplier is the only game in town. It's another to know you legally can't ask someone else to quote if the product or process related to it is proprietary. *That being said, Buyer's detest sole-sourcing.* This is due to the plain and simple fact that competitive bidding isn't legally or technically possible and the supplier knows it.

Sales Advice: If a product or service is deemed sole-sourced, the Buyer will work harder to keep that supplier happy and in business. *At least, that's what a smart Buyer would do.* But keep this in mind when you're pricing your proprietary or sole-sourced product: You may be the only supplier who can provide what the Buyer needs, but if your pricing or delivery is out of line, good luck selling *non-proprietary* products to the Buyer. He may be forced to place an order to you for widgets, but if you take advantage he will look elsewhere when he needs a doohickey.

SURCHARGE

Description: An additional charge to the client by the supplier in excess of a product piece-price.

Explanation: A surcharge is not usually a fixed cost that takes place on a monthly, quarterly or yearly basis. Its value is usually reliant on uncontrolled or unforeseen expenses created by external global forces. Surcharge examples are raw material and energy costs.

Sales Advice: Buyer's hate *surcharges*. Period. They understand they are sometimes necessary due to unforeseen changes in the cost of global raw commodities such as oil and metals. But keeping track of costs and having to change pricing within their database is a pain. If you are able to buy futures or maintain surcharges on an annual basis, it will reduce the workload of the Buyer and make them more inclined to give you the order instead of your competition. Imagine 'Supplier A' changing costs on a monthly basis due to material surcharges. Now imagine 'Supplier B' only changing on a yearly or bi-yearly basis. *If you were a Buyer, who would you prefer to conduct business with?* Obviously, price plays a role in sourcing the product and no Buyer should place an order to a higher-priced supplier just because they offer less surcharge instances than another supplier. Predicting surcharges throughout the year is a gamble if you don't hedge. *But if you can maintain a consistent price over an extended length of time it will improve your opportunities.*

Feedback: Discuss your ability to maintain costs over time with the Buyer. Most Sales Reps only discuss price and eminent surcharges that are out of their control. *Show your ability to stabilize costs where and whenever possible.* Educate the Buyer on your company's surcharges.

TERMS AND CONDITIONS

Description: Legal and binding language which is commonly used in contracts for the sale and receipt of goods and services.

Explanation: *Terms and Conditions*, or *T's & C's*, are usually found at the end of a purchase order. They are also known as *Boilerplate*. Specific or differentiated terms and conditions can also be included in the body of the contract, especially if the requirements for providing product is different than the standard corporate terms.

Sales Advice: If you've never read the T's & C's of your client's contract, do it now! Ask your legal department to point out potential areas of concern. Many suppliers assume the terms of their quote override the terms of the eventual order from the Buyer. But unless specific quoted terms are included in the body of the order, odds are you're legally under the conditions of the client's contract.

Feedback: When asked, I've rarely had a Sales Rep tell me they actually read the terms and conditions of any given purchase order I've awarded to them. Most claim they've never read them. *That's sad.* And while I appreciated their honesty, it's in the Sales Reps best interest to read, comprehend and ask questions about them. Ask your own legal department if you're not sure what they mean.

WARRANTY

Description: A legally enforceable promise or representation as to quality or performance of goods or services made by the supplier.

Explanation: Purchasing is free to negotiate for broad, strong warranties. Or they can accept your defined warranties and disclaimers.

Sales Advice: As a Sales Professional, it's important to know the difference between what kind of warranty the Buyer asked for and what your company offers. If the Buyer asked for a two-year warranty but you normally provide only a one-year, then quote and price according to the Buyer's request. And if the Buyer requested a one year warranty but you provide a two, your quote is now erroneously too high.

Feedback: Most product warranties are one year. *Unfortunately, that's all most Sales Professionals really know about it.* Most do not have a clue as to exactly what it covers, when it starts and when it ends. Most also do not know what actions on the client's part, or lack thereof, affect if not terminate the warranty. Educate the Buyer in the details of your product and service warranty. *I've rarely had any Sales Professional do that or even know the fine details of what their company's warranty is.*

FROM THE BUYER'S DESK: Discover, understand and use the everyday terminology and task descriptions of Purchasing.

SECTION 2

Sales From the Buyer's Perspective

- Sales From the Buyer's Perspective
- Don't Sell Me a Product, Sell Me a Solution!
- What Sales Books Preach That You
  Need to Avoid!
- Is Management to Blame?
- Be a True Sales Representative
- Are You a Sales Leader?
- Client Gift-Giving Advice

"Sales From the Buyer's Perspective."

Sitting on my side of the desk, I know that Sales is not an easy profession. Yet, Sales is so much apart of our everyday life. Not just our business life but our personal life as well. Wherever you are at this moment, take a look around you. Everything you see is there as a result of the sales process. From the roof over your head to the floor under your feet - and everything in between. Someone had a *need* and someone had a *solution*. All of our lives we are literally surrounded by the *influence* of successful Sales Professionals. That's what makes Sales a very necessary and noble profession. And that's why I sometimes try to sit *behind the Seller's desk* in an attempt to see things from their perspective. *Hopefully you're trying to see things from mine.*

In 2006 when Mr. Thomas Lasorda became the new President and CEO of then (Daimler)Chrysler Corporation, he gave a speech to an audience full of suppliers. And one of the things he said was, *"Some suppliers could greatly improve their sales approach by understanding how we think – what our Procurement and Supply organization needs to hear."* I completely agree with that statement. Because the best way to sell to any one is to mentally sit behind their desk, walk around in their shoes and try to see things from their perspective. What are their goals? What are their responsibilities? And what do they want and need to hear from you in order to make a decision about your company?

During my 20+ years of working on the supply-side before becoming a Corporate Buyer, I admit I didn't always understand why Buyers made the decisions they followed through with. When I was on the supply-side, we knew if we could just get our foot in the door we could show the

Buyers how we could improve their production, enhance their quality and save them money. *Why couldn't they understand that?* Why wouldn't they just give us a chance? **Does that sound familiar?** Aren't those some of the same questions you've asked yourself? Well it wasn't until I became a Buyer that I finally understood exactly *why* Purchasing thinks the way they do and makes the decisions they make. Hopefully by now in reading this book, you've gained some perspective as to what it's like to be employed in Purchasing, and what internal and external forces compel Buyers to place orders to specific suppliers.

From the Buyer's perspective you need to *re-think* your sales approach. Consider this statement: **You will develop more business relationships in two months by showing an interest in the client, than you will in two years trying to get the client interested in you.** And yet I have Sales Professionals who spend all of their time and energy trying to get me interested in their company.

The candid truth is, Buyers are not that interested in your company. Certainly not any more than you're really interested in that home improvement business who's installing new windows in your house. What interests you as a consumer is what those new windows are going to do for you and your family. They're going to improve the appearance of your property. They're going to save money on energy bills. And they're going to increase the value of your home. *That's where your real interests are, not in the company who sold and installed them.* And just as in your role as a private consumer, Corporate Buyers are more interested in achieving their own goals without much heartfelt, sincere interest in the companies they're buying from.

Again, *you will develop more business relationships in two months by showing interest in the client, than you will in two years trying to get the client interested in you.* That's the sales approach you need to develop and use. Yet so few Sales Professionals actually use that approach. So during your sales meetings, sell to the Buyers based on their own interests. Sell to the Buyers based on what they want and need to hear, and not necessarily what you can't wait to tell them about your company. **Because those could be two completely different things!**

I've been asked many times by Sales Professionals and Business Owners what the difference is between a **good** supplier and a **great** supplier in the eyes of Purchasing. From the Buyer's perspective, a **good** supplier will get me the product or information I requested by a promised date. A **great** supplier will do everything they can to get it to me earlier than the promised date. A **good** supplier will respond immediately when I contact them to resolve an issue. A **great** supplier will make certain I never need to call them because they're already working on resolving it.

A GOOD supplier will tell me what they can do for me. A GREAT supplier will ask what it is that I need. Read those last two sentences again and live it. Doing some research on your client or prospect to find out what they need will go a long way in impressing them. And with the Internet and business periodicals we have today, it's so much easier to research a potential client before you actually attempt to make contact.

FROM THE BUYER'S DESK: Ask and understand what the Buyer wants and needs in order for him to make a decision about your company.

BUYER'S WHO PREFER THIS: 93%
SALES REPS WHO DO THIS: 16%

"Don't Sell Me a Product, *Sell Me a Solution!*"

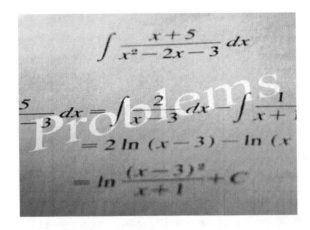

A few years ago I was approached by a Sales Professional representing an industrial parts washer company. He had heard of a new project that had recently been released and it was his desire to educate me about the washers his company could provide. I actually had washer suppliers coming out of my ears and was satisfied with the number of vendors quoting. *So the last thing I needed was another washer supplier.*

As a Buyer, I am responsible for the financial protection of my employer. It's my responsibility to know what suppliers are out there, what solutions they can provide, and of what value that solution is to my company. Unfortunately there were specific machines on this project that I was having difficulty in finding qualified suppliers. *But industrial washers was not one of them.*

Somewhere towards the end of the sales meeting, I happened to glance through the Sales Rep's product brochure and noticed the words *"high-pressure water de-burr"* in the list of machines they built. The words hit me like a freight train! *"You guys build high-pressure water de-burrs?"* I excitedly asked the Rep. He nodded his head. I informed him, *"I've been looking for companies who can build them. We need several for our new project!"*

Now just for your reference, a high-pressure water de-burr is a machine that removes excess material burrs from machined parts. Water is used at an extremely high-pressure to remove the surplus material. And because they're not purchased as often as a typical industrial parts washer, I was having difficulty finding a sufficient number of suppliers who could quote and provide them.

"Why didn't you tell me you guys can build high-pressure water de-burrs?", I asked. The Sales Rep shrugged his shoulders and replied, *"I don't know. Industrial washers are our main core of product. I just thought you'd be more interested in washers."* The truth was, the quantity of industrial washes needed on the project were numerous, while only a handful of high-pressure de-burrs were needed. Combined with the fact that the collective profit margin on the washers for this project was higher than the water de-burrs, it compelled the Sales Professional to only focus on selling his high profit, staple commodity over the solution I really needed. **But of course he didn't know what I needed because he never asked!**

Within the next few weeks I visited their facility along with our Quality and Engineering Group. We approved them both technically and commercially and ended up sourcing the high-pressure de-burrs to them. They also received an order for a few of the project washers as a bundled package . . . *no thanks to the Sales Rep of course.* **Because if I hadn't seen the de-burrs on their product list instead of what the Rep only wanted to show me, they would have ended up with nothing!**

Too many times Sales Reps try to sell me products they can't wait to show me instead of asking what it is I actually need. And too many times suppliers have lost out on business opportunities because they focused more on high profits in place of potential low-cost solutions. Since these Sales Reps were only focusing on their own aspirations instead of my needs at the moment, they lost out on potential business down the road due to what they couldn't wait to sell me at the time.

Think of it this way. Let's say you're a Sales Professional who hypothetically sells only two products: *blankets* and *life preservers.* And let's say both your profit margin and your company's focus was more on the blankets than the preservers. Now, imagine your prospect is drowning in the ocean. *Which product does he need? Which product would be easy to sell him at that moment?* The answer of course is the life preserver! Unfortunately, too many Sales Professionals attempt to get their foot in the door by trying to sell the prospect on the blanket, when it's the life preserver they need! Sell them the life preserver. Sell them what they need at the moment. And once the prospect is safely on shore and soaking wet, *then you can sell them the blanket!*

From the Buyer's and End-User's perspective, don't sell your prospect a product . . . ***sell them a solution!*** Remember that when you're selling solutions, you should sell based on what's important to the individual per their specific job responsibilities. If you're selling to the Buyer, sell it based on cost savings or other commercial goals the Buyer is responsible for. If you're selling to the End-User, sell it based on product capabilities. And if you're not certain what they're responsible for or what they need at the moment . . . **ASK!**

Many times the lower profit *solution* will eventually lead to high profit sales. Buyer's prefer to initially buy simple, low cost, uncomplicated products from new suppliers *to test the waters*, instead of expensive, highly complicated ones. *We need to feel comfortable placing orders to suppliers slowly and carefully.*

If you need to hire someone in your private life to put a new roof on your house, wouldn't you feel more comfortable giving him the job if you had first hired him to complete other, less complicated work around your house? You'd prefer to see how his workmanship is on minor jobs before giving him a high end project.

You job as a Sales Professional is to get your foot in the door. And the best way to do that is to offer *solutions* rather than focusing on just a product. *And if your product ends up being the solution, good for you.* But be sure to educate the Buyer on what that solution can do for him by asking what it is he actually needs in the first place. In the words of two End-Users I spoke to about this:

"Don't just hand me a quote, sell me on a solution!"

"First, give me exactly what I ask for. Then, offer a best solution. If I don't seem to know what I'm talking about or what I need, politely educate me."

FROM THE BUYER'S DESK: Don't sell the Buyer a product or service, *sell them a solution!* Find out what it is they need and offer a viable remedy.

BUYER'S WHO PREFER THIS: 87%
SALES REPS WHO DO THIS: 23%

"What Sales Books Preach That You Need to Avoid!"

Any football team would love to have a copy of their opponents playbook. To have a set of the plans, strategies and tactics the opponent is planning to use on your team would be beneficial to any organization. Not only would you know what the other team has been instructed to do, you could create your own internal strategies to counter any offensive play used on you.

That's why I enjoy a periodic weekend afternoon in a bookstore to sit, relax and breeze through the latest sales books on the shelves. I love to read about the latest strategies Sales Professionals are being instructed to use on Buyers like me by the authors. Sometimes I have a smile on my face because I'm reading tactics that are *Buyer-Endorsed*; that is, approaches that are preferred by those of us on the receiving end of sales strategies. But sometimes I shake my head in disbelief because I'm reading about a recommended approach that will not only upset the Corporate Buyer, it will drastically reduce future business opportunities for the Sales Rep.

I know that the advice given in any sales book or seminar isn't meant to reduce anyone's chances of making a sale. They all mean well. But until you've spent time sitting behind the Buyer's desk will you understand how and why some well-intended guidance *can give way to a negative outcome.* So from the Buyer's Desk, here are a few examples of **STRATEGIES** I've read in current sales books that you need to avoid, and the **REALITY** of their effectiveness on Corporate Buyers. *(Of course there are others and they're specifically discussed elsewhere in this book in more detail.)*

STRATEGY: Buyers are merely puppets of the End-Users and Management. They only place orders mandated by others. So don't waste your time building a business relationship or reviewing your quotes and capabilities with them.

REALITY: That all depends on what company or organization you're dealing with. It's true that in some companies Buyers are merely clerks completing cost studies, quote comparisons and order placements based on the direction from others. But in most companies, including the ones I've worked for, Buyers have 'cradle-to-grave' responsibilities. They're involved in budgets, supplier evaluations, contractual documentation, RFQ submissions, quote comparisons, supplier selection, cost-savings, commercial issues and other project responsibilities. So in most cases, supplier selection is a either a cross-functional decision or it's strictly decided by Purchasing. In either case, ignoring the Buyer is not a good idea. It's up to you to determine what the Buyers in any given company or department are responsible for and, therefore, how much time and effort is required on your end to develop a business relationship.

STRATEGY: Break the ice with the Buyer by starting your sales meeting with something funny.

REALITY: *Be careful!* If the joke falls flat it will set the tone for the rest of the meeting. You also stand the chance of insulting someone. This isn't a roast. You're not the Best Man or Maid of Honor giving a speech at a wedding. *You're a Sales Professional!* Be humble. Be down to earth. Most important, *be* professional. Try starting the meeting with, *"Thank you for the opportunity to present"*. Forget the joke.

STRATEGY: Start your cold-call communication with an engaging question. Something like, *"Did you know that most widgets breakdown right after the warranty ends?"*

REALITY: Sorry, I don't have time for 'Stump the Buyer'. Try instead to slowly give your name, your company name, and engage the Buyer by stating that you can only imagine how busy they must be. Ask if they have a few moments to discuss how your products may fit their current needs. *Do your homework!*

STRATEGY: Attempt to get around the lower-level person such as the administrative assistant to get to the Buyer.

REALITY: Lower-level people are there for a reason. It's to serve as the blockers against Sales Reps trying to get around the client's preferred administrative procedures. And Reps who by-pass procedures tend to upset not only the lower-level person who's been stepped over, but also those they report to. However if done correctly, a lower-level person can actually be an *advantage* in finding out who the right Buyer is for any given product. Be professional, courteous and complimentary, and that lower-level person will point you in the right direction.

STRATEGY: Bring lots and lots of information to the sales meeting. Overwhelm the Buyer with facts, figures and photos.

REALITY: One of the best sales calls I experienced was a Business Owner who brought in just one photo of a product they manufacture along with a signed testimonial from a recognized company they build it for. It wasn't even anything my company would buy. But it was a product that was so technically advanced to anything we would purchase from them that I immediately thought, *"Wow! If they can successfully build this product for this major company, they should have no problem handling my needs."* Also, in regards to your presentation, don't overwhelm the Buyer with too much information. Focus on the highlights, not the details of your capabilities. *I would rather recall three important things about your company than be given 100 that I'll never remember.*

STRATEGY: Agree to the price, capability and lead time of what your competitor quoted in order to get the sale.

REALITY: Never agree on any price, technical capability, terms, lead times or product outcome that you can't meet or aren't sure of. Discuss the requirements with your engineers, estimators and production people *before* agreeing with the Buyer. Don't promise something that your own internal people can't comply with. Too many times I've been contacted by frustrated engineers working for the supplier who told me they can't meet the product requirements or lead times that was promised by the Sales Rep. Be honest with your company as well as the Buyer.

STRATEGY: During a cold-call, stop and ask how the Buyer is doing.

REALITY: The second you ask the Buyer to answer a question, especially at the very beginning of the cold-call, you stand a chance of losing control of the initial conversation. You've just asked how they're doing. By doing that you've just given them the ball to run with because you no longer have control of the call. Instead, you can say, *"I hope you're doing well"* then proceed with your communication. In saying, *"I hope you're doing well"* you're not only showing an interest in their well-being, you're also keeping control of the call since you technically didn't ask a question and aren't expecting a direct reply.

STRATEGY: A testimonial from past or present clients is the strongest sales tool to *close the deal.*

REALITY: Testimonials on their own are like personal references; no one in their right mind is going to provide a poor one to the prospect. Most of us have the words "References available upon request" at the bottom of our resume. Somehow that's supposed to prove we're worth hiring. But the person doing the hiring only sees the references we give them, the ones that make us look good. If the hiring manager had a chance to speak with everyone we've ever worked with, I'm sure someone for whatever reason would say, *"Don't hire this person."* You can't please everyone. It's the same with testimonials. Suppliers get to weed out dissatisfied feedback from their customers and hand me the ones they most treasure. That's not to say that testimonials shouldn't be available for review as an addition to your other documents. I'm just saying that Buyers are a cynical bunch. We always accept testimonials with a grain of salt. For every 100 clients you made happy there's a few you didn't. We just don't want to be the next one. *So in the Buyer's mind, testimonials are NOT the strongest sales tools out there.*

STRATEGY: After you make the sale, move on to the next prospect.

REALITY: Too many times I've placed orders to suppliers, never to hear from them again. No follow up. No return of calls. No response to issues. It was as if they made a million dollar commission off that one sale and now they're sipping a drink on a tropical island enjoying retirement. In short, they act as if they don't need another order from me. *Well guess what, your wish just came true!* Yes I know you have other clients that need your attention. Yes I know you have other prospects to spend time with. *But don't play the role of 'The Invisible Man'.* Always leave even a little part of yourself with me. Let me know you won't disappear after receiving the order. Let me know you will respond to questions and issues within a reasonable amount of time. *Show me you'll be nearly as attentive after the order is place than you were trying to get it in the first place.* But if your one-time sale *did* made you a millionaire, congratulations! *Otherwise, please stay in touch.*

STRATEGY: Handle client issues by yourself. Don't ask your sales manager to do your job for you.

REALITY: You shouldn't have to ask your sales manager to do your job for you. But management should be willing to get involved, to offer advice and to join you during a corrective-action meeting with the client. Funny how I rarely get introduced to Sales Managers or Vice Presidents of Sales. That's because I'm rarely asked to meet with them. *Isn't that* *sad?* And when I do it's usually at their own facility, rarely mine. Getting assurance from the Sales Rep alone that the price is the best value, that the problem will be resolved, that delivery will take place as quoted is accepted with a grain of salt on my end. That's because I know the Rep's power and ability to make those things happen within his own company is limited. Having assurance from those higher up the ladder would make me feel a bit more warm and fuzzy about your company's capabilities and promises. *Unfortunately that's rarely done.*

A Sales Rep may promise a specific delivery date. But sometimes they make promises that other internal departments can't meet. At least a sales manager has access to their grade-level counterparts in production, assembly, quality and other departments and can make things happen. Having the sales manager show up once in a while, either with the Rep or on their own, shows concern for the client. It also gives me an opportunity to speak one-on-one with the manager in case I have issues with the Sales Rep that I'd rather not say in front of him or her. *(Oops, probably should have left that out!)*

STRATEGY: Send an invitation to Buyers and End-Users to connect on LinkedIn.com at their work e-mail address.

REALITY: 'LinkedIn' is a social networking website for people in professional occupations. It is mainly used for professional networking and job searches. (See the Section, *"Connect With Buyers on LinkedIn"*, pg. 25.) As of January 2013, LinkedIn reported more than 200 million acquired users in more than 200 countries and territories. Personally speaking I think it's an excellent source of finding and connecting with Buyers. *But that's not the problem.*

The problem is too many sales managers are telling their Sales Reps to e-mail Buyers at their place of employment and asking to connect. *WRONG! Why would you want to do that?* Are you trying to get the Buyer fired? Every Human Resource department knows that LinkedIn is an excellent tool to find a new job. Most companies forbid their employees to logon to the site at work, even during their lunch hour. *Why?* Because most companies don't want their people looking for new jobs on company time and using the company's computers to do it. Some companies run Internet searches on employee computers and check subject lines in employee e-mails. All perfectly legal. And due to the very nature of their position, *these checks are especially run against Corporate Buyers.* (Been there, had that done to me.) That's why most Buyers get nervous and upset when Sales Reps send them LinkedIn connection requests at their place of employment. I don't know how many times I've responded to LinkedIn requests from Sales Reps with scathing replies to never do it again! And when I ask why they even considered sending an invite to my place of employment they always respond, *"My manager told me to do it"*. On LinkedIn there is an area where people input their preferred contact e-mail. If it's at their place of employment that's one thing. But if it isn't, never contact them that way. *Buyers tend to get distraught when their called in to speak with HR!*

FROM THE BUYER'S DESK: Take care in the strategies that sales books and workshops teach. They may actually prevent opportunities from those you're trying them on.

"Is Management to Blame?"

The other day I received a cold-call from a Sales Rep hoping to sell products to my company. Since most cold-calls end up being pretty much the same generic conversation, I'm somewhat immune to *bad calls*. However this particular one was especially deprived. The following conversation is real but the names, companies, projects and locations have been changed. *The phone call went something like this:*

SALES: "Hello Mr. Locke. My name is Larry Martin and I work for Acme Products. I wanted to set up a meeting with you to discuss how we can provide our widgets in support of your ABC Program located at your manufacturing plant in Cleveland."

ME: "Larry, thanks for your call. Unfortunately none of the three things you mentioned have anything to do with me or my company. First of all, I'm not the responsible Buyer of widgets in my purchasing department. Second, our U.S. manufacturing plant is no longer located in Cleveland. It moved out of State nearly two years ago. Third, the ABC Program is not conducted out of our facility in the U.S., it's conducted at our global facility in Mexico."

SALES: "Oh, I'm sorry. So who could I talk to about widgets?"

ME: "Look Larry, I'm not trying to be rude. But I don't think it's my job as a Buyer to do your sales homework for you. What you should do is take the time to look up my company on the Internet, find out where our facilities are located, what they manufacture, and which areas might need your widgets. Then make some phone calls to those areas and find out who the responsible Buyer is. Quite frankly you should have done that before you bothered to call me."

SALES: "Okay. Thanks for the advice. Sorry to have bothered you."

ME: "No problem. Good luck."

At that point the cold-call ended and I shared the conversation with the Buyer sitting next to me. He shook his head and made the comment that the Rep obviously wasn't prepared to make the call with the hope of making a sale. Of course that wasn't a brilliant observation on my colleagues part and I'm certain everyone reading this book is thinking the same thing. *After all, only a 'green' Sales Professional would make the obvious oversights that Larry Martin made, right?* To me it really doesn't matter if Larry was 'green' or 'seasoned'. **Being 'green' shouldn't be an excuse for not knowing what to do or say!** And being 'green' won't make me want to bend over backwards to help you.

My question is this: *Was it Larry's fault or the fault of his Sales Manager that he failed to conduct even the most basic research before calling me?* Was he compelled by management to make as many calls as possible with the hopes of eventually making an appointment? Was he instructed to spend more time looking for new prospects instead of satisfying existing ones? Was he ever provided sales training that covered cold-calls? Or was he simply hired and thrown out to the wolves without the most basic of training? I did remain calm and polite during Larry's cold-call because I couldn't blame him for his ineptness. *I did, however, blame his manager.* After all, isn't it management's responsibility to coach, teach and mentor their sales team?

Now if you're in Sales Management please don't get bent out of shape. I didn't write this book to point fingers at Sales Professionals or their Management. The vast majority of professionals and sales managers out there are great people to work with. But if you could spend *one week* sitting on my side of the desk you would quickly realize that even the most seasoned Sales Reps make errors in judgment during the sales process; errors that may seem like the right thing to do on the Sales side, but from the Buyer's side it's contrary to our needs. And when I ask Sales Reps what compelled them to make the errors they made, their number one response is, *"It's mandated by Management."*

And therein lies a common yet major dilemma in the business world: *conflicting preferences between Sales Management and Corporate Buyers as to how Sales Reps should conduct business.* In other words, conflict between the Buyer's wants and needs vs. the Sales Manager's mandate. This leaves the poor Sales Rep in the middle trying to please both sides. For instance, some Sales Managers want their people to only and immediately focus on the next sale after the order is received, while Buyers want them to stick around and be available if issues arise or if questions need answering. Some Sales Managers want their people to postpone the communication of potential issues regarding products, while the Buyer needs to know that information immediately so they can make contingency plans on their end. In both instances, the Sales Professional must now make a choice: *upset the Manager and risk disciplinary action, or upset the Buyer and risk future business.*

The root cause of this dilemma lies in the fact that Sales Managers and Buyers are primarily concerned with *their own* goals and objectives which at times do not correspond with each other. The Sales Manager wants the best profit. The Buyer wants the best price. The Sales Manager wants the best usage of his Sales Rep with all of their responsible clients. The Buyer wants the Sales Rep's attention 100% of the time and doesn't care much about the other clients.

The good news is that this dilemma is fixable. But in order to do that, the goals and objectives of each party must be understood by both sides. Both parties must focus on what they DO agree on; *profitability and a long term relationship.* The final negotiated price must make profit for the Sales Manager and, at the same time, be within the Buyer's budget. Repeat business is preferred by the Sales Manager, and conducting business with a known supplier is preferred by the Buyer.

The real danger lies in those instances in which the Sales Manager directs the Rep to do something he or she knows will upset the Buyer. In that case, the Rep should be allowed to inform the Manager of potential consequences without fear of disciplinary action. The Representative should attempt to either change the Manager's mind or convince the Manager to join him at the next meeting with the Buyer. **Of the thousands of Sales Reps I've worked with, I've rarely had the opportunity to actually meet with their Sales Manager!** *Isn't that a shame?* Perhaps if more Managers periodically joined their sales team in the field, they'd be able to stay in touch with current or potential clients and hear for themselves what separates their own objectives from the Buyer's.

FROM THE BUYER'S DESK: Sales Management needs to take responsibility for their team and ensure they're balancing business between the goals of their company and the wants and needs of their clients.

"Be a True Sales Representative."

I once walked into a retail store to purchase a piece of jewelry for my wife's birthday. Standing at the jewelry counter with no one in front of me, I patiently waited for the sales clerk to finish her conversation with another clerk. They stood roughly eight feet away on the other side of the counter and could clearly see me waiting. The conversation I overheard had nothing to do with work; it was merely a discussion about their weekend. I raised my finger and said, *"Excuse me."* I was met with a half turn and the reply, *"I'll be right with you."* After another minute of weekend talk the sales assistant finally turned to me and asked, *"Can I help you?"* to which I replied, *"No, that's okay. I didn't mean to interrupt your conversation. I'll just look for something at other store."* As I turned and walked away from the counter the sales assistant yelled out, *"No sir, please, I'm sorry."* Too little, too late. Continuing my walk through the front doors of the store I said to myself, ***"I'll NEVER buy anything from here again!"***

How many times have you said that same line in your own private life while exiting a business? *"I'll NEVER buy anything from here again!" "I'll NEVER shop here again!" "I'm NEVER coming back here again!"* And sometimes we never DO go back, while other times we have no choice and end up returning - though not necessarily to the same department we had the bad experience with. And it doesn't matter if it's a retail store, on-line shopping, a restaurant or a home service company. **The fact is ONE employee's actions, or lack thereof, can ruin their company's chances of repeat business.**

So the question I pose to you is this: **Is it fair to judge an entire organization based on a bad experience you had with one employee?** Is it fair not to go back to a restaurant simply because the wait staff was inattentive? Is it fair to stop shopping at a specific retail store simply because one sales clerk ignored you? Is it fair to never use a home painting company again simply because their staff failed to show up when they said they would? I'm always one to give someone a second chance. But when wait staff, sales clerks and service people continue to provide inadequate representation, *I will go out of my way to ensure I NEVER do business with them again.* In fact, most of us do that. In our own private lives we will judge an entire company based on the inadequate representation of one sales or service professional. So whether it's fair or not, we sometimes evaluate an entire company based on the actions, or lack thereof, of just one individual.

Well guess what? *It's the same with Corporate Buyers!* Whether it's fair or not, Corporate Buyers may judge an entire company based on the actions, or lack thereof, of one Sales Representative. When a Sales Rep continues to provide inadequate service, poor response times, deficient communication and unprofessional demeanor, the Buyer may go out of his way to ensure he never does business with that supplier again. *I've talk with dozens of Buyers who tell me they won't buy products or services from a specific supplier simply because they don't want to deal with the Sales Rep.* Not that the products cost too much or are inadequate. They simply don't care for the supplier's sales representation. It may not seem fair, but it happens.

Lately it seems to Buyers that the title **'Sales Representative'** has a tendency to be taken too lightly by those who possess it. The term *'Representative'* refers to one who symbolizes what their company stands for and what their company is capable of. This is represented through dress, manners, knowledge and attitude. And if one or more of these qualities are lacking, there's a good chance the Buyer will look elsewhere for product.

"But that's not fair! Just because one person's behavior, capabilities or approach is lacking, it doesn't mean the entire company is like that!" True, but from the Buyer's perspective that may be all they have to go on in judging an entire organization's performance and capabilities. **It's important to understand that the Sales Rep may be the Buyer's only link to the supplier.** The Buyer may have never met anyone else at the company, nor traveled to their facility to see the operations. So the Sales Rep's actions, or lack thereof, may be *the only thing* the Buyer has to go by to determine what the entire company is like. This includes their corporate culture, their attitude towards their

customers, the capability of their products, and how communication is conducted. Especially during the initial sales meeting, if the Representative is unprofessional, has poor communication skills or doesn't appear to be trustworthy, *that's EXACTLY how the Buyer may perceive the entire company.* The less contact the Buyer has with anyone else at the supplier and the less intimate the Buyer is with the company's capabilities, management and corporate philosophy . . . the more important the role of *'Sales Representative'* will be. This is true whether the supplier is currently providing product or is attempting to secure business from the Buyer.

THINK LIKE A BUYER. If you were a Buyer, why would you prefer the Sales Reps you work with dress, act and conduct business in a professional manner? What do you expect from the wait staff, sales clerks and service people you encounter in your own private life? Do you expect them to sincerely represent the company they work for and what their employer stands for?

A typical corporate mission statement is as follows: *"The Corporate Mission of the Acme Company is to design, manufacture and provide high quality widgets for our global customers in a timely and cost effective manner."* So, is the Sales Rep actually doing that? Are they providing not only quality products, but *quality service* in a timely and cost effective manner? Are they supporting their company's mission statement in the way they present themselves and in the way they conduct business?

Sales Professionals should remain proficient, accommodating and down to earth. And they should also be appropriately dressed for the occasion. These days we're all use to casual attire at work but some Reps go a bit overboard and are a bit TOO casual. You don't always have to wear a suit and tie to your meetings but you don't have to look like you're ready for a tailgate party either. *First impressions are key with the Buyer because you may never get the chance for a second!*

From the Buyer's perspective, a true Sales *Representative* maintains the following characteristics: Is honest, down to earth and proactive. Does not emit the traits or attributes of a *'used-car salesman'*. Demonstrates a technical and commercial understanding of the products and services they sell. Responds to voicemails, e-mails and client requests within a reasonable amount of time. Can clearly communicate and work with the Buyer in a professional manner. Is not afraid to tell the Buyer the truth about the Rep's-own company's inabilities and errors. Shows respect for the Buyer's time. Listens to the wants and needs of the client and follows through. Educates the Buyer in terms of best value and most adequate needs.

As stated many times in this book, I've worked with thousands of Sales Professionals in my career. And in all that time I've *never* had a Sales Manager or Vice President of Sales ask me if I am actually happy with their Representative. I honestly don't recall anyone of authority calling or meeting with me in person to ask how the Sales Rep is doing, if they're providing what I need, and if they're doing it in a timely manner. **That's incredibly sad!** I *do* recall an instance in which the Sales Rep acted unprofessional in so far as to insult and even threaten one of the engineers at a previous employer. *Unfortunately his Sales Manager spent his time DEFENDING the Rep instead of spending time REPLACING him!* If you're a Sales Manager and you found out your Sales Rep isn't trusted by the Purchasing Department, how would you spend your time? *If it was me I wouldn't even ask questions!* Because no matter what you do or say, a cloud of mistrust will always hang around the Buyer's desk. *Personally I'd apologize and pull them out of that account faster than the speed of light!*

Beyond conducting business unscrupulously, sometimes personalities simply clash between Buyers and Sales Professionals for no apparent reason. Sometimes it has nothing to do with business and has everything to do with personality and chemistry. You could have the world's greatest, smartest, honest and capable Sales Rep working for you - *but if he doesn't get along with the Buyer for whatever reason, you need to pull him out of the account and put someone in that does!* **Unfortunately, if you're a Sales Manager, you can't do that if you don't even bother to ask the Buyer for feedback!** I guess it all comes down to what's more important to you as a Sales Manager: *defending your Sales Team no matter what, or improving business no matter what?*

FROM THE BUYER'S DESK: Be a true Sales *Representative* of your company through dress, manners, knowledge and attitude. If you're a Sales Manager, ask for feedback from the Buyers and End-Users regarding your company's representation.

"Are You a Sales LEADER?"

Here's some *Sales Advice* that you may not have been aware of: ***Buyers prefer Sales Professionals who are Leaders in their profession.*** Buyers prefer Sales Representatives who demonstrate and emulate the characteristics of a ***Leader.*** To a lesser extent, Buyers can be regarded as Leaders in the commodities they buy, the decisions they make and the projects they manage. But from a buying and selling standpoint they can't ensure a successful project alone, and certainly not from *'the Sales side of the desk'.* That's why Buyers prefer to conduct business with individuals who represent and follow through with the traits and characteristics of a true **LEADER; an individual who possesses a positive business influence in the direction and support of others that results in the accomplishment of a common goal.**

In order to be truly successful, Corporate Buyers need effective Leaders in Sales whom they work with on a regular basis. It could be the Business Owner, Sales Manager or the actual Representative the Buyer deals with. *Without Sales Leaders, Buyers are forced to work twice as hard to ensure things are effectively handled on BOTH sides of the desk.* Buyers need Sales Leaders who can see the big picture, who ensure product is of the best value, who deliver on time, and who can prudently resolve issues. Unfortunately, most business scholars will tell you that highly effective leadership is a rare commodity.

So how do you know if your own Sales Manager is a Leader? What characteristics does your Vice President of Sales retain that enlightens their leadership? And what traits do you yourself possess as a Sales Professional that lets the Buyer know his workload will be lightened and the success of the project is attainable? Here's a list of characteristics that Buyers look for in the Professionals they deal with:

1. True Sales Leaders are humble and are in business to serve. Buyers prefer Sales Professionals who are down-to-earth and unassuming about their accomplishments and abilities, as well as the company they represent. No one likes to buy from a loud-mouth. If you're selfishly focusing only on your own goals, thinking only from your side and not the clients, then you are your own worst enemy. Insincere compliments and actions are easy to recognize. Are you in Sales only for the potential money or are you also in it to assist your company and the client in reaching their own financial goals? *True Leaders in Sales are self-effacing and go out of their way to achieve customer satisfaction.*

2. True Sales Leaders are non-judgmentally motivated. Do you judge other people based on what they fail to do for you? Or do you try to see things from their perspective and attempt to understand why they make the decisions they make? Do you have a constant desire to learn and improve or do you simply justify your shortcomings? Do you think you have all the answers or do you consider other ideas with the contemplation that maybe their idea is the right one? Do you consider yourself an expert in your field without a need to improve, or do you constantly observe and learn from others? Do you listen and consider, or do you half-listen and do what you like? Do you expect others to go the extra mile to solve your own problems? Are you really interested in the facts and do you gather them unemotionally? Do you calmly listen to others or do you kick and scream until your way is accepted? *True Leaders in Sales remain positive when dealing with others and always consider the other point of view.*

3. True Sales Leaders aren't afraid to face and solve a problem. Buyers prefer Sales Professionals who aren't afraid to tell them the truth. For instance, your product isn't working per the contractual specifications, your product is going to be late, your service department can't meet their commitment, or your price by the end of the project will be over the client's budget. Now that you've admitted the problem, what are you doing to solve it and ensure it doesn't happen again? Are you waiting for someone else to fix things or are you going above and beyond the call of duty to resolve client issues, even if you have to complete tasks that are not your responsibility. Are you e-mailing people to gain information or give direction waiting for them to respond? Or are you personally and directly calling them on the phone and even communicating face-to-face? Are you getting the right people involved immediately? *A True Leader in Sales stays focused, uses effective communication, tells the truth and does what it takes to correct errors.*

4. True Sales Leaders continuously strive to improve. Buyers prefer Sales Professionals who refuse to accept how things have always been done when it simply doesn't work. True Leaders accept and promote change, accept and promote new paradigms, and are considered revolutionaries in their field. Leaders in Sales find ways to improve their sales meeting presentations and marketing strategies. They look for ways to enhance their quote packages. They challenge their own engineering and design teams to improve product and delivery. They challenge their estimating groups to go back to their own suppliers and find ways to lower or avoid costs. And they are constantly finding new ways to educate their clients, co-workers and their own sub-suppliers. *True Sales Leaders are constantly looking for a better mouse trap and always question the "we've always done it this way" mentality.*

5. True Sales Leaders are financially conservative on both sides of the desk. Buyers prefer Sales Professionals who look out for the client's bottom line, and not just the company they work for. Are your own profit margins excessive? Can specific components or services be removed or changed out for less expensive ones without affecting quality, performance and delivery? Will the client's budget suffer, thereby reducing financial opportunities for future programs? Are you going back to your own sub-suppliers and negotiating reduced rates in place of accepting their quotes at face value? Are you pointing out areas in the client's specifications where requirements are excessive or unneeded? *True Sales Leaders spend time, money and energy cautiously and in the best interest of the client.*

6. True Sales Leaders invest in their company. Buyers prefer to place business with suppliers who invest in their equipment, their facilities and their people. Buyers prefer to conduct business with Sales Professionals who also invest in themselves; invest in education, invest time and energy with the client, and invest in themselves within the company they work for. The most important investment a Sales Professional can make is in the education of their own products and services. Sales Reps must remain up-to-date on the technology and capabilities of the products they sell and not simply act as an order taker. Nothing is more frustrating to a Buyer than Sales Professionals who need to ask others within their own company for answers to questions they should have known themselves. Buyers also become frustrated when Sales Professionals ask questions about the Buyer's own company; things they could have found out on the client's website. *True Sales Leaders invest their time and energy in understanding the inner workings of their own company as well as the clients.*

7. True Sales Leaders communicate effectively and consistently.
Buyers prefer to work with Sales Professionals who communicate in a clear and concise manner. Voicemails and e-mails should be short but to the point. Issues over products and deliveries must be communicated honestly and immediately. Remember that Buyers would rather hear about problems upfront and as soon as possible. That way they can either assist the Sales Rep in resolving the problem, or develop a contingency plan on their end to accommodate the issue. Sales meetings must inform and educate the Buyer on what they want and need to hear. *Effective communication means informing the right people at the right time about the right topics with the right facts.* Equally important is follow up, feedback, responsiveness to issues and the on-time successful completion of promises. Communication is not just about speaking and writing effectively. Communication is also about behavior and integrity. If you say one thing but do another, your integrity will come into question. And once you lose trust from the Buyer it's difficult to get it back. *True Sales Leaders are not afraid to consistently and clearly communicate essential information within a timely manner.*

FROM THE BUYER'S DESK: No matter what your position or years of experience is, every Sales Professional is a potential Leader in their field - both in the eyes of their colleagues and the Buyers they work with.

"Client Gift-Giving Advice."

Before you know it another business year will be coming to an end. Halloween merchandise will be in the stores and the winter Holidays won't be far behind. And we all know what that means, right? *It's time to order your client's Holiday Calendars!* That's right, it's time to start thinking about ordering those calendars to give away to your existing customers and potential new clients during the winter Holiday season.

The question is, what theme should your calendar embrace? Will it be landscapes? Golf? Unicorns and rainbows? Or maybe photos of your own products? Either way, the calendar will be featuring your company name with the hope it will be displayed near the desk of your favorite Buyer. But no matter what your marketing department decides for this year's calendar, I'd like you to consider the following advice from the Buyer's Desk. And remember, this is from someone who is on the *receiving end* of those wonderful calendars. Ready? Here it is: **DON'T HAND OUT CALENDARS!**

Hopefully I'm not too late in providing this recommendation. Hopefully your company hasn't already dished out thousands of dollars on picturesque calendars featuring waterfalls, hot air balloons and puppy dogs. It is after all marketing's theory that if your company's name is staring the Buyer in the face all year long, at some point they'll think of you when sending out RFQs or when awarding Purchase Orders. *And for the most part, your marketing team is right!* Research has shown that people DO respond to advertising that leaves an impression. The best advertisements use images, jingles and stories to focus attention to their brand. Advertisers attempt to get potential clients to connect their brand name with a positive impression; an encouraging reinforcement that their products and services will bring satisfaction. That's why your marketing department is so insistent on ordering calendars with incredible scenery, calming subject matter, or leisurely pursuits such as golf.

But from the Buyer's perspective, the problem *ISN'T* the fact that you're giving me a calendar for the Holidays. ***The problem is the fact that EVERYONE is giving me a calendar for the Holidays!*** Nearly every Sales Professional mails their clients new calendars or hands them out while visiting the client's facility. On an average year, I receive dozens and dozens of calendars from the supply base, all with the intent of advertising their brand name with the hope of continued business. But consider this reality: ***How many calendars can I actually use? How many will I keep?*** How about . . . **ONE.** Oh, I might bring another calendar home for the house, but that's about it. *And odds are, neither one of them will be the one YOU gave me.*

So what happens to the rest of the calendars Buyers receive? One of three things will happen to them: (1) They end up in a pile on an un-used office desk for non-procurement employees to take. *And none of them will buy anything from you because they're not in Purchasing.* (2) They end up in a box to be donated to a local charity for kids or seniors who don't normally receive calendars. *And I guarantee they won't be buying anything from you either.* Or (3), they end up in the trash can. What a shame. What a waste of a thoughtful gift. *And what a waste of marketing expenses on your company's part!*

So what do Buyers recommend Sales Professionals bestow on their loyal clients and potential customers during the Holidays? How can a supplier stand out from their competition and offer something they'll be remembered by? From the Buyer's Desk, the first thing to consider in corporate gift-giving is to find out if you should even offer a gift! Many companies do not allow their Buyers (or any employee in the company) to accept gifts, lunches, outings . . . *or even a pencil.* Different corporations define different standards of *corporate ethics* including what a Buyer can and cannot accept. A Sales Professional should always be familiar with any given client's defined corporate ethics before offering the Buyer anything, much less a Holiday gift.

Most large companies have ethics guidelines on their corporate website. **Find them, read them and comply with them.** If you can't find anything about gift-giving policies on their website, ask for a copy of the 'corporate ethics code' and the 'supply-based ethical guidelines' from the Buyer or from their Human Resource department. NEVER tempt a Buyer or any employee within a client company with even the smallest of gifts if their ethics code does not allow it. *Never put anyone in jeopardy of losing their job!* Not only will it obviously upset the

Buyer to be called into HR, it will also guarantee that your company will never provide product to that client again.

Second, if you ARE allowed to give a gift to the Buyer per his company's approval, find out what the dollar value limitation is. **If it's $25 . . . keep it at $25!** Don't hand the Buyer a gold-plated pen set worth $100 with a wink and a smile and tell him it's only worth $25. Giving a gift beyond the true value limitation is just as bad as giving a gift when NONE are allowed. *In my opinion, it's WORSE!* Not only are you not complying with their corporate ethics guidelines, you're also trying to pull the wool over their eyes.

Third, once you are educated on the ethics rules and dollar value limitation, your next step is to rethink your gift-giving strategy. Due to the fact that nearly every Sales Professional and Business Owner hands out calendars, try thinking *outside the box* and consider other useful office products stamped with your company name. Keep in mind it should be something that could stay within the confines of the Buyer's general desk and/or office area and be noticed every working day. Pens are okay, but supplier's names are usually too small on it to be noticed. And pens usually have a habit of disappearing or being lost. A few times in my career I actually had suppliers provide pens that stopped working after a couple days. *That didn't say much about their company's technical capabilities!*

So from the Buyer's perspective, here are just a few inexpensive items you can hand out that could incorporate your company's name, items that will be used and noticed on a regular basis by the Buyer: Calculator, flash-drive, paperweight, tape dispenser, mouse pad, coffee or drink holder (forget coffee cups; they're as bad as calendars), paperclip magnet base, office accessory valet, desk clock, portfolio, business card holder, small dry erase board, cell phone case, etc.

These are great, practical gifts to hand out for a number of reasons: (1) They're used on a weekly if not daily basis by Buyers. (2) They're small enough to remain on or around the Buyer's desk. (3) Most would be at or under a minimal gift dollar value. (4) They're large enough to incorporate your company's name. (5) Most important, the majority of your competitors won't be giving them away!

Check out office gift catalogs on-line for items that can be personalized with your corporate name on it. Or, simply have professional looking stickers created with your corporate name and logo to place on the item. *Either way you're sure to make an impression on the Buyer or End-User with a thoughtful gift that won't be given away or end up in the trash.*

Here's the last bit of advice about corporate gift-giving: **Don't forget the Family!** So many Holiday gifts handed out by Sales Professionals only focus on the Buyer. In doing so, they miss out on a great opportunity to make a much bigger splash with someone *more important* than the Buyer, and someone who has *more influence* than the Buyer's manager: *It's the Buyer's Family!* Due to the fact that most Sales Reps give out calendars and golf balls, they overlook a prime market in the Buyer's own family. Find out if the Buyer is married or has kids. If so, present a gift or gift certificate that focuses on the family, i.e. a certificate for a salon treatment, golf driving range, pizza parlor, movie tickets, gift basket, etc. By giving a promotional Holiday gift to the Buyer's family you are secretly creating your own 'sales force' within the Buyer's house. *That's because it will create a memorable impression that the spouse and family will never forget.* But most important, *they'll never let the Buyer forget!*

FROM THE BUYER'S DESK: When it comes to corporate gift-giving, do something different for your clients and be remembered. Think *'outside the calendar'* and stand out from your competition.

BUYERS WHO PREFER NOT TO RECEIVE CALENDARS: 83%
SALES REPS WHO GIVE CALENDARS: 92%

SECTION 3

Introductions and Sales Meetings

- Cold-Call Sales Advice
- Buyer-Endorsed Voicemail
- What's the Prognosis, Doctor?
- The Condensed Introduction
- The #1 Sales Meeting Mistake
- Other Sales Meeting Mistakes to Avoid
- The Dog Ate My Homework!
- 10 Questions to Ask the Buyer
- 12 Things You Need to Let the Buyer Know & 12 Questions You Need to Answer
- The Hidden Power of Business Cards
- The Buyer-Preferred Commercial Brochure
- Sell Me On the Intangibles!
- Concluding the Sales Meeting
- Stop By and See Me Sometime

"Cold-Call Sales Advice."

Buyers are an obscure group of people. In most organizations they are difficult to understand and even more difficult to contact. You send e-mail after e-mail, leave voicemail after voicemail, and it still takes an Act of Congress to get them to respond, especially if it's a cold-call. Most Buyers like it that way. In fact, most Purchasing Departments purposely set up defense mechanisms to prevent continuous, direct cold-call communication. (Did you know that the day *call-waiting* was invented is actually a National Holiday for Buyers?) The fact that Buyers can now see who is calling *before* they pick up the receiver brings tears of joy to their eyes. *It's a beautiful thing.*

The truth is, most Buyers who have cradle-to-grave procurement responsibilities prefer to stay in control regarding cold-call communication. That's understandable since nearly every department within and outside of their company contacts the Buyer for something. We've discussed this earlier in the book, but due to the very nature of their position, most internal departments require information and assistance from Purchasing in order to move business forward. Accounts Payable calls the Buyer for information regarding the approval or rejection of invoices. Quality calls to discuss issues with a supplier's product. Material Planners call to find out what was purchased and when it's expected to ship out. Management calls for information regarding cost savings and commodity strategies. Engineers call for assistance when product requirements aren't met. Then there's the supply base; dozens of Sales Professionals calling during any given day or week for meetings, information and the resolution of issues.

Okay, I know I'm not getting any sympathy, but you get the picture. The bottom line is that communication with the Buyer is not always as easy as you'd like it to be, especially when it comes to telephone communication, and especially when it comes to ***cold-call selling.***

The majority of Sales Professionals would agree that the cold-call process is probably the most *reserved* part of selling and, with some, the most difficult and least liked. After all, *cold-call selling* is the process of contacting someone you've never met, who may not be familiar with you or your company, and attempt to sell them something. This is not to say that cold-call selling is the most despised part of Sales. Some Sales Professionals actually thrive on it, while for others it's a way of life.

What you need to know from the Buyer's Desk is that most telephone cold-calls are a turn off. This is due to the fact that the Buyer isn't hearing what he needs to know within a reasonable amount of time to make a decision about the supplier. So what's reasonable? **Think of it this way:** *how long is your own attention span when receiving a call at home from a telemarketer?* Not very long. Probably a matter of seconds. Well, the average attention span of a Corporate Buyer is a little longer than yours only because they get paid to take sales calls. *Think about that statement.* **Buyer's get PAID to take sales calls!** *(Am I getting any sympathy yet?)* Of course, a Buyers attention span has to be a bit longer than the normal person. Buyers have to put a little more effort into it because that's what they get paid to do. But the fact is you've got about 20 seconds to get the Buyer interested in your call before their mind wanders and they start thinking about things like the weekend or their golf swing.

The main reason why a Buyer's mind wanders during a cold-call from a supplier is because after a while, *all cold-calls tend to sound the same.* The main problem with cold-calls is that very few Sales Professionals really know how to do it right. That's because most are conducting their cold-call from the *Sale's perspective* and not from the *Buyer's perspective.* Cold-call selling should really come down to what the Buyer WANTS and NEEDS to hear, and not necessarily what you can't wait to tell him . . . *because those could be two completely different things!* Feel free to read that last statement several times. Memorize it if you need to because it's extremely critical. *In fact, it should be the new paradigm in Sales!*

It's important to be aware that if a sales meeting was the outcome of a cold-call, it doesn't necessarily mean that the Sale Professional used an adequate approach. It could be that the Buyer is so used to dealing with poor cold-calls that he simply overlooked an inadequate performance. If your cold-call is weak but The Buyer needs your product, you'll probably get the meeting. *But if your cold-call is weak and the Buyer doesn't necessarily need your product or already has sufficient suppliers, all the easier for them to turn you down.*

So let's discuss what it is that a Buyer wants and needs to hear. When you applied for your current job you most likely submitted a document either before or during your interview. That document was your RESUME. And experts tell us that resumes should be short and to the point. It should give the *highlights* and NOT the *details* of your career. That's because a resume is not meant to get you a job on its own merit. It's only meant to get your foot in the door so you can start working on securing the job. So when you call a Buyer for the first time, remember that you shouldn't be attempting to sell them anything. A cold-call alone will never get you a purchase order. It's only meant to get your foot in the door so you can start working on securing one.

With that in mind, what you need to do before you cold-call the Buyer is develop what I call a ***Verbal Resume***. In the world of Sales, some refer to this as their *Elevator Speech* or their *30-Second Commercial*. But again, an Elevator Speech usually only focuses on what the Sales Rep can't wait to tell the Buyer, and not necessarily what the Buyer wants and needs to hear in order to continue the conversation.

Just like a written resume, your **Verbal Resume** should be short and to the point. It should give the highlights and not the details of your company. It should not be developed to sell anything but to simply entice and engage the Buyer to get your foot in the door. Most personal resumes have a *Career Summary* statement at the top. Consider your condensed Verbal Resume as the *Career Summary* of your company.

Now, I'm not going to tell you how to develop or deliver your Verbal Resume. But from someone who's been on the receiving end of thousands of cold-calls I will tell you that you need to ***say it slow, say it clear, and keep it under 30 seconds***. Here's an example of a Verbal Resume that Buyer's would prefer to hear:

"Hello, Mr. Sherrow. My name is Connie Faber and I represent The Acme Company. I hope you're doing well. Acme is a provider of office furniture and equipment specifically for the industrial environment. We specialize in quality product lines, competitive costs based on our high-volume buys, and expedited deliveries. We currently sell a variety of office products to your competitors, including ABC Company."

In this example the Sales Rep told the Buyer more information in 30 seconds than he would normally get in a 30-minute sales meeting! In 30 seconds the Buyer was provided with the things he needed to know in order to continue with the cold-call. It included the supplier's product line, industry sold to, specialties and clients. From that information the

Buyer can then make a clear and conscience decision whether or not to continue with the call.

The advantage of a good Verbal Resume is that you'll impress the Buyer up front and make him feel more inclined to set up a meeting. In mentioning your products and services, think about your target prospect and what they're currently experiencing in their industry. You can find that information in industry publications and on the Internet, perhaps on the client's own website. What can your company do that could provide some key benefits to the target prospect? It could be increased production. It could be improved quality. It could be cost savings against their budgets. It could be expedited deliveries. Think about what the Buyer would be interested in achieving, find out what their current goals are, and focus on those needs. And don't forget to ask for a *Condensed Introduction*, discussed a bit later in the book.

The bottom line is that Buyers prefer Sales Professionals who take an interest in their company's needs. In turn they will be more responsive during your cold-call.

FROM THE BUYER'S DESK: Develop a cold-call *Verbal Resume* that will engage the Buyer based on what he wants and needs to hear, and not necessarily what you can't wait to tell him.

BUYER'S WHO PREFER THIS: 87%
SALES REPS WHO DO THIS: 12%

"Buyer-Endorsed Voicemail."

With the contemporary advent of voicemail, call-waiting and other telecommunication innovations, it's never been easier for Buyers to screen their calls, listen to messages without interruption, and be the controller of communication without even speaking directly with the Sales Professional. Cold-call messages are left by the Sales Rep with the hope of a returned call. Requested information is provided to the Buyer without a response. Calls to the Buyer asking for the progress of supplier selections are left unanswered. Not so good for the Sales Rep. But it's in a Buyer's nature *(and best interest)* to manage incoming calls and decide which ones will be replied to and which ones may stay unreciprocated.

Sometimes, cold-call voicemails from Sales Professionals and Business Owners are deleted by Corporate Buyers before they even reach the end of the message. This is not unlike you opening and quickly throwing out advertisements mailed to you in your own private life. You quickly sift through ads and junk mail to see if anything interests you based on your current needs. In short, what modern technology has done for the Buyer is to provide him with the ability to weed out unneeded, unprofessional and uninteresting communication without having to explain to anyone why.

So what can Sales Professionals do to help ensure their voicemail is accepted? How can the voicemail be more proficient and appealing enough to engage the Buyer? How do you keep the Buyer's attention and entice them to call back? How can Sales Reps use voicemail to their advantage? And what are some of the things suppliers do or fail to do while leaving a voicemail that irritates Buyers? *Here's some Advice from the Buyer's Desk.*

98

Let's say you're prepared for your cold-call to the Buyer. You've developed a proficient *Verbal Resume* and you know exactly what you're going to say. You pick up the telephone, dial the number and the next thing you hear is, *"Hi, this is Jennifer Wilson, Senior Buyer for the Acme Corporation. I'm either away from my desk or on another call. After the tone leave your name, number and a short message and I'll get back to you as soon as possible. BEEP!"* Dang! The Buyer's not there! Either that or she's just not picking up. *So what do you do now?* What are your options? Well, you could hang up at this point and try again later. You could leave a message to let her know you'll call back at another time. Or you could leave a message and ask for a return call.

From the Buyer's Desk, you need to know that if you're making a cold-call and can't reach the Buyer on his desk or main office phone, **NEVER, NEVER, NEVER** attempt to reach him on his cell or mobile number. This is *especially* true if the Buyer's desk phone message clearly states that his cell is for emergencies only. *Cold-calls are NOT emergencies.* And I'm sure you'd never do that, but trust me – it happens! If the Buyer is not picking up at his desk he's either in a meeting, traveling, working on something important or preparing to start his next job function. In either case, the last thing he wants is to deal with at that moment is a cold-call. There is a time, place and function for cold-call communication. *But over the Buyer's cell phone when he's not at his desk is NOT one of them.*

Proper telephone and voicemail communication is extremely important to both Sales Professionals and Buyers. So from the Buyer's perspective it's best not to clog their voicemail box with insignificant messages, or for that matter, cold-calls. Remember that the Buyer's voicemail box may only have storage for a limited amount of messages. So don't leave one just to say, *"Sorry I missed you. I'll call back."* Instead - just call the Buyer back! Also, if you leave a 'cold-call' message and ask the Buyer to reply, he probably won't. *Think about it. Why would a Buyer return a cold-call voicemail from a Sales Professional?* How many voicemails do you get at home from window replacement companies or insurance agencies asking you to call back? Probably several a month unless you're on the National-Don't-Call list. *Have you ever called them back?* No. So why would a Corporate Buyer return a sales cold-call?

If you need to get a hold of the Buyer, *keep trying!* Don't put the ball in the Buyer's court to call you back because that now puts him in control of the communication. If I had to return every cold-call voicemail I received from Sales Professionals requesting a call back I would never get my other responsibilities completed. *If you want the business, work for it!* If you want to get a hold of the Buyer, keep trying! Try different times of the day and days of the week. Most Buyers have specific times during any given day that they can't answer phone calls due to meetings or mandated tasks. Relying on the Buyer to call you back puts the control of business opportunities on the Buyer's side, **NOT YOURS!** And if the Buyer asked you to call back but he never picks up, send him an e-mail to let him know you've been trying.

In the event that you *really* need to leave a voicemail and *really* need the Buyer to call back, here are some Buyer-Endorsed techniques to help ensure that happens:

1. Make sure you first *clearly* and *S-L-O-W-L-Y* identify yourself, your company, and your phone number. Then, briefly state why you need the Buyer to call you back. *Don't leave a five minute message explaining why you need him to return the call!* Then give your phone number again before you hang up. From the Buyer's Desk I can tell you that the vast majority of Sales Professionals rattle off their telephone number SO DAMN FAST that either I can't understand it or can't write it down quick enough! Now I have to play the entire message back again just to get the last few digits that I missed the first time. *That's annoying and it happens way too often!* The best practice is to give your phone number immediately after giving your name and company name. Then give it again at the end of the message. And don't forget to entice the Buyer and give a good reason to call you back.

"Hello, Ms. Kean. This is Harvey Conrad from the Acme Company. My number is 555-123-7654. I have a question regarding the order we just received. Unfortunately we can't move forward until we understand specific information. Given your busy schedule, I'd appreciate a call back. Again, this is Harvey Conrad at 555-123-4567. Thank you."

2. Most Sales Professionals never even give their phone number at anytime during the message. So if I actually wanted to call them back I now have to take the time to look for it. Never assume the Buyer has your phone number memorized or immediately accessible. **Always leave it in the voicemail!** It doesn't matter if your number is tattooed on the Buyer's arm . . . *leave your telephone number!* Common sense and common courtesy! Imagine your dentist's office leaving a voicemail asking you to call them back because they need to change your appointment . . . but they don't even bother to leave their phone number. Now you have to spend the time to look it up to call them back. *It's frustrating and it wastes time.*

3. Another important thing to keep in mind is that when you leave a voicemail with the Buyer, **always leave your full name and company name**. It doesn't matter if the Buyer is your twin brother, BE PROFESSIONAL! I get voicemails from Sales Reps that say, *"Hey, it's me . . . give me a call back."* (Okay, who is ME?) Or, *"Hi, it's Bob, give me a call."* (Okay, Bob WHO?) Or, *"Hi, it's Bob Popson. Give me a call back"* (Okay, I recognize your name, but I deal with so many suppliers that I can't always remember who everyone works for. Sorry but it's the truth.) *"Hi, it's Bob Popson with the Acme Company."* AH HA! Now I know who you are! **Don't rely on the Buyer to have a photographic memory, especially if you're the one that needs the call back!**

4. Finally, give the Buyer a *good reason* to return the call. **Entice the Buyer to *WANT* to call you back.** You have product cost savings to discuss. You have a potential issue that could affect delivery. You have a question that needs answering before an order can be filled. You need assistance because you're not getting feedback from the End-User and it may affect timing. Most Buyers will call back if the reason for your voicemail has something to do with their responsibilities, budgets, delivery, or anything that could result in a poor appraisal on their end. *Convey the premise that you're calling to help them!* **Don't make it sound like the focus of their return call will only be to help you.**

When it comes to electronic communication, e-mails and voicemails are all critical tools in doing business with the Buyer. That's why it's essential for you to leave a message on YOUR OWN e-mail, desk phone or cell phone if you're on vacation, traveling, or simply out of the office for an extended period of time. *You cannot believe how many Sales Professionals do not do this!* The message should clearly state that you're out of the office, when you'll be returning, and who to contact for any emergencies. If you were a Buyer, why would it be important to know who to contact if the regular Sales Rep is out of the office? And as a Sales Professional, how can you remind yourself to ALWAYS leave an out-of-office message on your e-mail, desk and cell phone?

TRUE STORY: Several years ago while working for Chrysler I attempted to call a Sales Rep I'll call "Bill". Bill worked for a capital equipment company. I wanted to invite him to attend a supplier line-up meeting to quote on a new project worth millions. I left numerous voicemails and sent as many e-mails trying to get a hold of Bill to make sure his company attended. Unfortunately, Bill was in training all week. *But he never left a voicemail or e-mail message stating he'd be out of the office and who to contact in his absence.* I was *finally* able to get a hold of his Sales Manager. That's when I found out that Bill was in training all week. So the Manager sent another Sales Rep in his place. After all that was said and done, their company ended up with the order . . . *but no thanks to Bill*. Imagine if I hadn't been motivated enough to call his Sales Manager! They never would have had the opportunity to quote. *Can your company really afford to make that kind of simple oversight?*

Here's the type of message you should leave on your voicemail and e-mail if you're out of the office for an extended period of time:

"This is Diane Reed, Sales Rep for The Acme Company. I am presently out of the office and will be returning to work the morning of April 26. If this is an emergency please contact Mr. Tom Jones at 555-123-7654. Otherwise, please leave a message and I'll respond when I return."

Sounds like a simple, common sense thing to do, especially for a Sales Professional. And it's sad that I even have to include it in this book. But sitting on my side of the desk, you'd be surprised how many Sales Professionals fail to do this. But that's the reason for this book . . . *to provide professional feedback and point out the obvious things Sales Reps SHOULD be doing but often fail to do, thereby reducing their opportunities.*

FROM THE BUYER'S DESK: Call the Buyer back if he doesn't initially pick up. If necessary, leave a voicemail that will entice the Buyer to return it. Ensure you practice effective telephone and e-mail communication, especially when you're out of the office.

BUYERS WHO PREFER THIS: 82%
SALES REPS WHO DO THIS: 21%

"What's the Prognosis, Doctor?"

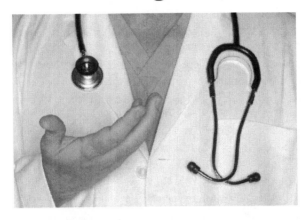

The other day I sat through yet another typical sales meeting with a prospective supplier. Two Sales Representatives sat on the other side of the conference table from me. During the hour presentation they talked about their company, pointed out items in their brochure, discussed their ability to provide good product at a competitive price, then asked if anything was coming up they could quote on. *Same old presentation, same old discussion, same old everything.* While I sat there trying to keep myself awake, I thought about a doctor's appointment I had the previous week. It was just a normal routine checkup. Nothing special. But it was the approach of the doctor that made me consider this sales meeting that I desperately wanted to leave.

The doctor did not immediately start the appointment by showing me a catalog containing various medicines and treatments available for any number of ailments. Instead he did what most doctors do at the start of an appointment . . . *he asked how I was feeling.* He asked if I had any issues since my last appointment. He inquired about my eating and exercise habits. He wanted to know if I had any concerns about my health or any symptoms I may have experienced in the last six months.

Like any good physician, my doctor did not start the appointment with an answer to my potential problems. He started it by asking exactly what my problems were. And he didn't assume I had the same medical issues as his last patient. Why? *Because every patient is different!* Every patient has different issues. Every patient has different symptoms. And based on those issues and symptoms, every patient has a different prognosis and treatment to correct it. *But there's no way a doctor can possibly recommend a treatment to any condition until he or she understands what's going on with the patient!*

Research. Question. Examine. Explore. These are the things doctors do in order to determine the best treatment for you. They don't immediately hand you a brochure when you walk into the examination room. They don't immediately talk about what they can do for your health. They don't discuss potential cures for what *might* be ailing you. They ask about your medical history. They review your historical medical records and question what your ailments are. Only then do they make recommendations and prescribe potential treatments. That's what doctors do. *And that's what the two gentlemen who were sitting across from me should have done!*

Not once did either Sales Representative ask how my company was doing. Not once did they ask what current and historical issues my company was experiencing, both internally and in the field. Not once did they inquire about the financial concerns of my budgets. Not once did they ask what apprehensions my company had in regards to supplier costs, capabilities, quality or delivery. Yet they were more than ready to hand me a brochure and inform me what their company had done for other clients without even knowing what my own issues were. They didn't conduct research on my company before their visit. They didn't examine the industry my company sells to in order to determine potential concerns, solutions, or how we could stand out from our own competition. They were ready to provide a solution before conducting sufficient research. In medical terms, *their focus was on the doctor and not the patient!*

Way too often, both *green* and *seasoned* Sales Professionals request an appointment, show up at my desk and make a sales presentation without first researching and determining what's ailing my company, my specific department, or the End-Users of the products and services I purchase. They are in full *Presentation Mode* without first completing their *Research Mode.* From the Buyer's perspective, there's no reason why any Sales Professional can't find something on the Internet, in business periodicals or on the prospect's own website to use in their presentation. As stated earlier in this book, *you will experience more business opportunities by showing an interest in the client then you will trying to get the client interested in you.*

Allow me to share with you an e-mail I recently received from a Sales Professional. Please note that I've made some edits to the content of her communication so as not to give the actual industry I'm in, nor my true competitors names, nor the Sales Rep's personal information. As you go through her e-mail, see if you can pick up on the type of research she completed before making contact with me, and what she did to entice me to set up a sales meeting.

Hello Mr. Locke,

I hope all is well. I left you a voicemail a few days ago and wanted to send you this e-mail as a means of introduction and follow up.

Adams Corporation is a global leader in machining high-precision complex components for the widget industry. We specialize in machining parts that require heat treatment, grinding, bore sizing, hard-turning, drilling and super-finishing to achieve precise tolerances for superior performance supporting customer applications.

Our focus is on producing the most difficult parts our customers design, primarily in the doohickey systems for widgets, including thingamajigs, thingamabobs and gizmos.

We know that from speaking with and providing product for competitors such as the Acme Company, Smith Systems and Johnson Incorporated, one of the biggest issues facing the widget industry today is excessive levels of contamination introduced by supplier components. Is this an issue your company is working to address? If so, we would welcome the opportunity to discuss this challenge and present documented verification of our contamination-free production.

I can only imagine how busy you are given your job title. I would greatly appreciate just ten minutes of your time to initially discuss our capabilities and improvements we've made for your competitors. Please let me know when we can speak for ten minutes to see if there is a fit between our companies.

For your review, I've attached our current equipment list that highlights our inventory of machines and quality measurement systems. I also invite you to visit our website at your convenience to learn more about Westwood; who we are and the industries we serve. We just added a new video that provides a nice overview of our company.

I look forward to speaking with you soon.

Sincerely,
Margaret Tienken
mtienken@adamsmach.web
555-927-1212

So what are your thoughts? Which sections of her e-mail reveal where she conducted her research before contacting me? Where did she review the *symptoms* and provide a potential *prognosis*? *From the Buyer's perspective, let me tell you why I had absolutely no hesitation to call her back for a meeting:*

- She completed follow up via e-mail when I didn't call her back from her initial voicemail. So she covered her bases, not knowing how I prefer to communicate.
- She concisely highlighted her company's capabilities and specializations.
- She conducted research to find out what industry my company serves and what applications we provide.
- She informed me that her company was able to handle even the most difficult product my company procures.
- Not only did she let me know that her company provides product for my direct competitors, she's actually met with them to review their industry and product concerns. Then she asked if I had the same apprehensions.
- Not only does she understand my industry concerns, she's addressed them by letting me know what her company has done to combat them.
- She let me know that she understands my position workload and only asked for a small part of my day to see if there's a potential fit between our companies.
- Finally, she allowed me to conduct research on her own company before we talk.

In short she **researched, questioned, examined and explored.** Like any good practitioner, she completed her Research Mode *before* jumping into her Presentation Mode. Her message was short and to the point. She effectively communicated her company's capabilities and her readiness to assist in my company's needs. Her e-mail wasn't pushy and it wasn't arrogant. And it flowed with a tone of support. Most important, **she engaged me!**

FROM THE BUYER'S DESK: Conduct sufficient research and show an interest in the company you're trying to conduct business with *before* you attempt to contact them.

BUYERS WHO PREFER THIS: 82%.
SALES REPS WHO DO THIS: 18%.

"The Condensed Introduction."

In my years in Purchasing I've sat through *countless* introductory meetings with Sales Professionals; meetings in which their company and product capability was presented for the first time with the hope of doing business. And except for a few instances, most of them covered the same material with the same details in the same format over the same requested time frame . . . *of 60 minutes*.

The meeting starts, we shake hands and exchange business cards. A brochure or media-based presentation is then covered by the Sales Professional either in paper form or on a laptop. Company history and key corporate information is explained, usually followed by product or service capabilities, usually followed by a list of current clients, usually followed by numerous photos of their products. The presentation ends and the Sales Professional sits back in his chair ready to answer my questions. There are even a few questions asked of me about future opportunities and potential orders.

After nearly 60 minutes the meeting ends with one of three outcomes:

1. I'm interested in the company and their products, and I have a current project for them to quote on.

2. I'm interested in the company and their products, but currently have nothing for them to quote on.

3. I'm *not* interested in the company or their products because either they're not capable of fulfilling my current needs, or they offer product that my company doesn't buy.

However, all three potential outcomes have managed to eat away an hour of my day. That's valuable time for any business professional. Of course if the meeting resulted in subsequent opportunities for my company then it was a good hour spent, though there's no way for me to know that ahead of time. But if doing business isn't the eventual outcome, then I can kiss that previous hour goodbye forever. *And that happens more often than not.*

The good news is that all three of these outcomes could have saved me and the Sales Professional valuable time if the requested *60-minute meeting* had been replaced with a proposed **Condensed Introduction**. Requesting a Condensed Introduction that only takes 10-12 minutes is preferred by Buyers because it allows them to quickly determine if the supplier can provide what they need without wasting much of their day.

One of the main reasons Buyers are reluctant to agree to a meeting with a new supplier is because it takes so much time out of their work schedule. Somehow, we've all got it in our heads that meetings *need* to be scheduled for an hour or it couldn't possibly be beneficial to either party. *Really? So who made that the law? Why are we so obsessed with 60 minutes?* As soon as the Buyer hears the words *"I'd like to schedule a meeting"* the first thing he thinks is, *"There goes an hour out of my day!"* But by offering to meet for a short but productive introduction, he no longer thinks that and will be more inclined to accept. *In fact, try to not even use the word "meeting" in your request because it automatically creates an adverse mood.*

As a Sales Professional you need to understand that it's *not* the *amount* of time you spend with the Buyer that's important. *Rather, it's the information provided during the time that's important!* A 60-minute meeting won't be beneficial if the Buyer doesn't receive the information he wants or needs to hear about your company. Here's how you could suggest a Condensed Introduction to the Buyer:

"Mr. Thornton, I can only imagine how busy your work day must be. That's why I'd like to suggest a condensed introduction that will quickly demonstrate our product line and what it can do for your company. Then at the end of the introduction we find there isn't a fit, I won't have wasted much of your time. When can we meet for a few minutes?"

Most initial sales meetings set up with Buyers run *WAY* too long. The Buyer schedules an hour meeting and it ends up being a complete waste of time. That's because part way into it, it's either clear the Sales Rep didn't do their homework or the Buyer isn't hearing anything he needs to know. But now the Buyer is stuck for the remaining 50 minutes because he committed that time to the Sales Rep. At that point, the Buyer most likely will not agree to a second meeting. However, if the Buyer had the opportunity to only commit perhaps 10 minutes of his day and found that the supplier *isn't* what he's looking for, then the meeting would end with minimal wasted time on either side.

Realistically, it doesn't matter if the initial meeting is 10 minutes or 60 – *if there's no fit, there's no fit.* But be aware that if after the introduction the Buyer decides he *is* interested in you, he may ask if you wouldn't mind extending the meeting (which you'll have to be prepared to do) or schedule another one when you both have more time.

The use of a condensed meeting isn't simply for cold-calls with prospects. It creates the perfect opportunity to keep your current clients updated on what's going on in your company that could be of interest to them. Too often, a Sales Professional will make that initial meeting with the Buyer to inform him of their products and capabilities, but never provides updates on their product line after they've received that first order. Your job as a Sales Rep is to keep in front of the Buyer with up-to-date information. And there's no better way to do that than with a condensed update meeting. Keep the Buyer updated on products and topics of interest to his company. Keep the Buyer updated on what your company has done for his in the last three months. **But get out of the habit of requesting 60 minutes every time you want to meet!** You shouldn't need more than 10-12 minutes for an update.

So think like a Buyer! If you were a Buyer, what advantages do you see for yourself with a Condensed Introduction? Why would it be beneficial that a supplier reviews and refreshes their capabilities at least once a quarter, and using only ten minutes to do it? As a Sales Professional, how can you research your own company to find out what new product information is available that would interest the Buyer?

Condensed Introductions are also valuable if you happen to be in town and don't have much time to spend with Purchasing. A few times I've had a Sales Rep call and say, *"I'm only in town for a few hours and I have some free time tomorrow. I know you're busy, but if you have just a few minutes I'd like to stop by to quickly discuss our product line and how it may be beneficial to you."* Phone calls like that usually work on me as well as the other Buyers I've shared notes with.

So the question is, how do you cover your products and everything you want to tell the Buyer about your company in 10 to 12 minutes? *Simple:* By covering the **HIGHLIGHTS** and *not* the **DETAILS** of your company. Think of it as submitting your resume. *(Sound familiar?)* Experts tell you that when applying for a job your resume should cover the highlights and NOT the details of your career. Because the purpose of a resume is to get your foot in the door with the hopes of eventually receiving an order. Initial sales meetings should be treated the same way. The purpose of a first-time sales meeting is to get your foot in the door with the hopes of eventually receiving an order. Covering the highlights of your company in a condensed time frame will quickly determine if the Buyer can use you.

Now imagine that at the end of your condensed introduction the Buyer wants to extend it because he's interested in your company and wants to go into more detail regarding your products or services. You have to be prepared in case it happens. Have all of the *detailed* information handy of what you *highlighted* in the meeting. But don't bring it out unless the meeting gets extended and the Buyer asks for it. If the Buyer wants to hear more but can't extend the meeting, then schedule another day when you both have time.

However, if at the end of your condensed introduction the Buyer says he has no need for your products, you can say this:

"Mr. Pullman, I appreciate the time you spent with me. I'm sorry we couldn't find a reason to do business at this time. Based on your experience in the industry, what could my company do to improve its opportunities in doing business with your company?"

At this point the Buyer may give you recommendations which you should write down to decide how realistic you can conform to them. Of course it's possible the Buyer won't give you any recommendations. He may end up being down-right rude or sarcastic, at which point you need to know when to stop and cut your losses. A Condensed Introduction isn't going to get your foot in the door if the Buyer is uncooperative. *No meeting will.* If the Buyer doesn't see any opportunities to do business with your company, you may need to cease and desist your pursuit for the time being so you don't ruin any future chances.

FROM THE BUYER'S DESK: Get your foot in the door and engage the Buyer by suggesting a *Condensed Introduction* to promptly provide the highlights of your company's capabilities.

BUYERS WHO PREFER THIS: 86%
SALES REPS WHO DO THIS: 5%

"The #1 Sales Meeting Mistake."

During my career in Purchasing I've sat through countless introductory sales meetings. Some were presented by 'green' Sales Reps and some by 'seasoned' Sales Professionals. Some presentations were productive and beneficial. *Most seemed to drag on forever.* Some engaged me by providing specific information I was interested in as a Buyer. Others contained nothing I could use to make a decision about the presenting company. I've also communicated with hundreds of Buyers from diverse industries for their input regarding the sales meetings they sit through. And we collectively came to the same conclusion as to what the number one sales meeting mistake is.

From the Buyer's Desk, I can tell you that the biggest mistake a Sales Professional or Business Owner can make during the all-important initial sales meeting is to give the same generic presentation to every company, every department and every individual they're presenting to. In other words, the Sales Representative creates a *one-size-fits-all* sales presentation and uses it on everyone they meet with; from Engineering, to Purchasing, to the eventual End-User of products and services. No matter what the prospect's roles, responsibilities and interests are, the same presentation providing the same product information is used over and over again. *Why would any Sales Professional want to do that?*

The reason this is the #1 mistake is because the initial sales meeting is the most important one you'll have with any given prospect. Because the outcome will make or break your chances of selling product to them. *This is your chance!* This is your *'first date'!* And if you blow the first date, good luck getting a second.

Now, imagine walking into a retail clothing store and every dress is a size 6 and every suit is a 40 regular. For some customers those selections will provide a perfect fit. But for most, the clothes will be too big or too small, too loose or too tight. But that's exactly what you're doing when you create a generic *one-size-fits-all* sales presentation. If you're using the same presentation on every company, department and individual you're hoping to sell to, it means that a portion of the information doesn't fit the wants and needs of any given individual sitting through it. Either you're providing product technical data to someone who may not be able to comprehend what you're talking about, or you're providing commercial information to someone who isn't interested. I have personally sat through countless sales meetings that not only bored me to death, but the Sales Professional did not end up receiving business from my company. And it was all due to the generic nature of their presentation. That's because those in attendance weren't hearing what they needed to know about the supplier and their capabilities based on their own role, responsibilities and interests. *A complete waste of my time and the supplier's!*

Having purchased capital equipment in the automotive industry, the majority of the sales presentations shown to me were filled with countless photos of machines, process systems and technical information. I admit some of the data went over my head. It's not that I didn't understand the basics of the equipment I was buying. It was the overboard, detailed description of every single electronic, pneumatic and hydraulic system within the machine; the inner workings of every machine component; the dozens and dozens of equipment photos . . . *PLEASE, SOMEONE JUST SHOOT ME!*

I'm NOT a mechanical engineer. I'm NOT a production supervisor. I'm NOT an eventual End-User of your products and services. **I AM A BUYER!** *Show me something a BUYER would be interested in!* What are your preferred terms and conditions? What is the 'value' of your equipment to my company? What is the financial shape of your corporation? Explain your warranty in detail. How does your project management ensure low-cost solutions and on-time deliveries? Yes, I do need to understand what you make, what your product is technically capable of and if it fits the needs of my current projects. *But don't forget to include the 'commercial' items that specific cover my role and responsibilities.*

My advice from the Buyer's desk is to develop sales presentations that are personalized to each specific company, each specific department, and even each specific person you're presenting to. Base it on the following criteria: their job title, their role in the company, the department they work for, their responsibilities, their yearly goals, their interests and needs. The next time you're starting to prepare a sales presentation for a new prospect, ask yourself the following questions:

"Who am I about to present to? What is this individual's job title? What are this individual's goals and responsibilities in their company? Therefore, what would most likely interest them in a sales presentation? And what would most likely NOT interest them?"

Because sales meetings are such a pet peeve to most Buyers, I decided to conduct an experiment while a Global Lead Buyer at DaimlerChrysler Corporation. Days before a new supplier was to present to my purchasing department, and without informing the other Buyers, I had the Sales Rep e-mail his planned presentation to me. It was formatted in *PowerPoint* and, unfortunately, contained the same old generic information every supplier gives. After reviewing it, I asked if he would allow me to work with him in redeveloping his presentation. He agreed so I provided him with the information I felt he would need to get the attention of my fellow Buyers; the information needed to engage their interest based on what they wanted and needed to hear. I had the Rep pull out non-essential information as well as numerous technical photos I didn't think would be necessary. All-in-all I ended up removing about 20 slides from his initial presentation. I also input specific data on the remaining slides based on the roles and responsibilities of my department. *Again, I never let the other Buyers know I had a major hand in creating the presentation.*

The Sales Rep subsequently held his sales meeting in front of the Buyers in my department. After its conclusion and after the Rep left the conference room, I asked my colleagues what they thought about it. One Buyer summed it up when he said word-for-word, ***"Man! That was the best sales presentation I've ever seen!"*** And do you know why he said that? Because unbeknownst to him . . . ***it was created by a Buyer!*** I removed everything our specific purchasing department didn't need to know and put in everything that we did. *But it really didn't take a Buyer to do it right, only someone seeing things from the Buyer's perspective.*

So how do you even know what the Buyer is interested in? How do you know what information would engage them or waste their time? How do you know what the Buyer really wants and needs to hear? The answer is simple: **Find out ahead of time!** A few days before your sales meeting, find out what information your prospect needs in order to make a rational business decision about your company. And the way to do this is by developing and e-mailing the prospect a ***Pre-Meeting Agenda.***

A *Pre-Meeting Agenda* is a Buyer-Endorsed prerequisite for any sales meeting. It should chronologically list the key topics you plan on presenting. It will allow you to inform the Buyer or End-User of your meeting intentions ahead of time to make certain it's what they want and need to know based on their job function.

Unfortunately, 95% of Sales Professionals don't send a Pre-Meeting Agenda before their presentation. Ninety-five percent of the Sales Reps we Buyers deal with simply walk into the meeting and start presenting without even knowing if its content is what we're interested in. So many times I've had to take control of the sales presentation only because I'm not hearing what I need to know about the supplier and their capabilities. It's embarrassing for the Sales Professional and it's not fun for me. But I'm not going to sit there and waste my time on information I don't need to know about. If I could receive a *Pre-Meeting Agenda* a few days before the presentation and be allowed to add or remove content from it, then the Sales Rep could spend more time on issues that interest me. Makes sense? *Then why is hardly anyone doing it?*

If you're presenting to a Corporate Buyer, here's a list of commercial items you could include in your Pre-Meeting Agenda as a start, some of which may or may not be applicable to your company or the prospect:

- The types of products and services you provide that are applicable to the prospect.
- A *brief* history of your company.
- The location of your main headquarters.
- Number of years the company has been in business.
- The strength of your corporate balance sheet.
- Your ability to comprehend and adhere to client specifications.
- Your industry certifications.
- Your ability to ship products globally.
- Your service and spare parts capabilities and locations.
- Your standard warranty and payment terms.
- Your capabilities in project management.
- The prospect's competitors that you currently sell to.
- Your company specialties and how they can save the client money, improve quality and improve production.
- How you are able to expedite product and service lead times.

Once you've completed your Pre-Meeting Agenda, e-mail it to the Buyer *a few days in advance* and invite any changes to it. Here's how your e-mail could look:

"Dear Ms. Dawson,

Just a quick e-mail to thank you again for the opportunity to meet with you. Attached for your review is a proposed meeting agenda covering possible topics for discussion. Please let me know if there are any items you would prefer to add or remove, as well as any specific technical or commercial information you need to know during the meeting."

If you get a response back from the Buyer with additions or removals, adjust your presentation accordingly. *There's nothing worse than asking a Sales Professional about something important I need to know during the meeting and they don't have the answer up front.* But if you knew ahead of time what I needed to know and what I might ask, you could bring the answers with you.

Of course if the meeting is only with someone from the *technical side* of the client, then you need to adjust your pre-meeting agenda and presentation accordingly. And if you'll be presenting to a *mixed crowd,* both Buyers and End-Users, then you'll need to contact each person or department and create your presentation to fit each of their interests and needs. The bottom line is to find out what the prospect wants and needs to hear BEFORE the meeting so that you're better prepared to present it.

FROM THE BUYER'S DESK: Make certain your initial sales meeting covers the things your prospect wants and needs to hear about your company. Find out what those things are *before* the meeting. Customize your presentation based on the prospect and not just your own company.

BUYERS WHO PREFER THIS: 84%
SALES REPS WHO DO THIS: 5%

"Other Sales Meeting Mistakes to Avoid."

During my time in Corporate Purchasing I've asked my colleagues to list their top **'pet peeves'** when it comes to sitting in sales meetings with Representatives and Business Owners. After all, the sales meeting is the most important function in spending time with a Buyer, especially if you currently don't do any business with their company. The sales meeting makes or breaks your future opportunities in picking up new clients and expanding your sales revenue. If the meeting is beneficial from the Buyer's perspective, you've got your foot in the door. But if the meeting doesn't meet the Buyer's expectations, *good luck getting a second chance.* So understanding what annoys Buyers and what reduces your chances of a successful meeting is incredibly important. And here they are in no particular order:

1. A major sales meeting mistake is arriving too late or too early. Before you leave for the meeting make certain you don't show up late, even if it means getting there before hand and having to sit in the visitor lobby or your own vehicle for an extended period of time before the meeting starts. Do whatever you have to do to make sure you're there on time, especially if you've never been to the Buyer's office complex before. One of the worst calls a Buyer can receive before a scheduled meeting is that the Sales Rep is stuck in traffic. *That definitely annoys Buyers!* What if the Buyer hadn't received the call and was waiting for the Sales Rep in the lobby or a scheduled conference room? The Buyer is only going to wait so long until he cancels your meeting. *Good luck getting a second one.*

Of course, most Buyers will understand if things were clearly out of your control; the plane was late, you got in an accident, etc. *But stuck in traffic is NOT an excuse, **it's poor planning.*** Too often I have Sales Professionals show up late for the meeting due to traffic which does one of two things. (1) It either pushes my whole day out, or (2) it gives the Sales Rep less time to talk with me about their company. So either my day expands or your meeting shrinks. *Neither scenario is good, though Buyers prefer the latter.*

Not only must you not be late, but don't be too early either! This especially applies if there is no lobby or buffer area to wait in. Even if you have to wait outside the Buyer's department area for a while, make sure you don't show up any more than 5-7 minutes before the Buyer is expecting you. That upsets Buyers just as much as being late. Sales Reps who show up too early and hang around the Buyers area makes for an uncomfortable time. This is especially true when the Buyer doesn't have a waiting area for the Rep. Then the Rep ends up hovering around the Buyer's desk while he's trying to get something done or is discussing confidential information with internal personnel.

2. Another meeting mistake Sales Professionals make is having too many people from their company meet with the Buyer. *Don't overpower the Buyer!* How many people are you bringing from your company for the meeting? I know you may think that the more people you bring the more impressed the Buyer will be. But the truth is, it's best not to show up with more than two company representatives if the appointment is only with one Buyer. Don't make the Buyer feel as if he's being ganged up on. Don't make the Buyer feel like he's on trial. *How would you feel if you were in a car dealership to buy a vehicle and you had three salespeople sitting across from you?* When a Sales Reps' Manager or Vice President finds out that a meeting with a specific Buyer has been arranged, they usually want to join in. *It's not a good idea if it means there will be more than two of you with one Buyer.*

It's always a good rule of thumb to ask the Buyer how many people he can accommodate for the meeting. Sometimes it's a matter of real estate as to how many people he can handle. A conference room may not be available and the Buyer won't want numerous supplier representatives crowding around his desk. So when you're setting up the meeting, ask the Buyer ahead of time how many people he can accommodate. Make sure he knows exactly who's attending the meeting, including their full name and job title. That's important information the Buyer will want to know ahead of time in case he needs to give your names to security.

3. Another mistake is failing to remove meeting distractions. Before you meet with the Buyer make sure your cell phone is either turned off or set to vibrate. Taking a call or returning a page during a meeting tells the Buyer there's someone more important than him. *And yes, it's happened to me more times than I care to remember!* If your cell phone is turned on and you ignore the ring, it will tell the Buyer you are willing to neglect a client. If you are expecting an emergency call, business or personal, inform the Buyer at the start of the meeting and ask for permission to take it if it comes in. *Think about how irritating it is when you're dealing with a sales clerk at a department store.* You're standing in line waiting for your transaction to be completed when the phone on the store counter rings and the clerk answers it right in front of you. It's annoying and unprofessional. And if your cell phone ringer is off but your vibrate is on, never pull it out during the meeting just to see who's calling. *That's as rude as answering it.*

4. The final meeting mistake verified by the Buyers I talked to is the use of a PowerPoint presentation. Starting up your laptop and opening the PowerPoint takes up valuable time. In addition, I've sat through many sales meetings in which the Sales Rep's computer either wasn't working properly or the PowerPoint wouldn't open. The Rep was without his presentation and fumbled through the meeting. Not fun for either one of us. If you're using a PowerPoint, either have it easily accessible on your computer or have a paper copy of it ready for use.

Another good reason not to use a PowerPoint on your laptop is that it's almost impossible for both the Sales Rep and the Buyer to look at the screen at the same time. Don't count on an overhead projector being available at the Buyer's facility. Even if you're planning on bringing a projector, you run the risk of eating up valuable time setting everything up, especially if you don't have access to the room prior to start time.

FROM THE BUYER'S DESK: Create a sales presentation geared towards the person you're presenting to. Arrive on time. Turn off your cell phone. Don't overpower the Buyer with too many representatives. Make your presentation easily accessible to view for the Buyer.

BUYERS WHO PREFER THIS: 79%
SALES REPS WHO DO THIS: 36%

"The Dog Ate My Homework!"

While working as a Senior Buyer at American Axle & Manufacturing in Detroit, I had a Sales Representative request a meeting to review his company's products. I happened to have a few hours open that week so we agreed on a day and time. The Rep was in his early 20's and must have been recently hired by the supplier. After introductions he started off the meeting by presenting his product brochure. He really didn't discuss it much nor how his products could benefit my company. *And less than ten minutes into the meeting he asked if I was ready to place an order with him.*

Now I don't know if this was his very first sales call or if I was the only Corporate Buyer he had ever dealt with. But I'm positive I was one of the first. *Regardless, you're probably grinning right about now.* I asked the Sales Rep if he knew what products my company manufactured. He shrugged his shoulders and replied, *"Axles."* I then asked him if he knew what *other* products my company produced. *He didn't know.*

I asked him if he knew where my company's manufacturing facilities were located. He pointed out the window at the plant across the street. I asked, *"What about my other facilities?" He didn't know.* I asked him which products featured in his brochure would provide the best value to my company based on the current business environment. *He didn't know.* I asked him what manufacturing and quality processes at his company could help provide technological success for mine. *He didn't know.* I then asked him to describe what steps his project management team took to guarantee best value, responsiveness to issues and on-time deliveries. You guessed it, *he didn't know.* At that point during the meeting I was honestly waiting for this Rep to simply admit, *"The dog ate my homework!"*

I leaned back in my chair and said, *"In that case, I'm going to do you the biggest favor of your career."* He immediately straightened up, took out his pen and prepared to write down a tremendous order. I said to him, *"I'm going to kick you out of my office. I'm going to ask you to leave the building and go back to your own company. And when you get there I want you to complete some research on my company and yours. Find out what products we make. Find out where our plants are located. Find out what the industry's direction is and how your products can support that direction. Find out what processes are within your company to ensure best value, best quality and on-time deliveries. Then give me a call back in two weeks to set up another appointment that will benefit us both."*

Now, please know that I didn't mean to be contemptuous. I didn't mean to sound funny or cruel. I thought the best way I could help this poor guy was to have him complete what he should have done before he made the appointment . . . **HIS HOMEWORK!** *I even offered him the opportunity to come back and start over again.* But instead of being embarrassed or apologetic for not being prepared and wasting both of our times, he stood up and shook my hand without saying much of anything. Then he walked out to the lobby and left the building. **And I never heard from him again!** He never called to make another appointment. He never e-mailed thanking me for the advice. It was as if he walked off the face of the planet. *I'm assuming he probably walked off the face of a sales career anyway.*

What took place is a true example of not being prepared for the sales call. And I'm certain that most Sales Professionals believe they are well equipped to meet with the Buyer. But from my side of the desk, from my experiences, suppliers do not conduct *enough* research on the prospects and their industry in general. Nor do they provide essential information about their own company's products, organization and capabilities that will prove advantageous to mine. *Again I'm not trying to come across as a whiner.* I'm only trying to provide some constructive feedback and advice on how to improve opportunities. **And this is an area that needs a lot of improvement!** In our private lives before we purchase a major item, we usually conduct research to determine the best product at the best value that best fits our needs. *In short, we do our homework.* So if we conduct homework on OUR end to BUY something, why doesn't the average Sales Professional conduct homework on THEIR end to SELL something?

In years gone by it was understandable why Sales Professionals may not have had the capability to conduct research before attempting the sale; *there was no Internet.* Today it's nearly impossible *not* to find some bit of information about the industry or the prospect. There are industry indicator reports, economic trends, manufacturing outlooks, pricing statistics and other types of electronic data available at the push of a button. And most prospects have their own website that provides beneficial information regarding the following: company history, business units, corporate vision, social media, facts and figures, products and technology, global business locations, research and development, integrity code, sales reports, presentations, industry news, press releases, case studies and contact information. The main purpose of a corporate website is to provide information in order to interest potential clients. *But as a Sales Professional you can use that same information to your advantage to develop your own sales strategies!* This goes back to a familiar theme that runs throughout this book: **Stop focusing only on *YOUR* company and start focusing on *MINE!***

Rarely do Sales Professionals bring up anything about my company to me. Based on the feedback from the other Buyers I've communicated with, only 12% of the Reps they deal with are prepared to discuss the Buyer's company as well as their own. Personally I find it to be more like 5%. *Isn't that sad?* Conducting research and being informed about your prospect will go a long way in impressing the Buyer. How many times have I said this statement already: *You will develop more business relationships in two months by showing interest in the client, than you will in two years trying to get the client interested in you.* And yet, so many Sales Professionals spend most of their time trying to get the Buyer interested in their company. **NEWS FLASH:** Buyers really aren't that interested in you or your company. The reality is, most are only interested in themselves and in what you can do for them.

Sales Advice From the Buyer's Desk: During your next interdepartmental team meeting, try to find and/or share Internet sites that would benefit the entire team. Have every Sales Rep come up with a couple of Internet sites a month that could be used to develop strategies and educate the client. Research your prospect's own website for valuable information to share with the team. Use that information to sell product that will help the client realize their corporate vision, their global presence, their research and development, and their cost savings strategies. The bottom line: *Don't let the dog eat your homework!*

FROM THE BUYER'S DESK: Conduct sufficient and applicable research before your sales meeting and show an interest in the prospect.

BUYERS WHO PREFER THIS: 82%
SALES REPS WHO DO THIS: 12%

"10 Questions to Ask the Buyer."

Okay, we've already established that Corporate Buyers are the 'Dark Side' of the sales process. At least, that's the inherent perception of some Sales Professionals. It's understandable how these perceptions could be created, and in some instances it may be true.

The point I'm trying to make here is that a portion of Sales Professionals are fearful of asking the Buyer anything that could potentially upset their business relationship. And again, that's understandable. But there are a few questions you could 'prudently' ask the Buyer that few, if any, Sales Professionals do. These are questions that the Buyer should be willing and able to answer without making waves. *If I was a Sales Professional, this is what I would ask:*

1. Ask the Buyer if there are any new projects on the horizon that you can quote on or at least provide a 'budgetary' quote for. This should be Sales 101, but it's *amazing* how many Sales Reps fail to do this. Most only ask that question during the initial sales meeting. Then they assume the Buyer will simply contact them if anything comes up. *Really? So you're relying on the Buyer to contact you about opportunities?* Sorry, but that's not the Buyer's responsibility, even if they tell you they will. So when you hear nothing from the Buyer you assume there's nothing new to quote on. Big mistake. Ask at least once a quarter if anything is coming up. If the Buyer knows of an opportunity they may be willing to share it. If they tell you they're not aware of anything to quote on they may be withholding information they prefer not to disclose at that point. *Or they have some hidden agenda and, for whatever reason, prefer not to include your company.*

2. Ask the Buyer about the roles, responsibilities and yearly goals of purchasing. Be careful not to ask the Buyer what *their* specific ones are, but ask the question in a general sense, *"I can only imagine how challenging your job must be. So what are the roles and responsibilities of a typical Buyer? What yearly goals do they generally have that companies like mine can assist in?"* Brown-nose a little. In asking about purchasing in a 'general' sense, they'll most likely respond in a more 'personal' sense. Finding out this information will help in developing your sales strategies.

3. Ask the Buyer to clarify their supplier selection process. That way you'll know who is involved in deciding which suppliers get asked to quote, and who you should be contacting that you may not already be in front of. *"Are you able to discuss the supplier selection process in a general sense? I can imagine there must be several departments involved."*

4. Ask the Buyer what internal or external forces could influence the supplier-selection process. Understand what and who you're up against in securing the order. *"Other than competition, what internal criteria could determine who is selected to receive a purchase order?"*

5. Ask the Buyer for their 'own' definition of a 'preferred-supplier'. It may be totally different from the Buyer sitting next to him. *"I'm sure dealing with suppliers all day long can be demanding. With your experience, what preferences do you have regarding the supply base? What do you specifically expect from suppliers and Sales Reps?"*

6. Ask the Buyer what direction he thinks the industry is taking in regards to technology, quality and cost savings. Again, ask in a general sense about the industry and the Buyer will most likely respond with a more personal reply. This way you'll find out what's important to his company and what the Buyer needs so you can help provide a solution.

7. Ask the Buyer about their corporate-mandated programs that suppliers should be involved in. They could be cost-savings, minority-sourcing, or some other client-mandated expectation. Show the Buyer, with both words and actions, that you intend to comply with those programs.

8. Ask the Buyer for a copy of their corporate supplier ethics code. Asking for a copy will show the Buyer you're interested in complying with their corporate principles. I would personally be impressed if a

Sales Professional asked me for a copy of it. *But in my years in Purchasing no one ever has!* Circulate a copy of your client's ethics code within your organization and live by them.

9. Ask the Buyer when THEY prefer you call them back for future opportunities. There is a fine line between calling the Buyer too much and not enough. It's obviously important to maintain contact. *The question is, when and how often?* This presents a definite dilemma for the Sales Professional: excessive follow up and upset the Buyer, or not enough follow up and lose a potential sale. Buyers would prefer to control the continuous in-coming calls from the Sales Representative, mostly because of the numerous suppliers calling on any given day. That's why it's best for you to simply say, " *I know you're busy and I know there's probably a fine line between keeping in touch and being a pest. So I'd like to ask, when would YOU recommend I call back?* " Let the Buyer make the decision. Let the Buyer set the parameters. That way when you do make contact again, you can remind the Buyer that you're calling per **his** recommendation. Remember, every Buyer has different preferences when it comes to their own time. And don't forget to ask if they prefer to communicate via e-mails, telephone calls, or a mix of both. Every Buyer is different.

10. Ask the Buyer what he suggests you do if you are having difficulty getting a response from the End-User or anyone else in their company. Maybe there's some important information you need, but no one is responding and it will affect your timing, thereby affecting their project. Hopefully the Buyer will recommend you call *him*. But if not, at least he can provide some feedback and point you in the right direction.

Again, these may all seem like elementary questions to ask. But they are important in conducting business with Corporate Purchasing. Surprisingly enough, *almost no one asks!*

FROM THE BUYER'S DESK: Ask the Buyer questions to gain insight and to show consideration.

BUYERS WHO PREFER THIS: 76%
SALES REPS WHO DO THIS: 9%

"12 Things You Need to Let the Buyer Know & 12 Questions You Need to Answer."

There are times to ask the Buyer questions and there are times to *educate* them. We Buyers may seem confident and sure of ourselves. But deep down we're as insecure as the next person. Given the fact that Purchasing is the most important department in any company when it comes to the 'control' of costs, Buyers are under tremendous pressure to protect their company both legally and financially. They're under pressure to keep costs down. They're under pressure to ensure product is delivered on time in order to support their own client base. And they're under pressure to resolve commercial issues.

From my side of the desk I can tell you that letting a Buyer know a few things up front will not only relieve some of that pressure, *it will also improve your sales opportunities.* So here in no particular order are some of the things you need to let the Buyer know; *things I would inform a Buyer if I was in Sales*:

1. Let the Buyer know you understand how busy they are and that you appreciate their time. Let him know this during telephone calls, e-mails and in meetings.

2. Let the Buyer know you understand it's not always easy to select the appropriate supplier. Be considerate and show tolerance if you lose the purchase order.

3. Let the Buyer know you understand how important trust is in a business relationship. Let him know you intend to do your best to uphold that trust in both words and actions.

4. Let the Buyer know that you're aware of his company's current news and events. Show an interest in the client. Bring up something specific that interested you about his company.

5. Let the Buyer know that like most of your competitors, you can provide the necessary *tangibles* of a product. You can provide the 'physical' attributes that he can buy from a number of your competitors. Then tell him about the *intangibles* your company can provide that others can't. (See the Section titled, *"Sell Me on the Intangibles!"*, pg. 136.)

6. Let the Buyer know of any new direction your company is taking in regards to technology, quality and cost reduction. Keep him updated!

7. Let the Buyer know about your company's ability to quote per their specifications and requirements. Make the Buyers aware of your comprehension of their company's unique qualifications.

8. Let the Buyer know the technical and commercial differences between his company's specifications and yours. Show how you can provide cost savings without reducing quality, product capability or lead time.

9. Let the Buyer know you understand the importance of taking care of problems, whether they're your company's fault or not. Be proactive!

10. Let the Buyer know who to contact at your company in case of specific emergencies. Provide a document that contains the names, titles, phone numbers and e-mail addresses of key personnel within your organization.

11. Let the Buyer know you will not *disappear* if the purchase order is awarded to your company. Let him know you will respond to e-mail and voicemail requests within a reasonable amount of time.

12. Let the Buyer know you will contact him as soon as possible in regards to major warranty and service issues associated with your products. Again, be proactive and take responsibility!

Just as there are 12 things you need to let the Buyer know, there are also 12 things you need to be prepared to answer, especially during the initial sales meeting. Be prepared if the Buyer asks you the following:

1. *"For what programs has your company already sold product to my company?"*

2. *"How can your company provide cost-savings against my company's program budgets? What specifications and requirements on my side are creating needless expense?*

3. *"What is your exact warranty coverage and time frame? How does it cover parts and labor? And what actions, or lack thereof, on my company's part would void the warranty?"*

4. *"What is your product delivery lead time and global shipping capabilities?"*

5. *"Do you have an understanding of my company's technical and commercial requirements? How do you ensure they'll be followed?"*

6. *"Have you completed product downtime and cycle-time studies on your products?"*

7. *"What are your installation, integration and qualification support capabilities at my end-user facilities?"*

8. *"What are your spare parts availability and lead times?"*

9. *"Explain the process of program management at your company. How will it ensure best value, quality and on-time deliveries."*

10. *"Explain how you respond to product and service issues at my end-user's facilities."*

11. *"What are your sales representation capabilities and limitations? Are you just an order taker or are you able to answer technical questions and negotiate price without management approval?"*

12. *"There are a lot of companies I currently deal with that provide the same products and services as you. As I'm actually looking to shrink my supply base, why should I consider you?"*

From the Buyer's perspective, you'd be surprised how many Sales Professionals, both 'green' and 'seasoned', cannot answer these questions without having to go back to their own company to conduct research. **Having the answer up front will impress the Buyer because most Sales Professionals don't.**

FROM THE BUYER'S DESK: Educate the Buyer on your company's internal capabilities and be prepared to respond to the tough questions.

BUYERS WHO PREFER THIS: 82%
SALES REPS WHO DO THIS: 27%

"The Hidden Power of Business Cards."

As a Corporate Buyer dealing with dozens of Sales Professionals at any given moment, you would think that my biggest pet peeve would be poor communication, incomplete quotes or being unresponsive. But surprisingly enough, one of my biggest pet peeves as a Buyer has to do with a 3" x 2" piece of cardstock called a *business card*. I have nothing personal against business cards. In fact I highly recommend their continued use. My pet peeve is that the majority of business cards given to me are not *'user-friendly'*. But you'd never know that much less care unless you had spent time sitting behind the Buyer's Desk.

The fact is, for being such a small piece of cardstock, a business card embodies more power than most Sales Professionals even realize! And yet most people treat it simply as a basic means of introduction. *"Here's my card. Call me if you have any questions."* From the Buyer's perspective, business cards are an important and necessary conduit to you and your company. **The quicker you realize that, the quicker your opportunities will improve.**

To reiterate, the vast majority of business cards are not user-friendly, not client-friendly, not Buyer-friendly. *And here's why:* Take a look at the front of your business card. **In fact, hand it to a complete stranger!** Are they able to determine what your company does? From looking at your card, can they tell what generic products and services you offer? Can they tell what industry you're in? If the answer is "no" to any of these questions, then it's time to redesign your business card.

What type of information is actually on your card? Well, most likely your name, your job title, your company name, company address, e-mail address and telephone number. *Wait a minute! What telephone number?* Is that your 'direct' number on the card? That's great, but don't forget to also include your company's 'main telephone number'.

There will be times I'll need to call someone at your company other than you; i.e. the service manager, accounts receivable, etc. But how can I do that if your direct number is the *only one* on the card? So now I either have to call you to get connected, or I have to look up the number on the Internet (time consuming), or I have to call your number and dial zero for the operator if you're not there. *That's annoying!* Make sure your main company telephone number is on your card, even if you have to write it down by hand.

Now, turn your card around and take a look at the back of it. What do you see? Most likely . . . NOTHING. The back of most supplier business cards are blank. That's too bad. Because the back of your business card is PRIME REAL ESTATE for important information the Corporate Buyer needs to know and use as a reference. *What kind of information?* How about your generic products and services?

You may ask, *"Why would I need to put my products on the back of my business card? The Buyer knows me! He knows my company. He knows exactly what products and services I can offer."* Really? You need to remember that most Buyers deal with *dozens* if not *hundreds* of suppliers at any given time. Buyers may have literally *thousands* of business cards in their possession. When a Buyer picks up your card he may have a hard time remembering exactly what type of products you sell, no matter how often the Buyer deals with you. *Don't count on the Buyer having a good memory when it comes to your career and income!*

It may shock you to know that Buyer's don't always remember your name, the company you work for or the products you provide. Unless I see you on a daily basis it's simply not possible to remember every single supplier I've ever dealt with. *Why?* **Because I deal with so many!** There are some Buyers who have fantastic memories, and there are some who can't remember anything. *Most fall somewhere in the middle.* I'm one of those Buyers. And I can't tell you how many times I've run into Sales Reps in the office or at a business function and I can't remember their name, who they work for, or exactly what they provide. *But putting your products and services on the back of the business card will help.* And don't forget, I won't always be the one buying from you. At some point another Buyer will take over and I'll hand them your business card. Now THEY have no clue who you are or what products and services you provide.

You might think, *"But wait a minute, what about that expensive color brochure I gave you? That has my products and services on it. And besides, printing on the back of my business card will cost extra money.* Though it's true it's more expensive to print on both sides of a business card, think about the money you're spending on those nice corporate brochures. ***Would you like to know what happens to them?*** I'm really not supposed to be telling you this, but the vast majority of those nice brochures you give Buyers usually end up either in the trash or in their filing cabinet never to be seen again. I don't have ANY brochures at my desk. I've thrown them all out. Why? Because I just don't have the room to keep them at my desk or in my cabinets. Besides I rarely use them as reference material. Most Buyers don't. I know because I've asked them. (See the next Section.) But Buyers ALWAYS keep business cards within reach, either in their drawer or right on top of their desk. And if they knew your products and services were on it, think about how much it could improve your chances of quoting. Even if the Buyer files your contact information electronically on their computer, *remember that they get that information off your business card!*

It's important to understand that your business card is the Buyer's main link to you so make sure it's updated. If you get a new card containing new contact or product information, make sure the Buyer gets one immediately and ask for the old one back. If you have a new phone number or e-mail address, don't call the Buyer or e-mail him with the new information. It simply isn't going to get updated. Mail him a new card or bring it in person and make sure the old card is thrown out. *This also gives you another opportunity to get in front of him.*

One last thought about business cards. Wherever you're having your cards printed, make sure the lettering is readable and at least text size 10. The vast majority of Sales Professional's business cards contain text so damn small it's almost impossible to read! *It's almost as if suppliers have a contest to see who can come up with the smallest text size.* Most cards have a lot of empty space on the front. *Use it up!* Increase the size of the text. And if the font color is too light against the cardstock background, it makes it even harder to read. If your card is white, use black ink for the text, not a light gray.

I know some companies and business card designers like to create fashionable, contemporary cards. *But if it's not informative or legible, what's the point?* Stop worrying about the design of your card and how pretty it looks. Focus instead on how Buyer-friendly it is!

FROM THE BUYER'S DESK: Don't make it difficult for clients to read your business card or remember what you have to offer. It could mean the difference between receiving an invitation to quote and not!

BUYERS WHO PREFER THIS: 79%
SALES REPS WHO DO THIS: 22%

"The Buyer-Preferred Commercial Brochure."

In a typical month I have numerous meetings with Sales Professionals who offer their company brochures and laptop presentations to show what they can do for me. ***Rarely does a Sales Rep ask what I actually need!*** Sometimes I have meetings with suppliers who don't understand why they rarely, if at all, receive a purchase order. They spend all of their time and energy criticizing the Purchasing process instead of focusing on correcting previous mistakes and improving their opportunities.

In either case I usually sit in my chair looking at the Sales Rep, thinking to myself, *"If I was in Sales, I know what I would do to get a potential customer's attention and increase future business."* I've said this before but if Sales Professionals could sit behind my desk for a week, they would come to understand that *Sales 101* is not as common as one would think. The fact is, relatively few Sales Professionals are actually doing the things that Buyer's *prefer*. And one of them has to do with those nice corporate brochures you hand out.

If your company insists you hand a brochure to the Buyer, you will want to reconsider the type and size of brochure to use. In reality, Buyers would prefer to receive a **ONE-PAGE COMMERCIAL BROCHURE**. That is, a brochure that doesn't *necessarily* focus on the *technical* side of your company but more on the *commercial* side, and summarized on one page.

You may ask, *"What about that expensive brochure I just gave you that covers all of our technical capabilities?"* Again, would you really like to know what happens to them? As stated in the previous Section, the vast majority of the corporate brochures you hand out to Buyers usually end up in the trash or in a filing cabinet never to be seen again. *Why?* Because most Buyers simply do not have the room to keep everyone's brochure in cabinets or in their general area. Buyer's rarely use them for reference material anyway. Oh, they may glance at them during the initial sales meeting and seem interested. But most Corporate Buyer's will never look at them again. *I know because I've asked them!* However, most Buyers would consider keeping your corporate brochure within reach if it focused on what they want and need to know about your company based on their own roles and responsibilities.

One of the problems with a typical supplier's brochure is that there's too much information and data to read. Buyers don't have the time much less the interest. Keep the information you provide short, to the point and on one page or one double-sided page if possible.

The main problem is that most supplier brochures contain too much *'technical'* information and not enough *'commercial'* content. Again, most brochures are geared towards engineering, manufacturing and the End-User of products and services. That's fine as long as the information is intended for them. *But remember that we Buyers are mainly responsible for the commercial side of the business; prices, warranty, lead times, terms and conditions, delivery or shipping terms, payment terms.*

Yes, it is true that some Buyers appreciate and may request some type of technical enlightenment. *It's your job to find out what they prefer.* In fact, have a one-page technical brochure *and* a one-page commercial brochure created and available and ask which one they prefer. *From the Buyer's Desk,* I'd recommend developing a single-page, double-sided brochure with the technical information highlighted on one side, and the commercial information highlighted on the other. Then your bases are covered no matter who you present it to.

THINK LIKE A BUYER. If you were a Buyer, why would you prefer a one-page commercial brochure outlining and associated with your responsibilities? And as a Sales Professional, what could you do to compel your company to create one?

At the very least, here's what your One-Page Commercial Brochure could contain, some of which may or may not be applicable to your company: Company name, address and contact information. Primary products and services. Parent company information (if any). Locations of manufacturing, sales and service. List of current clients. Standard product and service warranties. Maintenance and training capabilities. Preferred payment terms. Product delivery capabilities, company financial strength, quality certifications.

Once your Commercial Brochure has been completed, hand it to the Buyer and say:

"I'm sure you receive hundreds of technical brochures from suppliers. But as a Buyer, I thought you'd like one that's geared more towards your specific responsibilities. So we had one created especially for you."

THAT will get the Buyer's attention because now you're thinking in his best interest! And by the way, all of these items on the Commercial Brochure I've given as an example should be some of the same items you cover in your pre-meeting agenda and sales meeting with the Buyer! (See the Section titled, *"The #1 Sales Meeting Mistake"*, pg. 111)

THESE are the things Buyers WANT and NEED to hear from you. Technical and product capability information is good and should be available to discuss if requested. And I'm not saying that product capabilities should be completely void of discussion or representation for the Buyer. But the next time you're starting to prepare a sales presentation or design a company brochure, ask yourself the following questions:

"Who am I about to present to? What is this person's job title? What are this person's goals and responsibilities in the company? Therefore, what would most likely interest them in a sales presentation and corporate brochure?"

FROM THE BUYER'S DESK: Provide the Buyer with a Commercial Brochure to cover the items he wants and needs to hear about your company.

BUYERS WHO PREFER THIS: 85%
SALES REPS WHO DO THIS: 6%

By the way, creating and maintaining a Commercial Brochure also gives you a perfect and legitimate reason to get in front of the Buyer and update him about your current capabilities. On the next page is an example of what your Commercial Brochure could look like.

ACME PRODUCTS COMPANY
678 Baker Street, Anytown, USA
Main telephone: 555-123-7654
Website www.AcmeProdCo.web

ACME Products Company is a privately-owned manufacturer of widgets supporting the business environment. ACME specializes in quality widgets, expedited lead times and competitive costs to their clients. ACME focuses on proficient program management, prompt warranty service and expert training programs.

Main Headquarters: Anytown, Michigan, with sales offices located in Greenville, Indiana and Lakeview, Ohio.

Generic Products and Services: Widgets, doohickeys, thingamajigs, on-site installation and qualification services, maintenance programs.

Financial Capabilities: ACME typically receives orders ranging between $10,000 and $75,000. We have a strong financial balance sheet and up to $100,000 in loan guarantees from Anyplace Bank.

Client Specifications: ACME is thoroughly familiar with and compliant to industry specifications, including but not limited to mechanical, controls, safety, ergonomic and commercial.

Shipping and Delivery: ACME has global shipping capabilities and is able to manage the delivery of product, including but not limited to insurance, shipping fees, taxes, duty and import fees.

Service and Spare Parts: ACME offers full service and spare parts capabilities for warranty and non-warranty coverage, including a 24-hour hotline for emergencies. ACME understands the importance of quality and professionalism of on-site service to its clients and strives to maintain its focus on first-class customer service.

Standard Warranty: ACME's standard warranty is as follows: All parts and labor shall be guaranteed for a period of one (1) year and shall start on the date the client begins use of the product. ACME also offers extended warranty programs upon request.

Standard Payment Terms: Net 30. Specific cost reductions are available for progressive payment terms.

Program Management: ACME understands that proficient technical capabilities can be purchased from a number of our competitors. What makes us stand out is our program management and their competence in communication, timing, scheduling and project organization. Together they ensure on-time deliveries of qualified, best-value product.

"Sell Me On the Intangibles!"

A friend of mine whom I'll call Rick works for a home construction company managing the sales and designs of homes for potential clients. Some time ago, Rick mentioned that one of my co-workers, whom I'll call George, was interested in having a house built. Rick's construction company was one of two builders George was considering. As a favor I asked George which company he was leaning towards and he replied that it was Rick's competitor. When I asked why, George said, *"It's my perception that the other company is a better builder. Rick's price is lower, but I'm willing to pay a higher price for better quality."*

Now I don't know if George did research on his own or if he simply heard that the other company was better. Regardless of the reasoning, it was still George's perception that Rick's competitor provided a better value and was willing to pay for it.

So I told Rick that since price wasn't the issue, he should attempt to convince George to select his company by educating him on his company's *'intangibles'*. Rick asked, *"What do you mean intangibles?"* I answered him by asking, *"Did you ever explain to George how your company actually manages the build? The process by which you select quality products and materials? How you work closely with your clients every step of the design and build process to ensure they're getting what they asked for? How the house is put together using the latest benchmark manufacturing processes? How the house is designed to ensure energy efficiency and the lowest possible utility bills? How the construction is warranted and, if something does go wrong, you'll be responsive in resolving the issue?"*

It turns out that Rick never discussed these intangible topics with George. He only discussed layouts, options and pricing. In other words, he only discussed the **'tangible'** items, the **'physical'** things, the things that George could put his hands on, never knowing what it took internally within Rick's company to make that house a reality.

Think about sales in your own private life. When considering the purchase of an automobile there are so many products and options to choose from. And in most cases you either already have a vehicle in mind, or self-education compels you to change direction and buy something different than originally planned. Research is conducted and you make your final selection based on the manufacturers quality, out-the-door price, available options, warranty, service, technical capabilities and other factors. You also make your decision based on your experience with the show room personnel, especially the sales team.

Many dealerships have lost business, NOT due to the products they offer but due to the sales staff. My personal best experience in buying a vehicle was one in which the Salesperson asked what my needs were, took time to show me the options and advantages of the dealership's products, and explained how everything worked in the vehicle. He introduced me to the sales and service manager, and gave me a tour of the service department. He also informed me of their customer policies and how their staff responded to service, quality and warranty issues. *Guess where I bought my vehicle from?* The dealership Salesperson had conducted research on his own company's capabilities as well as my own desires and combined the two into a successful sale. *Most important, he sold me not only on the 'tangibles' of the vehicle, but the 'intangibles' within his dealership.*

One of the statements and questions I ask Sales Professionals during a meeting, and even over the phone during a cold-call, is one that most aren't prepared to respond to:

"I already deal with a dozen suppliers who can provide your products and services. And every one of them tells me they can supply me with good products at good prices. So why should I consider you?"

At that point, most Sales Reps either give me a deer in the headlights look or a verbal response regarding 'technical' capabilities. **What you need to understand is that as a Buyer, I can purchase technical capabilities from a number of suppliers.** A technical capability is a **TANGIBLE** item that I can buy. But what I cannot buy is the organization: The discipline, the sophistication, the corporate culture necessary to make that technical capability work seamlessly in the field. The reason I can't buy them is because they are **INTANGIBLES!** *Does that make sense?* You can't quantify or measure an intangible. You can't put your hands on corporate culture. You can't physically feel the inner workings of a successful project management team. These are *intangible* things that exist within your own company to ensure the product is what the client asked for, that it works the way the client expected, that it's delivered on time and is properly serviced in the field. ***Educate and sell to the Buyer on your company's 'intangibles' so they feel confident in buying your 'tangibles'.***

Not too long ago, a supplier's technical and tangible capabilities *alone* would have been the yardstick by which a Buyer measured and selected suppliers. But today, technical capabilities are almost a given. Today, technical capabilities count for LESS because other factors have grown in significance. In fact, from the Buyer's perspective, technical capabilities alone say less about you as a supplier than ever before. WHY? *Because just like in your own private life, a Buyer assumes the product will work!* That's what he's paying for. You don't go out and buy a flat screen television with the hopes it will work when you plug it in. You ASSUME and EXPECT it to work because that's what you paid for. ***It's the same on my side of the desk.*** As a Corporate Buyer I don't hand a purchase order to a supplier and say, *"Gee, it sure would be a plus if the product I'm paying for actually works in the field!"* It's expected to work. That's because global competition, industry quality measures and improved manufacturing processes have greatly enhanced the products we buy compared to years ago. These same improvements have also enhanced our expectations that the product will actually work.

The bottom line is that it's not the ***tangibles*** alone that will necessarily sell your products today. You need to educate me on the ***intangibles*** as well; how you ensure on-time deliveries, how you warrant sufficient technical support, how you provide capable program management, how you safeguard professional communication, how you define teamwork, how you ensure low-cost solutions, how you respond to issues, and how you guarantee price containment.

FROM THE BUYER'S DESK: Educate and sell the Buyer on the unseen *intangible* advantages within your company; ensure they feel comfortable awarding orders to you for the *tangibles*.

BUYERS WHO PREFER THIS: 84%
SALES REPS WHO DO THIS: 9%

"Concluding the Sales Meeting."

After years and years of holding meetings with Sales Professionals, I've noticed a few awkward things they do during and after the meeting that deserve mentioning. I'm absolutely certain that the specific Sales Reps I met with meant no harm. But unless you spend time sitting behind my desk you may not realize the potential implications of seemingly harmless actions.

After your meeting has concluded with the Buyer, if you don't have an appointment with anyone else, **leave the building!** Don't bother the other Buyers. Most Sales Reps want to stop and say hello to the other Buyer's they've done business with. Their hope is to get some face time while they're there. But if you see that the Buyer is on the telephone, eating lunch, working on his computer, conversing with a colleague, in a meeting with other Sales Reps or simply looks busy, **don't bother him!** You cannot believe how many times I've had Sales Reps leave a meeting with one of my colleagues, walk by my area, tap on my desk and say, *"I just wanted to say hi."* It didn't matter that I was in the middle of my own meeting. It didn't matter that I was on the phone. It didn't matter that I was in the middle of crunching numbers. They just HAD to interrupt me so they could say, *"I just wanted to say hi."*

Can you imagine every supplier who walks past a Buyer's desk on any given day, stopping just for a minute to say hello? Remember, you're not the only supplier the Buyer deals with. *Bothering the Buyer to make sure he sees you is not going to help you get an order.* **Showing up when the Buyer *does* need you will!** If every supplier who walked by my desk stopped me from what I was doing just to say *"Hello"*, I would never get my work done. Have you ever been trying to accomplish something at home or in the office but people keep interrupting you and you can't focus on what you're doing? *Aggravating, isn't it?* Well it's the same for Corporate Buyers.

Now if a Buyer ever says to you, *"Hey, I saw you in the office last week. Why didn't you stop and say hello?"* You can say to him, *"I saw you were busy, I know your time is valuable and I didn't want to interrupt you."* THAT response will score you more points than, *"I just wanted to say hi."*

Another mistake Sales Professionals make before the meeting is to hang around a Buyer's desk unattended. Whether you're coming in for a meeting or just leaving, never do anything that could be perceived as snooping around a Buyer's cubicle or office area. *Never wait for him right at his desk if he's not there.* The Buyer may have information open on his desk or computer screen that's considered confidential. This includes your competitor's quotes, commercial assessments and restricted information. So never sit down if the Buyer isn't there yet or attempt to read anything on his desk. I've even known Sales Reps who actually sat down on the Buyer's own chair to write him a note, or walk around their desk to leave their card on the Buyer's keyboard. **Unbelievable!** Hanging around an unattended desk looks suspicious to other Buyers and will get reported. Buyers look out for each other and watch for anything suspicious. *The best thing to do is to stay clear of the Buyer's cubicle or office in a neutral area until the Buyer shows up.*

The last bit of feedback regarding the conclusion of a sales meeting is knowing when to conduct follow up communication with the Buyer. *As stated earlier in the book, there is a fine line between calling the Buyer too much and not enough.* It's obviously important to maintain contact after the sales meeting. The question is when and how often? This presents a definite dilemma for the Sales Professional: Excessive follow up and upset the Buyer, or not enough follow up and lose a potential sale. We've covered this before but it's worth repeating. Corporate Buyers would prefer to control the continuous in-coming communications from Sales Reps. That's why it's best for the Rep to simply say to the Buyer, *"Mr. Coburn, I know you're busy and I know there's probably a fine line between keeping in touch and being a pest. So I'd like to ask, when would you recommend I call back?"*

FROM THE BUYER'S DESK: While conducting business in the Purchasing Department, don't do anything that could be perceived as unethical, suspicious or distracting.

BUYERS WHO PREFER THIS: 92%
SALES REPS WHO DO THIS: Unclear. Buyers are only aware of those who disturb them and are obviously unaware of those who were in the office but didn't disturb them.

"Stop By and See Me Sometime."

Many times in my career, I and various End-Users in my company have received invitations to visit a supplier's facility. *"If you're ever in the area, please be sure to stop by."* Obviously the supplier is thinking, *"If I can only get them to my facility and give them a tour they'll be more inclined to source business to us."* Unfortunately, taking a tour does not necessarily result in a purchase order. From the Buyer's perspective, taking a plant tour means, *"Okay, so you've proven your facility exists. Thanks for the sales pitch. But I still don't know if your products will work in the field. I still don't know what type of sales representation I can expect. I still don't know if your project management can get me the product on time."* However, I was part of an event that not only *compelled* me to visit a supplier's facility, *I never felt I was part of an actual 'sales pitch'.*

During my time as a Global Lead Buyer at DaimlerChrysler Corporation, one of the Tier-1 suppliers offered our Purchasing, Quality and Engineering groups an opportunity to attend various classes and informative sessions at one of their facilities. The idea was to provide expert training and educational classes on various functions and topics important to our industry. Topics included ISO Quality, Lean Manufacturing, Precision Machining, Finance and other areas of interest. *Each topic just happened to fit a core objective within our industry.*

The supplier had selected specific *experts* working internally for their own company as well as outside sources. The credentials of each expert was provided to ensure we knew that the information presented was direct from seasoned professionals in their field. Classes were held between one and four hour intervals with breaks intermixed. The breaks included refreshments and a lunch was provided mid-day. At the end of the event, educational brochures and data pamphlets were handed out.

The classes were proficiently structured and allowed for interaction with the attendees. Employees from various client companies, including DaimlerChrysler, were invited to attend and it gave us a chance to network with individuals in our own discipline working for other businesses.

What the Tier-1 supplier was able to successfully achieve in a practical yet professional way was the following:

- Host an event that attracted various departmental personnel from both current clients and future prospects.
- Compel clients and prospects to visit their facility and participate in a tour of the manufacturing and administrative areas.
- Allow the attendees to learn from veteran experts for free, thereby improving their knowledge of specific industry requirements and answers to specific industry concerns.
- Provide the attendees with educational handouts to both inform and use as a marketing tool.
- Implant in the brain of the attendees their company's recognition as an industry leader.
- Show the clients and prospects what they were technically and commercially capable of.

The supplier was very careful not to design the event as a *'sales pitch'*, but as an opportunity for the attendees to actually learn something of value. Not once did anyone try to sell us something. Not once did I feel like I was part of something like a 'time-share seminar' or 'industry infomercial'. I never felt pressured to buy anything from them after the event, though we did end up sourcing several products to them that we probably wouldn't have otherwise.

What this Tier-1 supplier had done was pull off an incredibly successful marketing campaign to entice clients and prospects to their facility. At the same time they prudently educated them on their technical proficiencies. To this day I still think it was a stroke of genius and unfortunately I've rarely had another supplier offer that same type of event. Too bad. *Because if I was in Sales, that's what I would do!*

Holding a training event that doesn't feel like a sales pitch, and inviting not just individuals from my company, but from various clients in the industry, will not only entice Buyers and End-Users to visit your facility, it will compel us to associate your company with quality products and processes.

So how do you go about setting up an event that would attract clients and prospects to show up? Your first step is to conduct research and find out what type of classes your clients would be interested in. This goes back to doing your homework and finding out what today's concerns are in the industry you sell to; quality, lead time, technology, tolerances, retail improvements, safety, product capability, commodity surcharges, cost reductions, government regulations, etc.

Once you've conducted research on your prospects and the industry, your second step is to find out if you're employing any *seasoned experts* in the areas you've defined. Perhaps one of your retired employees who was known to be an expert would be willing to facilitate a class.

Be aware that these internal experts must be able to run an *interesting, informative class* or you're better off not running it at all. If capable experts are not found internally, look for professionals outside of your company to provide training. It's possible that these experts exist within your own sub-supplier companies. Whoever you nominate or hire to provide the training, sufficient advertising of their credentials and related experience is key. *You need to convince the attendees that the people they are learning from are true experts in their field.*

Third, send out invitations to your clients and prospects. Make sure they know it's free. Advertise what classes will be held and who will be facilitating them. Again, you must make certain that your event is in no way perceived as a 'sales pitch' but rather as an opportunity to learn.

Finally, determine what type of snacks, refreshments and lunch will be catered. Define the class and breaks schedule. If no one within your company has experience in planning and facilitating such an event, research the Internet for ideas or hire an industry event planner to run it for you. *Make it as professional and energetic as you can because if you event turns out boring, ill-planned and misconceived it could do more damage than good.*

FROM THE BUYER'S DESK: Create a professional event to educate and inform your clients and prospects. Ensure it's perceived as an event to 'educate and help' and not as a 'sales pitch'.

BUYER'S WHO PREFER THIS: 83%
SALES REPS WHO DO THIS: 8%

FEEDBACK! Sales Advice from the Buyer's Desk

SECTION 4

The Quoting Process

- The Best Way to Improve Sales
- How to be Asked to Submit a Quote
- How to Get a Vendor Code
- Expediting the Quote Process
- Relationships vs. Economics:
  Where Did Our Love Go?
- How to Lower Your Quote Without Feeling it!
- Price vs. Value: Using TCO to Sell
- Get the Order Through Bundling!
- Lot Size vs. Annual Volume
- How to Submit the Perfect Quote
- A Buyer's Perception of Electronic Bidding

"The Best Way to Improve Sales."

A good friend of mine is a Lead Buyer for a major corporation. During his career he's purchased a wide variety of products and services. I recently asked him where he believes Sales Professionals can make the biggest impact in improving their opportunities. His answer was immediate and no surprise to me: *"Pay attention to my needs!"*

When I asked him to clarify his statement, it was his contention that most Sales Reps do not care about his requests as a Buyer. It was his experience that Sales Reps tend to focus only on their *OWN* needs. His reasoning came down to two things: (1) Not paying attention to the details in the Request-for-Quote, and (2) not asking about or showing concern for project requirements. *As a Buyer who has similar procurement responsibilities, I would have to agree with my friend.*

Do you remember the old Burger King commercial that declared, *"Have It Your Way"?* Nothing is more frustrating than giving your order to a fast-food cashier only to end up with something you didn't want, or some special request like *"no pickles"* that was ignored. In your private life it's aggravating when you deal with a retail specialist who tries to sell you something you don't need, tries to sell you options you didn't ask for, and who did too much talking and not enough listening. *Welcome to the Buyer's Side of the Desk!*

From the Buyer's perspective there is one foremost rationalization as to why Sales Professionals lose the purchase order. It's their inability to *pay attention* to the terms, conditions, requirements and associated specifications stated in the Request-for-Quote (RFQ). Whether the supplier is receiving an RFQ through e-mail or by attending a project line-up meeting, more times than not it appears to Buyers that their project needs are NOT being taken seriously.

Now I realize we Buyers can throw a lot at you during the RFQ process; an overload of specifications, product requirements and commercial conditions. At times it's difficult and time consuming for a supplier to sift through all of the documentation in order to give the client what they're asking for within a reasonable amount of time. But too often, directions and requirements that are clearly spelled out tend to lose their context by the time the Buyer receives the quote. Even the simplest of directions are bungled, *and it's the little things that count!* Understanding that insight from the Buyer's perspective, you need to make sure of five things when it comes to the RFQ.

1. You need to make sure that whoever receives the RFQ or attends the project line-up meeting takes proficient notes and asks the Buyer the right questions. Make sure they repeat what the Buyer requests to make certain they got it right; much like the wait staff reading back your dinner order to ensure it's what you asked for. Sometimes it's best to have two representatives attend an RFQ meeting to make sure nothing is missed.

2. Be sure to properly and thoroughly inform your company of the information provided and discussed at the RFQ meeting. You need to make certain that your estimating department spends a rational amount of time reviewing the documentation. Make sure they understand what needs to be quoted. If the Buyer asked for Net 60 payment terms and your company normally provides Net 30, include a price for both. Show the Buyer the price for his request as well as your ability to lower costs with your preferred terms. The bottom line is to *'quote accordingly'* per the terms and conditions of the RFQ, *even if it's not your standard terms and conditions.* It's a Buyers job to complete an *apples-to-apples* comparison of the quotes they receive. I'm certain that every supplier would prefer the Buyer completes a fair and unbiased comparison of each competitive quote. But if one supplier is quoting Net 30 terms and everyone else is quoting Net 60, then an apples-to-apples comparison can't be completed! Don't end up being the supplier quoting the wrong requirements. *Let your competitor be the one to risk having their quote thrown in the wastebasket!*

3. You need to create a *checklist* of the technical and commercial requirements stated in the RFQ to make certain all directives have been accurately met before the quote is submitted to the Buyer. Someone in the supplier's organization, most likely the estimating manager, needs to take the bull by the horns and take responsibility to ensure everything is completed on time and as requested.

4. **Review the quote on your own *BEFORE* handing it to the Buyer.** Normally when I point out an issue with the quote, a statement I hear way too often from the Sales Rep is, *"Well, I didn't actually read the quote myself. But I'm surprised the proposal team missed that!"* Really? You didn't even read it? A good number of Sales Professionals earn part of their income through commissions, *yet they rely too much on other people for that extra pay*, including departments and individuals within their own company. Don't count on internal groups getting it right. *It's your income! It's your career!* We all appreciate restaurant wait staff who check our meals before bringing it to us to ensure it was prepared to our liking. Well, Corporate Buyers expect as much from you. A true Sales Professional will ALWAYS review the quote themselves and compare it to the RFQ before handing it to the Buyer. *Never trust anyone else when it comes to your potential earning power!* One of the reasons why some quotes are not to the Buyer's specifications is because someone working for the supplier made the statement, *"I know what they want. I worked on their last job."* That is a VERY dangerous statement to make! Why is it dangerous? Because things change! Projects change. Requirements change. It's always best to work on a quote as if it's the first time you've ever prepared one for that specific Buyer or Client. Don't assume that it's probably the same specifications, payment terms, warranty, technical requirements or qualifications from the last job.

5. This is the simplest one. *Submit your quote on time!* We'll cover this in more detail a bit later in the book, but it needs to be initially mentioned now. Many times in my career I've been compelled to award an order to a specific supplier . . . *because theirs was the only quote I received in time!* Think about that. (See the Section titled, *"Expediting the Quote Process."*, pg. 161.)

Of all the interactions between Buyers and Sellers, the quoting process really seems to be the function that makes or breaks a supplier. Again, think about how many times you've ordered a meal at a fast-food restaurant and they failed to get it right. Now ask yourself, what could they have done to make sure the order was prepared based on the specifications you gave them? From the cashier taking your order to the grill cook preparing your meal, what should they have done to ensure your order was properly prepared? What communication and internal processes could they have taken to ensure everything was right? After you think about those solutions, you need to incorporate those same internal processes within your own organization.

Imagine how frustrating it is to a Buyer when they receive a quote that does not meet their requirements. The Buyer asks for a two-year warranty, but the supplier only quotes one year. The Buyer asks for FCA delivery terms but the supplier only quotes COD. The Buyer wants ten products in blue but the supplier quoted fifteen in red. *It's NOT the Buyer's job to ensure your quote matches the RFQ . . . IT'S YOURS!!!*

You need to understand that a quote properly prepared according to the Buyer's specifications *gets their attention* because the majority of proposals are not! I really shouldn't be telling you this, but would you like to know what happens to a percentage of quotes that are missing requested information? A poorly completed quote compels the Buyer to do one of two things. (1) It compels the Buyer to call and tell you what you missed. Again, it shouldn't be the Buyer's job to let you know what's wrong with your own quote. It's *YOUR* job to review it before submitting it. Or (2), it compels the Buyer to throw your quote in the trash! Been there, done that.

FROM THE BUYER'S DESK: Pay attention to a Buyer's wants and needs. Ensure a receptive and correct quote.

BUYERS WHO PREFER THIS: 94%
SALES REPS WHO DO THIS: 28%

"How to be Asked to Submit a Quote."

Obviously, the next step following your initial sales meeting is to work on selling the prospect your products and services. *That means you need to get the Buyer to invite you to quote.* And for that to happen there are several things you need to investigate and secure in your favor:

1. Is the project financially and technically approved?
2. Is the Buyer committed to placing an order to any qualified supplier?
3. Does the End-User already have a preferred supplier in mind?
4. Will the order most likely be placed with the incumbent supplier?
5. What does the Buyer & End-User honestly think about your company?

In some cases, suppliers are invited to attend a **Request-for-Quote (RFQ)** meeting (sometimes called a supplier line-up meeting) in order to bid on a specific project. And in most cases they'll get invited by the Buyer. But it's not always easy to get invited to quote even if you are already considered a preferred, pre-approved supplier.

So how do you make sure your company is asked to quote? **It may surprise you to know that very few Sales Professionals even *ask* if there is anything coming up they can quote on!** This should be Sales 101, but it's not done as often as you think. It should be done periodically throughout the year. As stated earlier, most Sales Reps ask if there's anything they can quote on during the initial sales meeting, then fail to do any follow up afterwards. That's because they assume the Buyer will simply remember them when something comes up. *Wrong assumption!* **Don't count on the Buyer to do your work for you!** Buyer's have lousy memories. Besides, that's not their responsibility, *IT'S YOURS!*

In order to increase your chances of being asked to quote anything, the first thing you need to do is find out what the prospect's supplier-selection process is in sending RFQs. This is a good question to ask during your initial sales meeting with the Buyer. Ask the Buyer how the process of supplier selection for RFQ's and eventual purchase orders works. What are the procedures and who is internally involved? *I've had relatively few Sales Reps ask me that.* Too bad, because it will give you a better understanding of how decisions are made. It will confirm who specifically makes the decisions so you can create a sales strategy to correspond with that process.

You need to know that most Buyers have a pre-determined list of suppliers to invite to quote on any given product or service. ***Think about your own private life.*** If you were looking to buy a new digital camera, you probably have a few brand names and retail stores that automatically run through your mind. It's the same with Corporate Buyers. When a product or service is needed they usually have a pre-determined list of preferred suppliers to contact. That list is reviewed, debated and scrutinized on a yearly basis by Purchasing and other internal cross-functional departments.

In some companies, Purchasing facilitates *supplier review meetings* with other departments who have first-hand experience with the supply base. These groups include but are not limited to Engineering and Design, Production, Quality, Finance and Material Planners. The intent of these meetings is to internally review each supplier technically and commercially. How well did they perform? What issues need to be resolved? Is their pricing fair and reasonable? Did they deliver product on time? Did their product actually work in the field? Was the supplier responsive to issues? Did the supplier support on-site service when it was needed? Is their sales representation sufficient? A list of criteria is usually reviewed by all parties and concerns are expressed. Suppliers are then rated in one of several potential categories, from poor to preferred.

The results of *supplier review meetings* are usually recorded in an internal supplier database. Some companies allow their suppliers to review their scores so they can work on what the client believes needs improvement. Other companies prefer to keep the supplier scores and ratings to themselves. Any smart company would allow suppliers to view their own ratings. How else can the supplier know what it needs to improve on? And if specific scores were erroneously or politically given, how else can the supplier defend itself against an unknown bias? As a Sales Rep it's up to you to ask if such a rating system exists and if it's accessible by the suppliers. *I can tell you that most do not ask.*

You also need to understand that it sometimes takes years of work on the end of the Sales Professional to be included on a preferred-supplier list. *It also takes just as much work to stay on it.* In some companies the Buyer and End-Users will sit down and discuss who should be asked to quote. If that's the method your prospect uses, there will be an increased chance that at least *one* of them will recommend you – but only if you've managed to get them interested in what you can do for them. *So not only will you have to do your homework on the Buyers, you need to cover the End-Users as well.* As stated before, the Advice from the Buyer's Desk is to find out who is involved in the supplier-selection process and get in front of as many of the decision-makers as possible based on what interests them. What are *their* goals? What are *their* responsibilities? What are *their* needs?

Another way to help improve your chances of getting on the RFQ list is to provide **budgetary quotes** for future programs. *There are a lot of good things that can come from this.* Not only do you get a chance to show off your capabilities but you may end up being the benchmark for the project. You also get a chance to review the client's specifications and project requirements ahead of time. That's a definite advantage, especially if you've never sold them anything in the past. Suppliers who have been doing business with the client for a number of years have the advantage of knowing their specifications inside and out. A new supplier just coming into the game isn't familiar with all the nuances and is open for more mistakes, which means they will need time to understand the specs in order to provide an acceptable quote.

If you've *never* delivered products to a company before, odds are you're not going to get a large order to start with. Sometimes you have to start small. If the End-User has a need for a hundred complex units, odds are a new supplier isn't going to get the order. *Too risky!* A few less complicated products at the most to start.

It takes time to build up a solid reputation and business relationship. *Unfortunately, it only takes one job to destroy it!* Today's Golden Child is tomorrow's four-letter word. Sometimes you have to take one step back to go two forward, which means sometimes you have to go above and beyond the call of duty in supplying products and services to get your foot in the door. Free service and maintenance, bare-bone pricing, free extended warranty, or a free product on trial basis are ways to entice the Buyer during the RFQ process.

Once you've been invited to attend an RFQ line-up meeting there are a few things you need to cover during and afterwards. *First, you need to convey specification differences.* This is a good way to get the client's attention during the quoting process. Demonstrate the positive technical and commercial differences between the client's specifications and your own in the quote. This could include options that deviate from the client's specifications, yet save them money and/or increase production with the same end result. The client needs to feel confident that if their specifications have been deviated it's not at the expense of lower quality or product capability. I've had several suppliers provide quotes that included a side-by-side comparison of my specifications vs. what they could provide. The comparison clearly showed the technical differences as well as the financial variance. *It was an eye opener and very impressive.*

Suppliers usually have their own standard specifications for products. Sometimes the client's specifications contain unnecessary guidelines, over-priced material and high-end sub-components. If that's the case, it's a good idea for you to review and demonstrate to the client the differences between your standard specifications and the client's corporate specs. *But again, you must clearly show that even though different specs were used, the product's qualified end result is the same.*

That being said, keep in mind that the Buyer does not always have the ability to convince the End-User to agree to the supplier's standard specifications. That's because the End-User is the person or department that usually receives the criticism from the corporate executive staff if production is not met or if quality is compromised. This is why a client's specifications may ask for an overdesigned, fanatical product when it really isn't necessary. Talking the Buyer into saving money by reverting to a supplier's specifications will be easier than talking the End-User into accepting your requests for deviations. And getting the differences out in the open will help lead to future progress. *It will also appear you're looking out for the Buyer's best interest.*

One thing you need to avoid telling the Buyer is that it would be the perfect time for your company to quote due to a lack of work at their facility. During difficult economic times, many suppliers use the reasoning of *"a lack of work"* to show they have sufficient room and available workers at their facility to focus their attention on the client's job if they get the order. *I've had several suppliers try this on me without good results.* It may seem like an advantage to the supplier. But the Buyer's concern lies in the fact that if the supplier has limited work, some workers may have been laid off or will be sometime soon. The Buyer may assume that the supplier will not have enough qualified people to complete the job on time. Or even worse, that a lack of business means a lack of revenue, thereby causing your doors to close. And as a Buyer, I'll also wonder why other potential clients aren't placing orders with you. *Is there something they know that I don't?*

Another poor tactic used by suppliers in the past, especially during difficult economic times, was to inform me if they didn't receive a purchase order they would have to lay people off. *This is the absolute worse thing a supplier can ever tell a Buyer!* First of all, that's not the Buyers problem! Never try to make the Buyer feel guilty about not awarding you with the order. Second, that tactic will never compel me to place an order with you. The order should be awarded based on capabilities and value, and *not* on people potentially being laid off. The Buyer is not responsible for layoffs at your facility and you should never attempt to make him feel that way. If your company is relying on one order to keep its doors open, it's already in more trouble than what one Buyer could ever create.

Another mistake a supplier can make during the quoting process is to be presumptuous about receiving the order, especially if they're the incumbent on the previous job. *A supplier should never assume they're going to end up with the purchase order based on prior experiences.* We all know that nothing is guaranteed except death and taxes. Some suppliers have a tendency to provide incomplete and un-descriptive quotes based on the assumption they'll receive the purchase order no matter what. Some suppliers believe themselves to be the only game in town and therefore expect the purchase order. Still others get arrogant and announce to the Buyer they either deserve the order or jokingly assert the Buyer should just award it to them now and save time. I've had that happen to me a few times. No matter how sure a supplier is of receiving a purchase order, they should never sacrifice the quality of a quote or the attention of an RFQ. And no supplier should ever become so bold as to demand the order from the Buyer, even with an impression of humor. *It's foolish and unprofessional.*

One last bit of advice regarding the quoting process. *The Buyer may not want to be bothered by suppliers while reviewing the quotes.* Therefore, when you hand in your quote, ask the Buyer how he would prefer to communicate during the review process. Unfortunately, many suppliers have a bad habit of constantly calling the Buyer to find out how the decision-making process is going. They also call to ask if the Buyer has any questions regarding their quote. You need to know that the Buyer may not be able to give detailed information as to *how things are going.* And certainly, most Buyer's will not wait for the supplier to call if there are any questions that need answering. I know that it's in your blood as a Sales Professional to say, *"I'm just calling to see if you have any questions about the quote."* Trust me, Buyer's know it's just a tactic to find out how things are going. But imagine numerous suppliers quoting on a project calling the Buyer, trying to find out if any decision has been made or if there are any questions. *It's time consuming and frustrating on the Buyer's end.* The best rule is to ask the Buyer up front when you should call or e-mail during the quote-review process.

FROM THE BUYER'S DESK: Periodically ask about opportunities to quote, even for budgetary purposes. Find out who is involved in selecting suppliers and develop a business relationship with each person or department.

BUYERS WHO PREFER THIS: 73%
SALES REPS WHO DO THIS: 24%

"How to Get a Vendor Code."

Whether it's called a **Vendor Code, Supplier Code** or some other term, congratulations are in order if you are one of numerous suppliers who have been assigned one by the client with the intent of buying your products.

For those of you unfamiliar with this term, a *Vendor Code* is a set of numbers, letters and/or other characters created by the client and assigned to the supplier in the form of identification. Purchase orders, invoices, payments and other processes are directly associated with the code assigned to you. In most cases, a supplier cannot receive an order without first being assigned a vendor code. In fact, some suppliers actually have multiple codes assigned to them based on their various business facility locations.

It's important to know that although having a vendor code is the key to receiving that first purchase order, it is *NOT* a guarantee you'll continue receiving them in the future. **As a supplier to any company, you must continue to EARN your vendor code every day you do business with them.** By that, I mean you must continue to provide whatever compelled the Buyer to award you with a vendor code in the first place. Whether it was product capability, customer service, cost savings or industry respect, you must keep up the energy, actions and the discipline that enabled you to receive that vendor code, *or stand a chance to lose it.*

I've been involved with many suppliers who busted their butt in order to be honored with a vendor code, only to have that same supplier eventually lose their enthusiasm, ignore requests and provide quotes that were either non-competitive or didn't meet requirements. **Having a vendor code doesn't mean you can relax.** Quite the opposite. Having a vendor code means you must work harder than ever to continue to ensure your quality, capabilities, communication, project management, sales representation and product/service value meets or exceeds the client's expectations.

The reality is that a vendor code is not a passport to the client's projects! Rather, it's recognition by the client that you are a preferred supplier capable of providing products and services to support their programs. Not every supplier who has a vendor code is guaranteed they'll be asked to quote. Nor should suppliers *without* a vendor code be barred from quoting. *The capability of a supplier's products and services should determine who will be asked to quote, and NOT whether or not they have a vendor code.*

Sales Advice from the Buyers Desk: If you ever encounter a Buyer who tells you, *"You're not allowed to quote or receive a purchase order because you don't have a vendor code"*, you need to prudently and tactfully remind him of three things:

ONE: No supplier was every 'born' with a vendor code. That's like telling someone they can't be promoted to manager because they've never been one before. *Well, neither was any current manager at one time!* At some point, none of the client's suppliers had a vendor code. They had to be given one by Purchasing. And they received their code either because the Buyer saw a need for their specific product, or the Buyer felt he didn't have enough competitive suppliers for a given commodity, or because the supplier was able to convince the Buyer there was a need.

TWO: If suppliers who do not have vendor codes are not allowed to quote, how will the Buyer fulfill his goals of knowing what suppliers are out there, what they can provide and how they can assist the Buyer's company to reach its goals? It's part of the Buyer's job to research and qualify new companies capable of providing the best product at the best value that best fits their needs. Suppliers selling current product can run the risk of going out of business. And if the Buyer doesn't have a qualified backup, he himself runs the risk of shutting down production or inhibiting his company to sell to their clients. If you don't have a vendor code or if the Buyer isn't willing to assign you one at this time, waiting in the wings for a supplier to close its doors or upset the Buyer enough to lose their own code can be your consolation prize. *But it shouldn't have to come to that.* If a key supplier shuts it's doors and you need to fill the void, there may not be enough time for your company's team to get organized, order material, get products qualified and provide them in time to meet the client's needs. Having a vendor code up front, gaining early access to the client's specifications and requirements, and even providing sample product will eliminate some of the time necessary to get up and running.

THREE: If suppliers who do not have a vendor code are not allowed to quote, how will the Buyer really know he's getting the best value? This is especially true if the Buyer continues to quote the same suppliers over and over again. In an economically poor business environment in which suppliers are closing their doors, putting their eggs in one basket is not a wise decision for any Buyer to make!

So the question remains, *why do some Buyers make it nearly impossible to get a vendor code?* The fact is, some companies actually hand out vendor codes like candy at Halloween. But in most cases it seems to take a miracle for a supplier to receive one. *So why is that?*

First of all, it makes perfect business sense for clients to be picky about giving out vendor codes. *In your private life would you just let anyone repair your vehicle?* Or would you prefer it be someone you've pre-qualified? If every supplier I could potentially do business with received a vendor code simply by asking for one, my entire day as a Buyer would be spent creating vendor codes with no time for anything else.

This leads us to the second reason why Buyers are stingy about handing out vendor codes: *It costs their employer money!* Before a vendor code is created and given to a supplier, there are commercial, financial, quality and technical reviews to be completed. This takes time, energy and money on the client's part. Depending on how in depth these reviews are, it can involve numerous people and cost the client thousands of dollars for every new vendor code created. It also takes time and money to maintain the supplier list. That's why one of the yearly goals of a Buyer is *'Supplier Reduction'*. In fact, some Buyers are rated during their yearly review according to how many suppliers they can logically get rid of. In most companies a dollar figure is associated with the reduction of one supplier. *Isn't that ironic?* Hundreds of suppliers at any given time are trying to get a vendor code, while Buyer's are constantly trying to *reduce* their supply base! In fact, a yearly supply base reduction of 10% is not uncommon in most Purchasing departments.

I've dealt with numerous Sales Professionals who have told me, *"I can save you money. Why can't I get a vendor code?"* There are times when it makes perfect sense to create a new vendor code for a supplier, yet it *still* takes an Act of Congress to make it happen. That's largely due to the paperwork, approvals and bureaucracy that some Buyers have to go through to get a new code created for a supplier. I shouldn't be telling you this, but some Buyers would rather *not* go through the time, effort and hassle of creating a new vendor code simply because of the amount of work it takes.

Here's another reason why a supplier might not receive a vendor code even if it means saving money. Let's say I've been buying widgets from Supplier A for some time. But all Supplier A has been doing is buying the widgets from Supplier B, marking them up and reselling them to me at a profit. It would make perfect sense for me to simply give Supplier B a vendor code and buy direct from them. But depending on how much money I can save my company will depend on how critical I think it's worth going through the trouble of getting them a code.

Let's say that I could save my company $5000 a year by getting a code for Supplier B. To some client companies, $5000 is not a good enough reason to create a new vendor code, especially if their revenue is in the hundreds of millions. Why? Because to some companies, putting the effort and expense of saving $5000 is like you going out of your way to save a dollar in your own private life; *it just may not be worth the time and effort no matter how much sense it makes.*

Another factor to consider is that the Buyer may not have the authority alone to create a new vendor code for a supplier. That final decision most likely has to be made by a Senior Purchasing Manager or Director who, depending on their own goals and agendas, may not be willing to do so. As stated earlier, most client companies are actually in the process of *reducing* the number of suppliers they conduct business with based on corporate objectives set by executive management. And when it comes to executive management, sometimes corporate goals takes precedence over something that may appear to be in the best interest of the company.

So from the Buyer's Desk, here are the best ways to convince Purchasing to consider you for a vendor code:

1. Inform the Buyer about your technical capabilities and product lead times. Suppliers are going out of business every day. Let the Buyer know how you would be able to provide products as a potential backup if their current source no longer can.

2. Give the Buyer some estimated costs of products so he can do a quick comparison against his current suppliers. If the estimated savings justify having a new vendor code created, he may show some interest.

3. If you have a wide variety of products available, see if the Buyer can justify buying them all from you instead of from various other companies. Introduce the concept of 'one-stop shopping'. See if you're able to provide a number of products he's currently buying from several other suppliers. Buying five different products from one supplier instead of buying them from five separate companies will provide the Buyer with potential cost savings as well as supplier-reduction opportunities.

4. Find out if any of your current clients simply buy your products and resell them to someone else, even as a sub-component of their end product. If the savings justifies the expense in creating a new vendor code, you may be able to convince the Buyer to purchase them directly from you, thereby cutting out the middleman and saving the Buyer money from needless markups.

5. Finally, ask the Buyer what it takes to get a vendor code. How easy is it? How difficult is it? What is the process? Who are the decision makers? As much as suppliers would love to have a vendor code from my company, *I've rarely had a Sales Professional ask me what it actually takes to get one!* Too bad. At least with that information they'd know what they're up against.

FROM THE BUYER'S DESK: As a Sales Professional or Business Owner, find out the processes and requirements in securing a vendor code. Point out positive reasons why it's in the prospect's best interest to consider you.

"Expediting the Quote Process."

I recently sent a Request-for-Quote to a supplier for a somewhat uncomplicated product, much like one they had manufactured for a previous program. Due to a recent design change and revised project timing, the product needed to be sourced as soon as possible. *I clearly expressed that expedited need in the RFQ.*

After a week and with no word from the supplier, I sent an e-mail asking for a status of the quote. I again expressed the urgent need for the product. I received a reply from the Sales Rep that the RFQ needed to be processed through specific internal departments before they could provide the pricing and lead times. *Within the next five days I sent three additional e-mails asking for the status of the quote.* I finally received a response after my third e-mail. The supplier said I could expect the quote by the end of the week. *Of course, the end of the week came and went with no quote and no communication from the Rep.*

I then sent two more e-mails asking for the quote status. No response. It had now been nearly three weeks since I sent the RFQ for an expedited quote with little response from the supplier and precious time ticking away. I finally sent an e-mail explaining that if I didn't receive status by the end of the day I would be compelled to move forward with our other options for that product. *That got a response!* The response was that they were doing everything they could do to expedite a response. *(What the hell did that mean?)* I thanked them and asked if they could just provide me with a *best-guess* lead time for the product so I could plan accordingly. No response. I again e-mailed asking if they were able to at least provide an estimated product lead time. Because if the lead time was beyond my project schedule, I wouldn't have them move forward with the quote. The reply came back that the lead time would be provided in the quote that was still being internally worked on.

They apparently didn't understand my request and there seemed to be no sense of urgency on their end. I then asked if they had any existing product from the previous job sitting on a shelf somewhere or at least the raw material so we could proceed with the project. Of course, no response.

Now it was my understanding that this supplier was in financial distress. That surprised me based on their seemingly lack of motivation to provide me with a quote so they could sell product. (Or should that news have surprised me after all?) But whether the supplier was experiencing monetary issues or not, the main question is this: *What type of internal process did the supplier have that apparently inhibited them from providing a quote within a reasonable amount of time, especially knowing that it was urgently needed?* Was every department informed the quote was hot? Was the Sales Rep concerned about my immediate project needs or the financial needs of his own company? Were their own sub-suppliers tasked with the same pressing need for costs and timing? And are their mandated internal processes constraining their ability to improve sales?

Too many times, internal corporate guidelines inhibit companies from realizing their true potential. How many of us are forced to comply with strict mandates set forth by executive management that are not in the best interest of the company? For that matter, which guidelines actually prevent the company from standing out from its competitors? How many times do we sit at our desks and say to ourselves, *"This process is totally screwed up. It doesn't make any sense. We could do things much quicker if we were able to bypass one or more of these mandated steps."* As employees we owe it to our company to prudently point out written procedures and everyday practices that impede our ability to legally, ethically and financially prosper. But too many times we find that ego, politics and the *"we've always done it this way"* mentality stands in the way.

My *Advice from the Buyer's Desk* is for your Sales Team to meet with all applicable departments and individuals in your company, as well as your sub-suppliers, and go through the complete process of quoting. Scrutinize every step in the process; *does it provide value?* How is the RFQ received by the supplier? How long does it take the RFQ make it to the estimating department? How quickly are questions sent back to the Buyer? Are sub-suppliers contacted and requested for their own quotes with the same urgency the client has? Can pricing from previous projects be used based on *common sense estimating* and *progressive cost increases* instead of starting from scratch? Are communications from the Buyer being addressed within a reasonable amount of time, even if it's only to say, *"We're still working on it?"* Does the information being provided in the subsequent quote actually match what the RFQ requested? How many steps, days, personnel and work can be pulled from the quoting process and still provide an adequate quote per the Buyer's request?

Improving the quoting process even by one day can greatly increase a supplier's ability to improve sales. Streamlining corporate procedures, finding faster ways to determine pricing and lead times, and adherence to the terms of the RFQ the first time will also give your company an advantage over your slower competitors.

IMPORTANT: We briefly covered this a couple Sections ago. But from the Buyer's Desk I can tell you that countless times in my career, I have awarded purchase orders to acceptable suppliers for the plain and simple fact that theirs was the ONLY quote I received in time to meet my project milestones. Let me repeat that: **I've awarded business to suppliers because theirs was the ONLY quote I received in time!** My project needs were urgent and I didn't have time to wait for the other suppliers to submit their quotes. I gave each bidding company ample opportunity to meet the deadline. But time had run out and only one pre-qualified supplier managed to submit their proposal on time. In most cases the initial price was reasonable and the Sales Representative was immediately awarded the business - never knowing that theirs was the only quote I received. *If that isn't an incentive to improve your internal quoting process, I don't know what is.*

We live in a business environment in which timelines are short and design-to-build schedules are even shorter. In fact with some projects I've worked on, placing orders to suppliers who were the ONLY ones to provide a quote in time was the NORM *and not the exception.* Make sure your company and your own suppliers, reorganizes, restructures and streamlines your quoting process to take advantage of those opportunities.

FROM THE BUYER'S DESK: Research ways to expedite your quotes without sacrificing its content. Make certain they are to the Buyer's requirements and provided in time.

BUYERS WHO PREFER THIS: 88%
SALES REPS WHO DO THIS: Not sure of the percentage since it's a supplier's internal process. But the percentage of suppliers who submit inadequate quotes and/or later than the requested date is 57%.

"Relationships vs. Economics:
Where Did Our Love Go?"

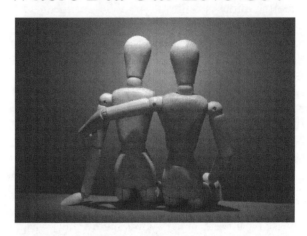

I recently read an interesting article written by a Sales Professional. The individual claimed that the **Relationship Buyer** has been in steady decline in past years. According to the article, a *Relationship Buyer* is one who shows trust in the supplier and, in return, the supplier determines what and how the Buyer wants to conduct business. In short, a business transaction that's a win-win for both Buyer and Seller. Everything is warm and fuzzy. No games. Group hugs.

The author went on to state that the Relationship Buyer from the past is now being replaced by the **Economic Buyer**. The *Economic Buyer* trusts no one and only buys based on best price, not best value. The Economic Buyer plays games and is more interested in the bottom line than a silly relationship with the supply base. *Essentially, the Economic Buyer is a ruthless pain in the butt!*

After reading the article I have to say that I categorically agree with the author. He has defined today's business relationship between Buyers and Sellers . . . *but only if you read his article from the bottom up!* Because regarding the progress from *Relationships* to *Economics* the author has his facts straight, **it's just his timeline that's backwards.** We're not moving from a Relationships to Economics business trend. Rather, in my opinion, it's the other way around.

For those of you who have been in business for a few decades, think back to the golden era of buying and selling in the 1970's where purchase orders were corruptly awarded at the 19th hole. How about the 1980's where recessions and economic failures resulted in reduced budgets, price over value decisions and supplier bankruptcies. Or how about the

1990's where business people like General Motors' global purchasing chief, J . Ignacio Lopez, started wars with the supply base by imposing unilateral price cuts *thereby destroying supplier relationships.*

Now think about today's global business environment. Global competition has made companies rethink their buying strategies in terms of partnering with vendors. Technological advancements and quality initiatives have compelled Purchasing departments to buy from capable companies and not necessarily the cheapest ones. Customer expectations have precluded Buyers from buying on price alone, thereby thinking of future sales. All of these events have changed the way procurement departments think and act. **Best Price** has been replaced with **Best Value**. Putting the supplier out of business has been replaced with ensuring suppliers remain financially sound to continuously provide product. Buying the cheapest from third-world countries has been replaced with buying the most efficient even if it means a local supplier.

Yes, I know there are always exceptions to the rule. There are still Purchasing Departments that maintain the 'Lopez' strategy. There are still companies who prefer larger bottom lines to an adequate supplier relationship. There are still procurement groups out there who are willing to sacrifice quality for third-world pricing. And guess what, *there always will be!* Personally, I have no intention of working for a company like that because odds are they won't be around long. But compared to the strategies and practices of yesteryear, the vast majority of companies have traded *Economics buying* with *Relationships buying.*

That's not to say that the relationship is always healthy. What relationship is? But when measured against the past, it's certainly better than it was. And if you weren't around in the '70s, '80s or even the '90s, ask one of the old-timers about the not-so-good ol' days in sales.

Client companies have slowly woken up to the fact that low-quality products based on the cheapest component pricing results in low volume sales and lost customers. They've come to realize that browbeating the supplier for every penny can result in either shortcuts made by the supplier which results in poor quality, or a financially-strapped supplier who can no longer provide product because they've closed their doors. *And a bankrupt critical supplier is one of the biggest fears of a Buyer!*

Of course you yourself will judge my opinion with your own experiences. Some will read this and agree, and some will indignantly shake their head and disagree. I think what it comes down to is the complexity of the product and the sophistication of the Buyer's customer base. After all, retail companies who buy in high volume employ Buyers who continue to nickel and dime the supply base to death. *Retail selling can be brutal.* Yet as customers of these retail stores, we all enjoy paying bargain prices for life's necessities, don't we? And when we're buying these inexpensive items, we're not even thinking about what the poor Sales Rep had to go through to get the order and provide the products we just placed in our shopping cart. Maybe that's why I have such a high regard for Sales Professionals.

Now then, how about that group hug?

FROM THE BUYER'S DESK: Purchasing Departments in today's business environment are leaning towards best 'value' and a healthy Buyer-Seller relationship in place of best 'price'. Those who aren't are headed for economic disorder.

"How to Lower Your Quote Without Feeling It!"

The perception of most Buyers is that product *capability* is expected and can be bought by a number of your competitors. In other words, Buyer's expect products to work when they're purchased, just like we do in our private lives. And most Buyers believe that specific products are available from a number of qualified suppliers that will fit their needs and perform without issue. Bottom line: *You're NOT the only game in town.* So unless you happen to be the only supplier in the world who can provide a specific product or service, **price** has become even more important to you during the Buyer's decision-making process.

Think about this statement: It's possible that every competing supplier of a given product could convince the Buyer that their product will work. Every competing supplier could convince the Buyer that their product will do exactly what is specified and expected. But only ONE supplier will be able to convince the Buyer that they have the **BEST PRICE**, whether it's from being the initial or eventual low bidder, or through the educational process of *Total Cost of Ownership* or TCO *(to be discussed in the next Section).*

So how do you convince the Buyer the best price or best value is coming from YOU? Well, convincing through TCO takes education and energy; things the Buyer may not have time for. So best value aside, convincing the Buyer by being the initial low-bid supplier is the *fastest and most straightforward way.* What most Sales Professionals don't realize is that *they may have been the initial or eventual low bid supplier without even knowing it and without having received the order*! There are a number of reasons why this could happen.

So *From the Buyer's Desk*, the following list contains the Top Ten ways suppliers can lower the price of their quotation without hardly removing a penny from it:

1. Read and understand the RFQ. Don't give the client more than what they've asked for. That is, make sure you're not *over-quoting*, thereby *over-pricing*. Anything above and beyond what's been asked for should be in the *'options'* section of your quote. Don't give away the farm! Make sure you understand *exactly* what the client wants. For instance, if they want pricing for *one* set of widgets, make sure your quote doesn't provide a price for *more* than one set. That will increase your overall base price substantially and without warrant! *From my side of the desk, this happens all the time!*

2. Provide 'progressive-payment-terms' pricing. Most of the purchase orders created by Buyers are set up either with a full one-time payment plan or a 'progressive' payment schedule. A progressive schedule means the client will pay the supplier a percentage of the total order value either ahead of time or when specific milestones have been met. For instance, an order could be set up as 50% down and the remaining 50% paid once the product has been received or the service has been completed. Another example is a purchase order set up with numerous line items representing various stages of project completion. As one stage is completed the supplier can invoice against the order and receive payment against that specific line item.

Obviously if a supplier has to spend money for raw material, design, manufacturing, overhead and other expenses before getting the full amount, they may have to borrow from a financial institution to pay for it. At the very least it reduces the supplier's cash flow. Interest rates and other financial means are then calculated into the price of the quote. *But the more money the supplier can receive up front or during the progression of the order, the less they have to borrow or the better their cash flow, which means a lower overall cost to the Buyer.* This creates an advantage to the supplier if they can convince the client to set up *numerous line items* on the order, each representing a specific milestone.

Unfortunately some Buyers will not set up progressive payments on an order because it's too time consuming for those who need to review and/or approve the invoices. But if your pricing for progressive or line item payments provides sufficient cost savings, the Buyer may have the ammunition to convince accounts payable to accept progressive terms. As an example, a supplier's quote could state: *"$10,500 with a single-payment or $8,500 with progressive payment terms."*

You can also accomplish a lower quote if you can convince the person generating the *requisition* to create it with specific line items to invoice against once each item is completed. Convince them not to total everything in your quote on one lump-sum line item. For instance, design and engineering could be on one separate line item. So when that part of the job is competed, you can invoice for it now instead of waiting until the entire job is finished. That will allow you to lower the initial price of your quote since you'll be receiving percentages of the funds ahead of time to help pay for expenditures on your end.

3. Make sure you understand what is to be priced as an option and what is *not*. If on-site service, training or delivery costs are to be quoted as options, make sure you didn't include them in the base price. For instance, the RFQs I send are based on FCA delivery terms, which means that my company is paying for the freight and insurance of the delivery of your product. But too often a supplier will *include* freight and insurance in the piece-price of the part so they end up being higher priced than their competitors. Sometimes that added cost is hidden in the piece-price and sometimes it's itemized. But it's not up to the Buyer to try to figure that out especially when it shouldn't be there in the first place. Not paying proper attention to the RFQ terms and conditions is a major reason why supplier's overprice and lose the order!

4. Make sure you know the absolute financial bottom line that you're willing to *lose* the job! Most suppliers only lose the order by a small percentage and could have received it at a lower profit. Sometimes a lower profit is better than *no* profit at all. It's my experience that some suppliers lose orders by only a few percentage points. Knowing where you're absolutely willing to walk away is essential.

5. Increase your communication with the Buyer during the quoting process. The more you can meet with the Buyer to review their requirements and educate him on the value of your product, the better chance you'll have in receiving the order. It also provides a chance to propose low-cost solutions that can reduce the base price of your quote.

6. Review your last quote with the Buyer, especially if you *lost* the order. How far off were you from the low bid and why? If the Buyer can't give you an exact dollar amount, ask for a percentage instead and figure it out from there. If you quoted *exactly* what the successful supplier quoted, why was your price higher? What's your competitor doing that you're not? What technical or financial advantages do they have? Are their sub-suppliers providing better pricing than what you're getting? Are your overhead or markup percentages too high?

7. Negotiate now with your *own* suppliers for better pricing. Don't go back to the Buyer after you've submit your quote to say, *"We met with our suppliers again and were able to get their prices down."* Why wasn't that done the first time? Does your estimating group just accept sub-supplier pricing or do they subsequently negotiate for the best price?

8. It's not difficult for a Buyer to make a mathematical error! Going through every supplier's quote and making sure they have *every* dollar accounted for is not an easy process for a Buyer, *especially* if the quote is unintentionally misleading or confusing. Ask to meet to ensure the Buyer knows *exactly* what your price is. If they don't have time, make sure the quote is clear and logically based on their *preferred* format; a **benchmark quote**. (See the Section titled, *"How to Submit the Perfect Quote"*, pg. 179.) Show the base price, followed by the itemized pricing. Make sure items are clearly marked as *base price* or *option*. I had a few suppliers at Chrysler who consistently included their itemized pricing *immediately* after the base cost, *but never clearly separated the two from each other*. Other Buyers in my group would tally their quote incorrectly by adding some of the itemed costs into the base cost. This made the supplier's price appear higher than what their actual price was.

9. Make the Buyer aware of *bundling opportunities*. Your company may be providing several quotes to the same client, but to different Buyers and even to different global purchasing departments. If that's the case, make sure each Buyer is aware of everything you're quoting to their company and what savings could be realized if you received two or more of the orders. (See the Section titled, *"Get the Order Through Bundling"*, pg. 174.)

10. Make sure you're not marking up specific purchased items with an unreasonable percentage, if any. Many purchased items or services are marked up by the supplier using an unwarranted or gluttonous percentage when they should have received little or no markup at all. There should not be a supplier markup for things that are not directly changed before it's provided to the client; i.e. transportation.

FROM THE BUYER'S DESK: Pay attention to how your quote is priced. Ensure a clear, concise quotation based on what the Buyer asked for, then quote and clearly label everything else as an option.

"Price vs. Value: Using TCO to Sell."

A long time ago, in purchasing departments far, far away, Buyers were busy negotiating with Sales Professionals for the lowest possible price. Every nickel and dime was squeezed out of the suppliers and the one left standing with the best price won. It didn't matter how long the product was designed to last. It didn't matter if it met End-User specifications. As long as it was the lowest price, the Buyer was happy. Of course the eventual End-User of that product was miserable and had to live with what Purchasing bought. But for the Buyer, life was good. He met his yearly goals and was awarded accordingly. And it wasn't that the Buyer necessarily chose the low bid on his own. *He may have been mandated to do so by Purchasing Management.*

Fast forward to present time. The economy has changed. The business environment has changed. Companies are going out of business for making poor decisions, especially when it comes to procuring lowest-cost, poor-quality products and services. After all, generally speaking, two-thirds of the cost of products sold by companies are *purchased items*. And if sourcing decisions made by procurement departments are based on *best price* alone, the purchased items going into the product they sell will eventually fail.

Decades ago companies could afford to make poor sourcing decisions. This was due to the fact that there was limited competition, especially from overseas manufacturers. Products had inferior quality and consumers were stuck with what they bought. And companies could afford to buy new equipment every year if needed because it was cheap and their profits were extreme due to non-global competition.

Then the business environment became *global* and competition grew stiff. Overseas competitors starting producing quality products thanks to innovators like W. Edwards Demming. Businesses could no longer afford to buy the cheapest. Consumers became better educated and demanded better quality. And those companies who refused to change would eventually close their doors. *That's the beauty of a market economy; it slowly but surely weeds out poor decisions.* That's not to say there aren't procurement organizations out there who still source to the low bid no matter what. It's to say that those who continue down that path will eventually end up insolvent.

As the economy continues to shift and global competition increases, procurement departments are realizing they can no longer afford to buy poor performing products, sub-components, materials and service. Like consumers, Buyers have also become better educated in their decision-making process. They realize they can no longer afford to buy the same cheap product year after year. The products and services they buy need to last to the end of their project or to the end of its intended use. **PRICE has now taken a back seat to VALUE.** This is the future of Strategic Sourcing. *And conversely, it's also the future of Sales.*

But here's the problem. If the Buyer firmly believes every supplier is offering the exact same quality product, *then price becomes the only decision factor he has left to award the order!* If you were a Buyer requesting quotes for pencils from five different suppliers and you believed every pencil was exactly the same, you'd be stupid NOT to buy from the low bid. But if someone educated you on the difference between their pencil and their competitors', then you have something else to use as a comparison: **VALUE!** *Value is what the Sales Professional must use to educate and entice the Buyer.*

The difference between *price* and *value* can be anywhere from zero to infinity. Price is not necessarily determined by its value. Price is normally based on the crossroads of supply and demand. As a Corporate Buyer, my perceived value of any given product can be based on a number of things: how quickly I need it, how emotionally involved the End-User is, how many qualified competitors are out there, how superior it is to similar products, the length of time I need it to work, etc. *So as a Corporate Buyer I'm willing to pay more for the **price** if I've perceived its **value** to be worth it.*

More and more Purchasing Departments are using the Value Method of **Total Cost of Ownership** to determine which product to buy and which supplier to buy it from. In a nutshell, **Total Cost of Ownership**, or **TCO**, is a financial assessment used to help Buyers determine direct and indirect costs of a product. TCO takes into consideration a variety of factors when deciding who to source business to. It includes expenditures such as start-up costs, one-time or non-recurring costs, overhead costs, logistics, scrap, taxes, location, documentation, utilities, tooling, training, warranty, maintenance and other direct and indirect costs. *The more complex the product, the more factors and costs that are included in the TCO calculation, the more homework the Buyer must complete on his end.*

There is one other essential factor used in the calculation of TCO, especially when major projects or product usage life-cycles are involved. **That factor is TIME.** Rather than just simply looking at the price of a product, TCO considers the complete *cradle-to-grave* cost over time; from product development to disposal. Time involves the total cost of the product to be incurred during its life-cycle. *That's because TCO is the effect of one decision over another over the lifetime of the product.*

As a Sales Professional it's imperative for you to know the expected time regarding the use of the product the Buyer would like to purchase. You need to ask that question when an RFQ is received. *Because if you don't know the length of time it's needed for, you won't be able to educate the Buyer on the TCO value of your product.*

Here's a quick example: Let's say a widget from Supplier X costs $100. Your widget costs $125. The Buyer assumes both widgets are exactly the same and decides to buy it from Supplier X thereby saving $25 up front. *Let's try this again, only this time you've done your homework on the Buyer's program as well as the competitor's product failure rate.* You found out that the Buyer needs the widget to last two years. And you know that the widget from Supplier X only lasts one year. Based on your internal data you also know that your higher-priced widget will last two years. So in educating the Buyer you tell him that at the end of two years he'll actually need to buy *two* widgets from Supplier X at a TCO cost of $200, while your widget that lasts two years costs $125. *Therefore, buying your product will save the Buyer $75 by the end of his program.* Now this example is elementary but it shows the importance of staying educated on your competitors products, your own internal product failure modes, and the client's product-cycle needs. Several economic decision tools like a *Cross-Over Chart* can be used to educate the Buyer and justify the sourcing decision in your favor.

FROM THE BUYER'S DESK: Educate the Buyer on the 'value' of your products over time, not just the 'price'.

BUYERS WHO PREFER THIS: 81%
SALES REPS WHO DO THIS: 21%

"Get the Order Through BUNDLING!"

While working as a Senior Commodity Buyer for a previous employer, I received two competitive quotes from a Sales Professional I'll call "Janice"; a quote for Product-A and quote for Product-B. I had intended to source Product-B to another supplier. But I had Janice's company in mind for Product-A. However, the price of Product-A was 12% higher than my budgeted cost. And in order to get it through management approval I knew I had to negotiate that price down. So I contacted Janice and requested a 12% reduction on Product-A. Janice responded with a counter offer. She said, *"I'll give you a 12% reduction on Product-A, but only if I receive the orders for both A and B."* Janice was willing to take a little less profit on one product in order to secure the sale of both. What Janice had offered is a *classic* negotiation tactic: **She *bundled* the prices of the two quotes in order to get both purchase orders.** In other words, *"I'll give you what YOU want if you give me what I want. Let's make it a WIN-WIN."* And it worked.

Janice's company was happy because it received an order for both products. My management was happy because the price of Product-A came in at budget. And I was happy because my management was happy. It ended up being a WIN-WIN-WIN.

But the entire bundling scenario made me think about that 'classic' negotiation tactic. *If that strategy is so 'classic', then why don't more Sales Professionals use it?* During my career in global purchasing I've only been approached by a handful of suppliers bundling quotes on various products; that is, *offering to reduce the cost of one product in order to secure the business for more than one.* Of course you won't have a chance of winning any order if the Buyer or End-User doesn't think your products are capable of meeting their needs. And it won't work if other suppliers are *collectively* lower than your bundled costs over all the products. *But the fact is when it comes to bundling it's been my experience that most Sales Professionals don't even try!*

One of the reasons why most Sales Reps don't try is because they're unaware that bundling opportunities even exist! They think to themselves, *"Well, I personally don't have other products to bundle with my quote"*, not thinking that just maybe someone else in their sales office does. And maybe no one in their own sales office *is* quoting anything to that specific Buyer or client. But if the Sales Rep's company has other sales offices in other parts of the State, country, even other parts of the world, they need to find out if *anyone* in those locations are quoting *anything* to that specific Buyer, or that specific Purchasing Department, or even to another Buyer within the client's own global locations.

Remember, bundling quotes doesn't have to be tied to just one commodity, one project or one sales office. *Expand your horizons and think outside the sales box!* Bundling quotes can include multiple commodities within any sales organization in your company from any part of the world. Unfortunately most Sales Reps tend to only think about what's going on in their *own* environment without considering the rest of their company's local, national or global sales organizations.

Another bit of advice is to ask the Buyer if he knows of any bundling opportunities within his *own* company. Let's say you're a Sales Rep and you've been given an RFQ from the Buyer to quote on widgets. Thank the Buyer for the opportunity, then remind him that besides widgets, your company also makes trinkets and doohickeys. Ask if the trinket and doohickey Buyers have any projects to quote on. Let the Buyer know that bundling your widgets with one or more additional commodities could lead to a reduced cost on his quote if more than one order is awarded to you. Sounds like a good idea. *But in my years in Purchasing I've rarely had any Sales Professional do it!*

When I was a Lead Buyer at the DaimlerChrysler headquarters in Michigan, we developed a database to keep track of our current and future projects around the world. Project information on the database was input by the responsible project Buyer. We could see what other Buyers in other procurement organizations around the world were currently sourcing, as well as what they were planning to source on future programs. Information on the site included the responsible Buyers and their contact information, the global project names and definitions, the products and services needed for each project, the quantity of each product required, the project budgets, and the names of the suppliers who would be asked to quote.

This information was incredibly advantageous to the Buyer! We could collectively contact suppliers from around the world and negotiate price by offering to source more than one project to their parent company. So it was absolutely imperative that we Buyers kept project information updated and that we stayed in touch with each other. *The important thing to note here is that it didn't matter that our desks were separated by an ocean.*

As an example, let's say I had planned to source 100 widgets for my U.S. project. And based on the quotes I received, I had a preferred supplier to source the widgets to. By researching our internal database I found out that the same preferred supplier had a sales office in Germany and was quoting 50 trinkets on a German Project. I contacted the German Buyer and we agreed that if the supplier could 'bundle' and lower their quotes for both of us, the supplier would receive the order for my 100 widgets *and* the order for his 50 trinkets.

It's important to point out that it didn't matter if the bundling took place between two separate sales offices located in different parts of the world. It didn't matter that the bundling involved more than one global project. And it didn't matter that the bundling involved more than one commodity. What mattered is that the supplier's parent company was able to bundle both quotes and received both orders, while the German Buyer and I enjoyed better pricing for both of our projects.

The database at DaimlerChrysler was a huge success. It compelled us to seek savings opportunities based on the rest of the global organization, not just within our own little world in Michigan. Well, that same success can be achieved at your own company either with a similar database or through simple face-to-face communication with your domestic and/or global counterparts. But it amazes me that when I ask a Sales Rep, *"Is your company quoting anything else to my company right now?"*, most of the time the Rep doesn't have a clue!

Remember, it doesn't matter if your company is global or not. It doesn't matter if you have more than once sales office in the same town or in different national or global locations. Even if you only have ONE lone sales office located within one building, here's my question to you: *Is your Sales Team talking to each other and sharing information that could provide bundling opportunities for any given client?*

FROM THE BUYER'S DESK: Improve your business opportunities by researching and bundling potential sales.

BUYERS WHO PREFER THIS: 87%
SALES REPS WHO DO THIS: 7%

"Lot Size vs. Annual Volume."

Based on the theme of the last Section, there's one more type of **bundling** opportunity to discuss that's much easier than researching local, nationwide or global projects in order to increase sales. I call it **Annual Volume Bundling**. And the best way to explain it is to first give you the narrative of a prior experience.

I once took over a commodity of parts from another Buyer in order to expand my horizons and gain experience in production buying. A few weeks into the new role I received a quote from a supplier informing me he was *increasing* the prices of specific parts. According to the supplier, prices had been held for the past six years and an increase of material costs, labor and burden had forced his company to increase prices.

Unfortunately, some of the new prices were nearly double what they were before. The Sales Rep shared with me the actual material quotes from his own suppliers, as well as cost and pricing data from his estimating group. The documentation he shared certainly justified their need to raise prices. *I had no choice but to agree to their increases.*

But before I updated the purchase order prices, I researched the yearly demand for these specific parts from our own clients. Then I compared the *yearly demand* against the *lot-size* pricing on the supplier's quote. *And what I found intrigued me.*

For one specific part, my company had been paying $14.16 per unit. And unfortunately, the price increase had raised it to $21.60 per unit. That would have been a huge cost adjustment to swallow based on our annual volumes. Looking at the supplier's quote, the $21.60 price was based on a lot-size of **100 units**. Any less than 100 ordered at a time and the price would go up even further. However, my research showed me that we had an average demand of **10,000 units** per year for that part.

I thought to myself, *"Why would I only want to buy 100 units at a time if the yearly demand from our clients is 10,000 units?"* Not only were we ordering 100 units of the part 100 times a year, we were also spending more on freight and overhead in order to have 100 separate shipments arrive at our plant instead of just one or a few. Similar research on most of the parts requiring increases showed comparable scenarios. The fact is, we were consistently buying in *low volume* in order to meet *high volume* yearly demand. *It didn't make sense.*

So I called the supplier and asked him to go back to his estimating group and recalculate new prices based on our actual *yearly sales volume* instead of their own *minimal lot sizes.* As if by magic, the part with the initial $14.61 price tag that had increased to $21.60 . . . was now reduced to only $13.32 per unit. *Amazing!* By bundling the part per our yearly volumes, not only had I offset the price increase, *I actually got the unit cost below what it had been years ago!*

It turned out that a few of the parts did not provide a cost reduction, even at the higher yearly volumes. So I kept the lot-size of those parts at the initial minimum quantity in order to keep inventory as low as possible. But by finding out what my yearly demand was and comparing it to the initial lot-size costs from the supplier, I was able to keep the prices of most of the parts below their original quote.

Now, I know that this strategy will not work with every commodity, product or service. But if your quotes involve selling in *"lot-sizes"* or *"minimal quantities"*, you need to ask the Buyer what their actual yearly demand is, or what the previous year demand was. Then, offer a new price based on that volume demand. Show the Buyer a comparison between your normal lot-size price and the yearly demand price.

Be aware that he may not be able to accommodate all of the inventory at his facility for an entire years worth of product, which is probably why the Buyer is only ordering in minimal lot sizes. But if you can arrange something on your end in releasing a quarter or half year at a time, or if the price savings justifies shipping the yearly demand at once, the Buyer may agree to it. Not only will it show the Buyer you're looking out for their bottom line, but you'll guarantee a year of sales for that product. *And I bet that most of your competitors aren't offering this type of bundling savings to the Buyer.*

FROM THE BUYER'S DESK: Improve your opportunities by bundling potential sales based on yearly volumes instead of minimal lots.

BUYERS WHO PREFER THIS: 73%
SALES REPS WHO DO THIS: 11%

"How to Submit the Perfect Quote."

During my career in Corporate Purchasing I've received, reviewed and analyzed tens of thousands of quote packages; quotes covering everything from capital equipment to office supplies to on-site services, *and everything in between.* Some quotes were a direct response to my Request-For-Quote (RFQ) while others were considered 'budgetary' for future projects. And if there's one thing I've learned over these many years as a Buyer it's the fact that *supplier quotes are like snowflakes . . .* **NO TWO ARE QUITE ALIKE.** What really makes each supplier's quote different is how it's *formatted.* By that I mean formatted how the quote is laid out; how it's chronologically arranged based on pricing, commercial terms, product information, etc.

Of course it's understandable why every supplier's quote format is different than any given competitor. It's the same reason why RFQs from different purchasing organizations are different; *everyone has distinct preferences when it comes to formatting their documents.* Supplier quote formats have evolved through the ages in every company. Some formats have remained the same for years while others have changed based on the input of the sales team and their management. Some formats are specified per strict corporate standards, while other companies let the members of their sales force create their own quoting format based on their own preferences. And depending on the commodity or project requirements, quotes can range in size from a single page to a mountain of information. **The bottom line is that most quotes are a mixture of personal taste and internal procedures.** In other words, most quotes are only created from the *supplier's* perspective *. . . and that's the problem!*

Since no two quotes are alike it shouldn't surprise you to learn that *the majority of quotes received by Buyers tend to be misleading or confusing.* Either the format of the quote makes it difficult for the Buyer to find vital information, or the itemization of pricing and other data is ambiguous. Whatever the reason, suppliers can make it very difficult for Buyers to read and comprehend what is trying to be communicated. At times, the Buyer has a hard time understanding where everything is, especially the commercial information needed to complete an apples-to-apples comparison of competing suppliers. Information is sparse or overwhelming. Prices are provided but not itemized. Optional costs are not clearly marked or separated from the base costs. *And trust me when I tell you, it's not difficult for a Buyer to make a mathematical error due to a poorly prepared quotation!* Going through every supplier's quote and making sure every dollar is accounted for is not an easy process, especially if the quote is unintentionally misleading or confusing to the Buyer.

Advice from the Buyer's Desk: **Don't count on the Buyer to be able to fully understand your quote!** Don't count on the Buyer to be able to find the information he needs to make his sourcing decision. Don't count on the Buyer to understand what your price is and exactly what's included in that price. For the vast majority of quotes, commercial terms and conditions are either missing or fly in the face of the Buyer's RFQ. Technical data is omitted or too advanced for the Buyer to understand. The quote is unorganized and confusing. All of these scenarios cause the Buyer to do one of three things:

1. The Buyer will contact the supplier for clarifications or corrections.

2. The Buyer will complete a quote comparison without contacting the supplier, thereby unknowingly using misleading information in the comparison without really knowing who the low cost provider is.

3. The Buyer will throw the quote out. *And trust me, I've seen that happen more times than I care to remember.*

Fortunately there are two remedies to this problem; two solutions that can greatly improve your opportunities in securing more business and ensure the Buyer understands the content and format of your quote. And both of them require proactive action on the part of the Sales Professional. These two remedies are (1) an **Executive Summary** and (2) a **Benchmark Quotation**.

EXECUTIVE SUMMARY. The best way to avoid any confusion in a quote, especially if it's several pages thick, is to create an **Executive Summary** of your proposal and insert it at the front of the package. *An Executive Summary is an abridged overview that includes key information from your quote, condensed on one page.* The Executive Summary should provide all of the key vital information and pricing the Buyer needs up front in order to make a decision. An example Executive Summary could include the following information: your company name and address, your vendor code (if any), the client's RFQ number, the payment terms and delivery terms, the quote validation date, the warranty period, the delivery date, your corporate quality certifications, the total price or piece-price, and the total cost of any non-recurring or one-time expenses. If you're not sure what the Buyer would like to see on an Executive Summary . . . *ask him!*

The final items you should have at the end of your Executive Summary is your name and contact information. You'd be surprised how many quotes I've received that has the Sales Rep's name at the end of it with the statement, *"Please feel free to contact me for any questions"*, with no contact information provided. *That definitely annoys Buyers!* It doesn't matter if you think the Buyer has your phone number or e-mail address memorized, leave it with your name! Be professional.

After you've created your Executive Summary feel free to share it with others for their input, *including the Buyer's!* Let the Buyer know you thought it would make life easier for him if you created an Executive Summary of your quote. Then ask for his input on the Summary's format. Since it's for the Buyer's benefit he may want to review it to add or remove items based on his own preferences. Providing an Executive Summary and making sure the Buyer knows it's there will make you stand out from your competition. This is because most suppliers don't even provide one unless the Buyer stipulates it.

BENCHMARK QUOTATION. In regards to format and presentation, the best way to ensure your quote is to the Buyer's preference is to ask him for a Benchmark Quotation. *A Benchmark Quotation is a quote created in a specific format that is preferred by a specific Buyer based on its layout as well as the chronology of the information provided.* Some Buyer's like the pricing up front. Some like it at the end. Some like to see specific product information. Some do not. What you need is feedback from the Buyer or Purchasing department of their own preferred type of quotation layout and format. Ask the Buyer what their ideal quote would look like and see if he can give you an example copy.

If the Buyer can't provide you with an example of his preferred Benchmark Quotation, bring him your last quote and have him mark it up according to his preferences. Where does the Buyer prefer specific information and how does he prefer it's presented? How does the Buyer prefer the pricing to be itemized and totaled? And what areas of your quote were confusing? Then take the marked up quote back to your office and have your estimating group clone it for future quotes for that same Buyer. Even if your quotes are normally one-page, ask the Buyer to critique it. *What would he prefer to see on the next one and how should it be presented?*

Remember that every Buyer from every department and from every company will have a different preference for quote formatting. So you may end up with dozens of benchmark quotations electronically on file for the dozens of Buyers you deal with. *It may create extra work, but it will also create more business opportunities.* Because it will allow each Buyer to easily find the information he needs to make a sourcing decision. And it will show the Buyer you're thinking in his best interest.

In my years in Purchasing I've asked numerous Buyers if they would prefer to receive a quote based on their preferred format. **Nearly 100% of them said "YES".** Then I asked how many Sales Professionals had actually offered to create a quote template based on their preferences. **Every one of them said "ZERO".**

FROM THE BUYER'S DESK: Find out what the Buyer's own benchmark quote looks like and adhere to his preferred format.

BUYERS WHO PREFER THIS: 93%
SALES REPS WHO DO THIS: 0%

"A Buyer's Perception of Electronic Bidding."

As a Corporate Buyer I do not claim to be an expert in the process of Electronic Bidding, or *E-Bid*. But I do know that many Sales Professionals today are either submitting quotes through the E-Bid process or may someday be compelled to do so by the client. So I thought I'd share my experiences on E-Bid and provide a true Buyer's perspective on the practice.

Prior to my employment in Corporate Purchasing, I was actually employed on the supply-side of the business for over 20 years, working for a number of engineering companies. During that time I attended Request-For-Quote (RFQ) meetings and put together quote packages for potential clients. And having worked on the supply-side I understand the amount of time, effort and cost involved in the quoting process of a single product or entire program. *Now, on top of all that comes the paradigm shift of Electronic Bidding.*

When I first started out in the industry back in the late 1970's, everyone wore a tie to work. And if you didn't wear a tie, people in the office would say, *"Oh . . . casual day?"* Now in today's world if I wear a tie to work most of my colleagues say, *"Oh . . . got an interview?"* Now that's a small but perfect example of how the way we do business has changed. ***When it comes to business, change has NEVER been the exception. Change has ALWAYS been the rule.*** Many years ago the majority of us never heard of ISO 9000, Total Quality Management, Lean Manufacturing or any number of technical and administrative advancements that have evolved over the years. Today, they're the rule. Desktop and laptop computers, e-mail, voicemail and cell phones didn't even exist when I started out in the industry. Now they are common place and no company can do without them.

The bottom line is that if a company doesn't keep up with technology and the latest industry trends, they need to get out of the way because they're going to get run over by someone who will. It reminds me of the old golf saying, *"In the game of golf, you'll always miss 100% of the shots you don't take."* The pendulum of change is constantly in motion. And in some industries, with some client companies and with some purchasing departments, the pendulum is swinging towards Electronic Bidding if they're not already there. So I'd like to share my experiences with E-Bid; how the process works and what the positive and negative aspects are for both suppliers and Corporate Purchasing.

To start, I'm honored to say that I was the *very first* Senior Buyer at DaimlerChrysler Corporation to facilitate on-line E-Bid auctions for their power-train purchasing group. It was an interesting experience. It's important to know that no supplier was forced at DaimlerChrysler to use E-Bid in order to submit a quote package. Every supplier was allowed to submit their normal quote package without the fear of being penalized. And yet only a hand full of suppliers chose not to participate in E-Bid. In addition, no supplier was charged anything to bid on the on-line auctions because DaimlerChrysler covered the E-Bid facilitation costs.

What's also important to note is that every supplier went through sufficient training to learn how to place their bids electronically. Each Supplier also went through real-world practice sessions a few days before the actual bidding took place so they could become familiar and play with the on-line options. *By the way, this is highly recommended for every client company to offer their supply base.*

In a nutshell, 'E-Bid' is sort of like using 'E-Bay', except for the fact that the price is going DOWN instead of UP. For our E-Bid sessions, the supplier logged onto their own computer, they logged into the E-Bid website with their own created password, they found the specific DaimlerChrysler auctions, and they started bidding at the specified time. Each auction lasted for ten minutes, which is not a long session. And that's why Sales Professionals had to do their homework before the day of the E-Bid. They had to know what their absolute bottom line was so they could spend the time pushing keys instead of wasting time planning a strategy.

At the end of the ten minutes the low bid supplier was considered the 'winner' of the E-Bid, though I hesitate to use that term because the low bid supplier did not necessarily WIN the purchase order. If the technical content of the quote package was not acceptable by engineering, or if commercial content was found to be erroneous, they didn't 'win' anything.

But unlike E-Bay, it was impossible for a supplier to hold off until the last possible second to submit their lowest price and beat out the other suppliers. That's because there was an automatic 'overtime cycle'. If any supplier submitted a bid within the last three minutes of the auction it was automatically extended for an additional amount of time. And if within the last three minutes of the extension period a supplier submitted yet another bid, the auction was again extended. But if at the end of the last three minutes of the auction or the last three minutes of the extension there was absolutely no activity from any supplier, the auction ended.

At DaimlerChrysler we used two separate types of E-Bid auctions. One auction was called the **English Reverse**. With this process, suppliers were allowed to submit a bid as long as it was below the current low bid from another supplier. Unfortunately if a supplier couldn't beat the current low bid, then they couldn't submit a bid at all. The other auction was called the **Dynamic Reverse**. With this process a supplier could submit a bid even if it wasn't below the current low bid from someone else, but as long as it was lower than their own last bid.

Part way through the E-Bid process, we realized that the English Reverse was not a good method of bidding for either us or the supplier. *That's because we weren't allowing suppliers to submit their own final best price.* Previously the supplier was only allowed to submit a price if it beat the another supplier's current low bid. Well, maybe they *couldn't* beat the current low bid but maybe they *could* have beat their own last bid. And if we ended up sourcing that supplier, we may not have received the best price they could have offered. That's why we finally decided to only use the Dynamic Reverse auction and allow suppliers to submit their best price, even if it wasn't below their competitor.

But again, best price did *not* necessarily secure the purchase order. Other factors played into receiving the order, including the technical and commercial content of the quote package. Sometimes the LOW bid supplier received the purchase order, and sometimes the HIGH bid supplier did. From the Buyer's perspective this is the only fair, common sense approach to E-Bids.

By now you may be thinking, *"Well, if a high bid supplier was able to receive a purchase order, than why do E-Bid at all?"* There are positive aspects to E-Bids for both the Buyer and the Seller. For the Buyer it saves an incredible amount of time in the negotiation process. Especially on the projects I worked on with hundreds of products to purchase covering over 50 commodities, and hundreds of suppliers to potentially negotiate with. E-Bid made my life as a Buyer a hell of a lot less stressful. The other positive aspect for the Buyer is that it obviously helps to reduce the cost because suppliers are directly bidding against each others pricing.

But there are positive aspects of E-Bid for suppliers too. During the auctions the suppliers were able to see what the current bid was, just like on E-Bay. But they were not able to know *who* that low bid competitor was. No company names were shown to any bidders. But the suppliers *could* compare their current price with the current low bid and align their price either below it or just above it with the understanding that low bid does *not* necessarily win the order. Another positive aspect for the supplier is that they were able to see for themselves what the true *current market value* of a specific commodity was. They were able to find out whether or not they had been bidding too high or too low in prior programs. Remember that with a regular paper or sealed bid, the supplier has no way of knowing where the current market price is based on competition. E-Bid was able to provide them with that valuable information.

E-Bid isn't perfect. There are some obvious drawbacks for both purchasing and the supplier. For the Buyer we lose whatever face-to-face negotiating power we may have had. We lose a portion of the personal working relationship we built up with the supply base. And at a time in which supplier relations are key to program success, E-Bid sort of dilutes it during the quoting process. For the supplier, E-Bid is sort of like playing poker except for fact that all of the cards are turned up and everyone's wearing a mask. *Everyone knows what you know, even though they don't know who you are.*

At DaimlerChrysler we had our share of issues with Electronic Bidding. Some suppliers accidently got disconnected from the E-Bid website so we had to start the auction over again. Some suppliers improperly lowered their price during the auction by pulling sub-components and program requirements out, so we no longer had an 'apples-to-apples' auction taking place. *In those instances we had to run the E-Bid again, minus I might add the supplier who tried to cheat the system.* We had suppliers claim the website didn't accept their last bid seconds before the auction ended. We even had a supplier bidding on-line and going head-to-head against another bidder . . . until they realized that the other bidder was someone from their own company! *We all got a good laugh from that one.* At the end of the day, we at DaimlerChrysler Corporation were 100% fair and ethical in the way we ran our E-Bid auctions. I was very proud of that.

All in all, E-Bid saved a lot of negotiating time for both the Buyer and the supplier. And it redefined commodity market values for everyone. It may surprise you that the majority of the feedback I received from the suppliers was positive. Some suppliers absolutely loved E-Bid. Some did not. *The question is, does E-Bid create an effect on the current market price for a commodity?* Have E-Bid auctions been successful in reducing the price of a suppliers normal quote? We can all speculate but I don't think anyone has the absolute answer right now because of the current economic environment we're all trying to survive in. Whether a client uses E-Bid during an economic downturn or not, the price IS going to come down because that's what the economic and financial markets dictate. That was verified by the handful of paper quotes received on the program that weren't put through the E-Bid process. I believe time will verify that E-Bid does have a tendency to lower prices, though not as much as during an economic decline.

E-Bid is not for everyone. It's not for every Buyer and it's not for every supplier. *It's certainly not for every commodity.* There has to be a good fit. In fact there are four key factors in making a process like E-Bid work for both the Buyer and the Seller.

1. The Buyer *must* be absolutely clear and specific as to what the supplier needs to include in the E-Bid price, as well as what needs to be left out. The end result *must* be apples-to-apples. If the commodity is too customized, E-Bid is *not* the direction to take.

2. The supplier *must* be allowed to opt out of the on-line bidding process and be allowed to simply submit a typical paper quote package without the fear of being penalized. It may not be to the supplier's advantage to do so, but it needs to be allowed. Otherwise Buyer's may lose good quotes from good suppliers who simply don't want to E-Bid.

3. The supplier *must* be allowed to eventually submit their own best price during the E-Bid, even if they can't beat the current low price from a competitor.

4. The supplier needs to know what their absolute bottom line is before the on-line auction starts. If the supplier doesn't know their bottom line going in and doesn't know when to quit, that supplier is headed for trouble! Then again, my Dad always said, *"Winners never quit, and quitters never win. But those who never win and never quit are idiots."*

The future for E-Bid is unclear. I think in more positive economic times it will be better defined and show the true savings potential for the Buyer, as well as the true market value of a commodity for the supplier. I do believe that E-Bid will be around to stay in one form or another in specific commodities that make sense, especially when it comes to large programs. Or, when a Buyer is procuring large quantities of a straightforward, well-defined product like a hammer or a pencil. But if a Buyer is only planning to purchase a few, highly critical, highly complicated items, then the process and setup of E-Bid, in my humble opinion, is not worth it for either side.

FROM THE BUYER'S DESK: There's a time and place for Buyers to utilize electronic bidding. There are both positive and negative aspects of E-Bid for both sides of the desk.

SECTION 5

Negotiating With Buyers

- Buyer-Endorsed Negotiating
- It's the Price, Dummy!
- Bargaining Behind the Buyer's Desk
- How Buyers Defuse Negotiation Strategies
- Prevailing Over the Incumbent Supplier
- What To Do if You Win the Order
- What To Do if You Lose the Order
- Don't Bad-Mouth the Competition

"Buyer-Endorsed Negotiating."

If it has been determined that your quotation is technically acceptable, that your product is capable of fulfilling the needs of the End-User, you will most likely enter the *negotiation phase* of the sales process. And depending on which company, organization or Buyer you're dealing with, negotiating can be anything from easy to complex, and from fair to biased. Some clients use the on-line bidding process to negotiate as explained earlier. Others use traditional face-to-face negotiating. And some processes are done through sealed bids. *The bottom line is that you need to find out what kind of negotiating will be taking place so you can prepare for it.*

In order to better understand how Corporate Buyers view negotiating, let's first review the process in our private world as a consumer. *There are three types of time-influenced negotiating we deal with in our own lives.* Each has their own purpose, strengths and weaknesses. Each utilizes their own sales strategies. And each produces a unique reaction from you as a buyer.

The first type of time-influenced negotiation is a **One-Time Sale** strategy. In this instance, the company is focusing on selling their product to the consumer *just once*. They may not expect nor care to sell product continuously to the same customer. What kinds of companies rely on the one-and-only sale? Infomercials. Time-shares. Used cars. And what type of negotiating do they use?

- High-pressure; limited-time only.
- Psychological games; convincing through shady routines.
- Interest in the seller's needs only.
- Minimal interaction.
- Disappear after the sale

These types of sales strategies are usually a turn off for you as a consumer. You don't like to be pressured into anything. You don't care for sales people who will do or say what it takes to make that one-time sale. You don't care for companies who put their own wants and needs before yours. And you certainly don't appreciate the Sales Rep's lack of desire to call you back or make things right if you're not satisfied.

The second type of time-influenced negotiation is **Cyclic Sales** based on a 1-5 year timeframe. Not something you'd normally buy more than once a year. What kinds of products and services fall into this category? Computers. Televisions. Appliances. New cars. Home remodeling. The sellers of these products and services use similar types of sales strategies as the *one-time sale*, though perhaps not as obvious. The difference is they're counting on the fact that there's been so much time in between purchases, hopefully you've forgotten about your less-than-perfect experience when you first bought a product from them. And sometimes it works. But sometimes you do remember and you vow never to buy anything from that store or company again.

The third type of time-influenced negotiation is **Perpetual Sales**. That is, the sale of products and services involving multiple buys throughout the year. These types of strategies cover products and services such as retail, groceries, personal hygiene, personal services, clothes, home goods and general maintenance. Think about what type of negotiating strategies you would prefer to deal with in your own private life when it comes to Perpetual Sales? How would you prefer the company representative to work with you during the negotiation process? How about someone who:

- Provides solutions without pressure to buy.
- Asks you questions without playing psychological games.
- Shows interest in your own needs as a consumer.
- Provides consistent, professional communication and support.
- Creates a trustful negotiating environment.
- Is available and responsive to your after-the-sale needs.

It's important to note that from the Buyer's perspective, most Sales Professionals only seem to negotiate price during the actual quoting process. *Well, when else are you going to do it?* Sales Professionals should be negotiating price on the *very first day* they have contact with the Buyer. It should start from that first initial telephone call, e-mail or meeting, *and it should never end.* You should think of that *first* contact with the Buyer as being the *first* step of many in getting to the negotiation stage. And every step of the way you should be creating a trusting environment so when you finally get to the point when you tell the Buyer, *"That's the best price I can give you"*, he believes you. (See the Section titled, *"Gaining and Maintaining a Buyer's Trust"*, pg. 30.)

Think of it this way. If I had proposed to my wife on our first date, her obvious answer would have been **"NO!"** *Why?* Because she didn't know me well enough. She didn't know my background, my strengths, my weaknesses or my intentions. There was no time to develop and build a relationship based on trust. There wasn't enough time to determine if there was a good fit between us. There wasn't enough information for her to make a decision on whether to commit or pass on the proposal. And in developing a relationship, especially one based on trust, it sometimes takes weeks, months and even years before the other party is willing to commit.

Unfortunately, too many Sales Professionals want to *"propose"* on *"the first date"* – otherwise known as *"the initial sales meeting"*. Too many Sales Reps expect an opportunity to quote or even receive an order following the initial sales call. And my answer to them is usually, **"NO!"** *Why?* Because I don't know them well enough. I don't know their company's background. I don't know their company's strengths, weaknesses or intentions. There hasn't been enough time to develop and build a business relationship based on trust. There hasn't been enough time to determine if there's a good fit between our companies. And I may not have enough information to make a decision on whether to commit in allowing them to quote much less award them with an order.

Unfortunately, many suppliers believe it doesn't matter what they do. They believe that the Buyer is going to make his decision based on price alone. But as stated earlier in this book, *if the Buyer isn't **educated** by the Sales Rep on the **value** of their product, then price is the only thing the Buyer has to use as a selection criteria.* If you were a Buyer and you perceived that every product is exactly the same, you'd be crazy not to pick the lowest price! In order to successfully negotiate, the Sales Professional needs to sell on the value of the product after developing a trusting business relationship. *And that's true no matter if you're selling a multi-million dollar system or a $5 pen.*

FROM THE BUYER'S DESK: Negotiate based on the specific type and time-influenced selling taking place. Determine if you really want repeat business or prefer to just sell and run.

"It's the Price, Dummy!"

Price, price, price! Seems Buyers are only interested in your price. *"Is this your best price?" "Can you lower your price?" "I can't live with that price."* If you had a dime for every time you heard the word "PRICE" coming from the Buyer's mouth you wouldn't be reading this book. You'd be relaxing on a tropical beach sipping a fancy drink. *But unfortunately, price is a reality that demands attention no matter what side of the desk you're sitting on.* So if it has now been determined that your quote is technically acceptable, you will most likely enter the *negotiation phase* of the quoting process. And as stated earlier, depending on what company or Buyer you are dealing with, negotiating can be anything from simple to difficult, and from fair to subjective. Some Buyers use different types of negotiating processes, depending on the product or service being negotiated; from on-line bidding to traditional face-to-face negotiating. And as recommended earlier, you need to find out what kind of negotiating will be taking place so your company can prepare for it.

So what's the best way to negotiate with Corporate Purchasing? Not an easy question to answer. In previous Sections of this book we've discussed how important it is to build *trust* in a business relationship. Because when it comes to negotiating with Buyers, two things are extremely important: (1) *trust*, and (2) *knowing your absolute bottom line*. With that in mind, negotiating really comes down to two rhetorical questions:

1. How do you convince the **BUYER** that your final price is the best price you can offer?

2. How do convince **YOURSELF** that your final price is the best price you can offer?

Let's cover the topic of trust a bit further as it's perceived from the Buyer's Desk. Developing trust early in the business relationship is essential, especially when it comes to negotiating. When you're buying a retail product like a television, appliance, computer or automobile, you'll sometimes ask your friends and family, *"Where do you shop"* or *"Who do you buy from?"* Essentially, what you're really asking them is, ***"Who do you trust?"***

So take a moment and think of someone you absolutely trust. Think of someone you know that if they were selling you something, you'd believe them if they told you, *"This is the best price I can offer."* It could be your spouse, your partner, a family member, a good friend or even another sales professional. *Now that you have someone in mind, what is it about that person that makes you trust them?* What is it about your relationship with that individual that compels you to believe he or she is telling you the truth? Have you known him for a long time? Has she ever lied to you? Do others view him as an honest person? Is there something in her character or demeanor that ensures you she's honest? Has he conveyed a sense of trust throughout your relationship with him? Have you ever done business with her before that resulted in a positive, trusting outcome?

To some, the ultimate relationship is **marriage**. And what is the relationship of marriage based on? *Continuous trust, uninterrupted commitment, constant assurance, unbroken faith.* Of course, a business relationship is emotionally far removed from the bond of marriage, but it still entails some of the same attributes: *Continuous trust, uninterrupted commitment, constant assurance, unbroken faith.* You're looking out for the client's best interest. You're on the client's side. You're solving the client's problems. You're interested in the client's needs. You're creating a constant environment of preferred communication and support. In short, ***you've earned their trust!***

Now that you've maintained trust in the business relationship with the Buyer, let's cover the two rhetorical questions stated earlier. ***First, how do you convince the BUYER that your final price is the best price you can offer?*** That's where the element of trust plays into the negotiating process. What is it about your own character, demeanor and business history that will make people trust you when you tell them, *"This is the best price I can give you"*? Go ahead and ask your business associates. What is it about you that compels anyone to believe you're telling the truth? Have they known you for a long time? Have you ever steered them down the primrose path only to later throw them in the thorns? Is there something in your own personality, body language or demeanor that assures others, *"I can trust this person"*?

Now let's take on the second rhetorical question. *How do you convince YOURSELF that your final price is the best price you can offer?* Have you done your homework? What have you done to ensure it's the best price? How closely have you worked with your estimating department? Do you simply accept from others what the price should be? Have you conducted enough research on your own to accept the cost and the logic behind it? How well do you understand the materials market? Have you reached your absolute bottom line? Do you even know what your absolute bottom line is? Is it based on cost-plus-markup? Do you know what your competitors are charging for the same product or service? Have you questioned every aspect of your price as well as those from your own sub-suppliers? As stated earlier, so many times I have Sales Professionals say to me, *"Let me go back to my own suppliers and see if I can negotiate a better price."* *Really? Why didn't you do that the first time?*

Again, from The Buyer's Desk, the two key things in negotiating best price is **TRUST** to convince me you've offered the best price, and **HOMEWORK** to convince yourself you've offered the best price.

FROM THE BUYER'S DESK: Convince yourself you're offering the best possible price before you try to convince the Buyer.

"Bargaining Behind the Buyer's Desk."

Everyone has an opinion as to how to negotiate. There are hundreds of sales books in the stores and on-line, each with their own ground-breaking negotiation tactics and approaches that worked for the author. And you've heard of, if not attended, seminars and workshops that provide hardcore strategies when negotiating what you want or what you want to offer. Personally I don't discount any of the books or classes out there because each has something positive to offer to the Business Professional. I've always thought that if you can get something of value from any form of sales instruction, the price paid will have been worth it, *even if it only resulted in one additional sale.*

So in this Section, I've included some of the *contemporary* negotiation tactics described in today's books and seminars – those currently used by Sales Professionals on today's Corporate Buyers. In the description of each strategy I've included not only the Buyer's perspective, but what to do if Buyer's use that same tactic on you. **Remember, we Buyers are reading the exact same books and are attending the same brand-name seminars you are!**

GIVE AND TAKE. A classic negotiation tactic from the sales side of the desk is to concede something in exchange for something you want:

"I'm willing to offer you an extended warranty if you agree to my initial price for the product."

"I'll give you a free year of service if you accept my quote today."

"I'll give you 10% off the price if the order will reflect my preferred payment terms."

One of the brand-name negotiation workshops puts a great deal of emphasis on this strategy – and rightly so. The key to a successful *Give and Take* negotiation is to ensure that what you're giving is of little importance to you, and what you're taking is of practical benefit to your company. In order to make this happen, the Sales Professional or Business Owner will inherently provide a list of things they can offer to concede to the Buyer. Usually these things have little to no value to them or their company.

However in a twist of that tactic, be aware that the Buyer may ask for things in the RFQ that *he* really doesn't need, like prolonged payment terms or extreme specifications; things that would prove difficult for the supplier to accept anyway. Then when the Buyer agrees to drop his *(superfluous)* demand in trade for a cost reduction, the Sales Rep feels like he got something back; *cost avoidance.*

The problem with the *Give and Take* method of negotiating is that there's no guarantee the other party will actually need what you're willing to give away. *"I don't need an extended warranty. You'll have to find another way to reduce your price."* In a previous Section titled, *"The #1 Sales Meeting Mistake" (pg. 111),* we talked about the need for the Sales Professional to ask themselves the following questions about the person they're about to present to:

"What is this person's job title? What are the person's goals and responsibilities in the company? Therefore, what would most likely interest them? And what would most likely NOT interest them?"

Those same basic questions hold true when trying to determine what you can offer for the things you want during the negotiation process. The secret in finding out is asking ahead of time during the initial quoting process.

"Based on your responsibilities on this project, what are some of the things most important to you?"

"Are there any specific expectations of the product that will help to achieve your departmental goals?"

"What will you need from the preferred supplier in order to ensure the product's success?"

Find out the Buyer's wants, needs and interests in sourcing the product. Maybe price isn't the key motivator in awarding the order. If the price is low but the normal product lead-time is beyond the need, then price is insignificant. In that scenario, the ability to hold your price and guarantee expedited delivery is your bargaining chip. So your job is to find out what counts, what matters most to the Buyer. Is it price, quantity, delivery, quality, capability, function or something else? Have the Buyer rate the importance of each area. Then determine what you can offer in potential low cost concessions to support what matters most. *"During the initial project meeting, you said that having the product in four weeks is absolutely imperative. Unfortunately our normal lead-time is six weeks. But if you'll agree to our current price, we'll guarantee a delivery in four."*

ASK FOR MORE, EXPECT LESS. Buyers will often request price reductions or percentages off costs that are *well below* what they really need. Your initial price for the service is $5000. The Buyer's target price is $4500, or 10% below your quote. So he asks for 20% off with the anticipation of ending up at 10%. Many times in our personal life we'll offer a price way less than what we're actually willing to pay, hoping the seller will agree. Real estate is a prime example. Sometimes it works and sometimes you end up *"splitting the difference"* with the home owner.

But here's the secret: The main reason the Buyer goes overboard in asking for price reductions is because they think you've *automatically* gone overboard in pricing it. They're assuming a *'buffer'* has been included in the cost with the *expectation* of future negotiations.

In order to defuse that tactic you need to let the Buyer know up front, well before you submit your quote, that you intend to give him the best price you can offer with the initial submission. Before you even hand in the quote, tell the Buyer you had it in your hands to review a few days earlier but knew he wouldn't be happy with the price. So you *already* went back to your estimating group and your *own* suppliers to improve processes and find ways to negotiate a better deal. Explain that your intent was to not waste the Buyer's valuable time; *that you've **already** found ways to reduce costs without sacrificing the quality or requirements expected.*

Of course this counter tactic will never work if you haven't already cultured *trust* in your business relationship with the Buyer. The element of trust is discussed in a few Sections in this book. It's the most effective way to convince Purchasing that your initial or final price **IS** the best price you can offer.

EXAGGERATED RESPONSES. One of the oldest maneuvers a Buyer will use when they see or hear a *"shocking"* price from a supplier is to overreact with words, facial and body expressions. The purpose is to make the Sales Professional feel awkward and inept about the price they just presented. It's a psychological game used by Purchasing to intimidate the poor Sales Rep who *had the nerve to waste the Buyer's time with such a ridiculous price!* I've personally never used this tactic. I prefer to swear.

Regardless, if the Buyer tries to intimidate you in such a way, don't fall into their trap. Don't counter their overreaction by trying to apprehensively or irately justify your price, or by offering an immediate cost reduction. Instead play it cool and say, *"You know, that's the same reaction I had when I first saw that number from my estimating group. I was shocked. Then, we sat down and they showed me exactly what it takes to provide that product. In fact, I have the documentation with me if you'd like to review it."*

In the Section titled, *"Talk the Language of Purchasing"* under the designation, *"Cost of Goods Sold"* (pg. 50), we discussed the advantage of sharing your cost and pricing data for any given product or service with Purchasing. Included in the data should be your cost for items such as raw material, outsourced components, in-house manufacturing, work hours, transportation, documentation, hourly rates, SG&A and profit. When everything is clearly and chronologically spelled out in black-and-white and the Buyer is educated on the time, material and expenses it actually takes to get the product to market, they'll be more willing to accept your initial price or at least negotiate to a reasonable level you can both live with.

KNOW WHEN TO HOLD 'EM AND WHEN TO FOLD 'EM. In the previous Section titled, *"It's the Price, Dummy!"*, we asked the rhetorical question, *"How do convince yourself that your final price IS the best price you can offer?"* Have you completed your research, probed every process, and scrutinized every aspect of internal and external costs? Is your profit margin set in cement? Are you confident that the final price you're prepared to offer *IS* the best price?

Once you reach that all important final number, you need to have management unconditionally agree that one less dollar or one less concession means you're folding your hand and walking away from the poker table. Many times I've found myself sitting at a Vegas slot machine with a bucket full of quarters and a resolved strategy to walk away when I'm down to $50. That's before I get caught up in the emotion of a potential jackpot. *"Well, what's another $10? As long as I* *walk away with $40, I'm good"* Minutes later. *"Okay, so I'm down to $40. I can afford to lose another $10. No big deal. Besides, I should win something by then anyway."* A few minutes later. *"Okay, so I'm down to $20. It's only $20. It's not going to break me."* Five minutes later I'm walking out of the casino with an empty bucket. I didn't have the will power to quit despite my well-conceived plan to stop at a set amount. I gave away the farm. Sold my soul to the devil.

The other danger in not knowing when to walk away is allowing the Buyer to become too accustomed to discount pricing. They get used to winning concessions based on the supplier's desperation or the fear of losing the order. Once he gets a taste, he'll expect it every time. And once the Buyer becomes addicted to the supplier caving in, it's extremely difficult to wean him off that expectation. Knowing your absolute 'walk away' point and sticking to it will not *only* put the leverage of negotiation in your favor (even if you don't end up with the order), it will keep the Buyer in check the next time you're sitting at the poker table.

KNOWLEDGE IS POWER. The individual sitting on either side of the desk with the most accurate and comprehensive information about a product's expectations, timing and competition will usually do better in negotiations. The individual who understands more about the other company's capabilities, internal processes and motivations stands a better chance of succeeding in getting what they want.

If the Buyer is pressuring you to immediately reduce your price because timing is tight, but you know that project kick-off is a month away, then the leverage of negotiating is on your side. If the Buyer tells you he has plenty of other suppliers to source product to, but you know that the other competitors are either financially strapped, aren't capable of providing the product or didn't even quote, then the leverage of negotiating is on your side. If the Buyer tells you your quote isn't even close to the target price, but you know that the overall project is well below budget, then the leverage of negotiating is on your side.

Knowing what to ask the Buyer, and developing a relationship with all of the decision-makers within any client company is the key. It's the key to gaining the information you need to offset these types of tactics used by the Buyer. There are several Sections in this book that talk about the importance of building a working, trusting relationship with the End-Users as well as the Buyer, especially those who collectively decide which suppliers will be allowed to quote and which will end up with the order. And you do that by engaging the End-User based on their own specific roles, responsibilities, wants and needs. Not only will it strengthen your sales opportunities, but some End-Users have a tendency to provide the actual facts about projects, products and competitors; things the Buyer would never tell you. That's because End-Users are more concerned with end results then they are with commercial details.

It's the End-Users who live with the everyday struggles in the field. And when in the right frame of mind, most will vent and provide insight into the very things the Buyer doesn't want you to know. *"What's the reason this product or service is needed?"* *"What concerns do you have with the incumbent supplier?"* *"What issues are you experiencing and what is the solution you're looking for?"* *"And when do you need this solution to happen?"*

The more knowledge you have about the struggles the End-Users are experiencing, the more negotiating leverage you'll have with the Buyer. *"It's my understanding the project won't be kicked-off until next month."* *"It's my understanding Supplier X's products aren't meeting production expectations."* *"It's my understanding that cost savings in support services has opened funds in the budget for my product."*

TWO EARS, ONE MOUTH. Zeno of Citium was a Greek philosopher born in 334 BC. He was the founder of the Stoic school of philosophy in Athens and lived to be 72. As far as I know he was the first person to assert, *"We have two ears and one mouth, so we should listen more than we say."* In other words, we should listen more and talk less. A wise viewpoint coming from someone who was born more than 2,300 years ago. And if you took the basic Dale Carnegie course like I did, you'll recall that one of the principles in winning people to your way of thinking is to let the other person do a great deal of the talking. *In fact, I say let them talk first!*

So when negotiating, why would you want the Buyer to talk first? Isn't that giving him control of the negotiations? Actually, there are several reasons why you should let the Buyer open the discussions. First, most people feel they have the power and the leverage if they talk - and talk first. So go ahead, let them feel commanding. Let them feel in control. It certain won't hurt at the start of the meeting, especially when nothing has been collectively debated yet.

Another reason to let the Buyer talk first is in the hopes he'll start the bidding war. Too many Sales Professionals I've worked with started negotiations by laying all of their cards on the table before I even show one of mine. They had no idea what price I even needed them to come down to. They just volunteered the information, never knowing if it met or exceeded my needs. But if you can get the Buyer to start the conversation, he may let you know where he needs to be, which may be higher than what you were going to offer.

A third reason to let the Buyer talk first is that it gives them a chance to vent. All day long they've been waiting to say something about your quote, your product and your price. They can't hold it in anymore. So let them blow off some steam. In doing so it will position two things in your favor. One, it will make the Buyer feel better to have gotten everything out. The weight and pressure of what was building up will have subsided and they're now in a better disposition to negotiate. Two, it will allow you to better understand where they're coming from. What are their issues? What are their concerns? What price do they want you to come down to? What do they want you to concede? What do they need in order to award you with the business?

As a Buyer I normally try to get the Sales Professional to open the discussions and vent first. In doing so it usually gives me more information about the supplier's situation than I had before. What are *their* concerns? What data do *they* want to present? *Knowing these things before I talk may change my entire negotiation strategy on the spot!* As new and previously unknown information is presented by the Sales Rep, it changes my negotiation plan. Many times I was ready to agree to specific cost reductions and concede certain options based on preconceived assumptions on my end. But when I let the Sales Rep talk first and heard what his actual concerns were, my reductions ended up being more than I had hoped for and I conceded nothing.

SILENCE IS GOLDEN. Some negotiation books and workshops will discuss the power of *silence*. The Buyer asks you to reduce your cost by 10%. You tell him you can't. The Buyer then quietly sits in his chair, stares down at his desk in a state of reflection and says nothing for a few moments. The silence builds and you're beginning to feel a bit awkward. The longer the silence on his end, the longer you feel obligated to say something, even offer something up. A consolation prize. A concession. A potential solution. Maybe even the price reduction you just said no to. Whatever you're feeling at the moment, don't give into it. It's the Buyer's obligated turn to say something and he knows it. Just stay as silent as he is. If his silence continues, ask if he would like a day or two to think about it. *If he continues to remain silent, he's just being a jackass.* Don't give into it.

A silent Buyer is a powerful negotiation tool. And sometimes the silence can go on for days. While a Lead Buyer at DaimlerChrysler, I negotiated with a Sales Professional I'll call "Tony". Tony was quoting on a project and knew there were other competitors involved. When he handed me his quote he explained, *"This is my final offer."* I had some time on my side before I had to select a supplier so I thanked him and said I'd be in touch. A week went by without contacting Tony. On the seventh day, Tony called and said, *"Hey, we gained some additional concessions from our own suppliers. I can offer a price reduction of 12% but that's as low as I can go."* I thanked Tony for the information.

Another five days of silence on my end. The next morning another call from Tony. *"Hey, we were able to reduce the manufacturing time so we can offer you another 7% reduction."* I thanked him again. This was followed by three more days of silence. The subsequent afternoon I received yet another call from Tony. *"Okay. I spoke with our estimating group and they agreed to another 5% price reduction."* I thought to myself, *"Hell, if I remain silent for another two weeks I'll end up getting the product for free!"*

Tony's actions resulted in a few things against him. One, it told me *never* to believe him when he says, *"This is my final offer."* (Especially the fourth time around.) Two, it told me that his initial price was too high, especially after a total reduction of 24%. Three, it told me that his company's method of cost estimating was inadequate. Regardless, Tony ended up getting the order. He was happy because his negotiation strategy (whatever it was) worked - at least in his mind. And I was happy because I got 24% off the initial quote. And I did that without even saying a word. Silence *is* golden.

TIME IS ON MY SIDE. The 1963 song *"Time Is On My Side"* by the Rolling Stones is one of my favorites. And it happens to be one of the official theme songs of Corporate Purchasing. That's because *time* is the one factor that's normally in our favor when it comes to negotiating. I'll either let you know that *I'm out of time* and I need your final reduced price now . . . or I'll inform you that *I have plenty of time* to see what your competitors will offer. Both tactics are used in an attempt to get the preferred-supplier's price down.

In a previous Section titled, *"Buyer-Endorsed Negotiating"*, we discussed time-influenced approaches some Sales people use in our private lives to compel us to buy their product. These approaches involve either high-pressure, limited-time-only tactics like vacation timeshares . . . or the seller will claim he's in no rush to sell and will wait for the right buyer and price. In either case, the seller is holding the consumer hostage. It's either, *"Buy now or lose it forever"* or *"You're offer is too low and I have other people interested."* Well, there's nothing saying that the *BUYER* can't use that same tactic on the *SALES REP* when it comes to buying a product. That's why it's best to avoid any type of deadline ultimatum from the Buyer. And here's how to do it.

If the Buyer is pressuring you to provide your best price

immediately, don't make a snap decision. Don't let the heat of the moment get the best of you. In previous segment titled, *"Know When to Hold 'Em and When to Fold 'Em"*, the emphasis was knowing your bottom line before entering the negotiation phase. At what point are you willing to walk away? Tell the Buyer you would personally appreciate the order, but you've been given strict instructions by Sales Management to pass on the opportunity if it means going below your final offer. Put the blame on someone else. I do it all the time. *"Gee, I'd love to buy those earrings for my Wife, but I'd never hear the end of it if she knew I paid that much for them."* In putting the final decision into the hands of someone who's not there, the Buyer loses his ability to negotiate further. And it either buys you time to go back to your manager, or the Buyer was serious and the negotiations are over.

If you do have a little wiggle room in your price, don't offer it all up at once. Baby steps and small percentages is what you should offer. Buyers won't expect any Sales Professional to give away the farm right away. One pig at a time. Maybe a couple of chickens. Minimal reductions will tell the Buyer you may be close to, if not already at, your lowest price. But a dramatically reduced price will tell him you've been holding back. I once had a supplier provide a price of $250 for their product. I asked for a reduction. It came down to $247. I told him I needed another reduction. It came down to $246.53. In seeing such a resolved number it was my perception that I got the *absolute* best price the supplier could offer. I was no longer squeezing nickels and dimes out of them, *I was now squeezing pennies!* That was enough for me.

On the other hand, if the Buyer is pressuring you because he has plenty of time with other suppliers waiting in the wings, ask yourself, *"Then why is he wasting time with me?"* The reason he's wasting time is because **he wants your product!** If he has plenty of time, then why is he pressuring you to make an on-the-spot decision? Now it's possible he has other suppliers in the wings. But who are they, what can they provide, and at what cost? *"You'd better give me the price I want! I have other suppliers pounding on my door waiting to offer me a better offer."* You should be thinking (but not saying), *"Good for you! Let them in! And let's compare their product against mine. Let's compare their 'value' against mine."* If the last price you gave IS the best price you can offer, turn things around on him. Then, use the *'time'* approach and let him know how *long* your offer is good for. Hopefully he doesn't waste the time left negotiating with those in the wings. Tell the Buyer, *"The reason I can only offer this price until Friday is because we received that same time limit from our own suppliers. If I can let them know by Friday that we've been awarded the order, they promise to hold* *their costs. After that we'll be compelled to raise our quote only due to their price increases."* There you are again, blaming it on someone who's not there; someone the Buyer can't negotiate with. *Good for you!*

CARNIE GAMES. If you've ever attended a carnival or State Fair, you've no doubt seen if not played the games located near the Midway. Target shooting, ball toss and balloon darts are just a few of the games available to lay your money down and attempt to win the big prize. In reality, most people do *NOT* win the big prize and that's how Carnie's make their money. But one tactic Carnie's use in keeping the sucker, I mean player interested is offering a "consolation prize". So instead of winning the big stuffed bear worth $200, you end up with a plastic souvenir worth 2 cents. Somehow that's either supposed to keep you trying, or at the very least make you feel like you got something out of it. For some players, the consolation prize is a minor 'trophy' and they feel satisfied. For the Carnie, it's a 'reward' that cost them practically nothing.

That's a tactic some Sales Reps use on Buyers and, for the most part, it works. If you've truly hit rock bottom and cannot lower the price of your product, offer the Buyer a consolation prize. *No, not a plastic souvenir worth two cents.* But something they'll consider a minor "trophy" that will cost you practically nothing; at least something that's far less than the cost of reducing your quote. *"We are unable to lower our current offer. However, we can include free on-site service for three months."* Find out from the Buyer what it is you have that he could use. A small investment that will help secure the order. Then the Buyer can tell his manager, *"I wasn't able to get the price down but I talked them into some free services."*

You can also offer another type of consolation prize. Have you ever seen the cable show, *"American Pickers"*? One of my favorites. I love to watch those two guys negotiate with the sellers. Next time it's on, watch what they do. Learn from their strategies. One of the guys likes to "bundle" things for sale. If he doesn't agree with the price of one item, he'll temporarily leave it and look for something to bundle it with. *"Okay, you want $100 for the old clock. That's high for me but I'll agree to pay it if I can get this vintage oil can for $10."* If you can't come down in your price, find out if the Buyer or anyone in his department has another product to quote on. We've discussed the bundling process earlier in the Section, *"Get the Order Through Bundling."* (pg. 174). Offer a discount on Item #2 if you can't lower your price on Item #1. This increases your business opportunities and, at the same time, keeps your final price . . . *final.*

WE AGREE TO DISAGREE. Many sales books and seminars will tell you it's best to enter negotiations with the mutual understanding that some point-of-views will not be aligned between Buyer and Seller. Not everything will be agreed on and not everything will be accepted by the other party. It has nothing to do with right or wrong, truth or lies. It has everything to do with perceptions, circumstances and personal preferences. Neither side is willing to change or give up their slice of the pie. *"Well, I guess we'll just have to agree to disagree."*

One of the best ways to negotiate items based on these types of disagreements is to 'break bread' with the other party. By that, I mean getting to know each other personally before professional responsibilities cloud the issues. Like most guys, one of my favorite movies are "The Godfather" series. And my favorite line is, *"Keep your friends close but your enemies closer."* But as a Buyer I prefer to say, *"Keep your co-workers close but your suppliers closer."* This is in no way a negative connotation. Quite the contrary. I prefer to have good business relationships with the Sales Reps I work with for a number of reasons.

In the Section titled, *"Buyer-Endorsed Negotiating"* (pg. 190), we discussed the importance of developing a relationship based on trust *before* diving into the business relationship. That's *exactly* the Buyer's strategy with this tactic. In allowing Sales Reps to *first* know me as a human being, they find out I like the same brand of beer, we share stories about our kids, and we talk about our plans for the weekend. I'm no longer the *'dark side'* of the sales process. I'm no longer a rude, obnoxious Buyer. I'm just a regular Joe. I'm now one of them. Group hugs and all that stuff. And most important, because I've shown my *soft side*, I genuinely seem to have both my company's and the supplier's best interest in mind. I now stand a much better chance negotiating before we even sit down to bargain. And when prices come down and concessions are given, they're given to a colleague in need, *not* to a greedy Buyer. *Because it's easier to negotiate with allies than it is with adversaries.*

From that point it's also easier to find out what items we agree on, where we're on different sides of the fence, and which of *those* are most important to us. Hopefully the ones most important will be resolved accordingly. For the others, *"We'll just have to agree to disagree."*

FROM THE BUYER'S DESK: Contemporary negotiation strategies are studied by both Buyers and Sellers. One's ability to successfully negotiate what they want and need will be determined by how well versed the other party is in the same tactics, and what their own wants and needs are.

"How Buyers Defuse Negotiation Strategies."

Whether they learn from experience, through professional training, from management or as a natural-born instinct, Corporate Buyers best protect their company both legally and financially through the process of **negotiating**; legally by negotiating the terms and conditions of the contract, and financially by negotiating the best value.

In many ways, Buyers have the advantage over Sales Professionals when it comes to the eventual outcome of negotiations. That's because the vast majority of the time, the Buyer gets to negotiate with *several suppliers* for the same product, whereas each Sales Rep is only negotiating with *one Buyer.* It sometimes comes down to odds and statistics; the more suppliers the Buyer has to negotiate with for the same product, the more chances he'll reach his target price. If the Buyer has five qualified suppliers to negotiate with, odds are at least one of them will agree to the price the Buyer needs. Whereas the Sales Rep only has one Buyer to negotiate with and has the potential to lose the business to one of the other four suppliers.

The other advantage the Buyer has is actually knowing the magic number; that is, the final price the Buyer is willing to accept. *That's the last card that remains face down on the poker table.* The advantage comes in the fact that the Buyer can win the hand without ever having to show that last card. *Imagine playing poker and accepting the other person's word that they won the deal without ever seeing their last card.* The odds are not in your favor. Even if you win the purchase order, you may never really know if your accepted price was above or below the number on that last unseen card, or by how much.

But regardless of who has the advantage in negotiating, Corporate Buyers have another tactic up their sleeves when it comes to concessions and arbitrations. This specific tactic is designed to discourage Sales

Professionals from actually using any negotiation strategies against the Buyer. And if this tactic is used properly it can quickly turn the negotiations in the Buyer's favor. I really shouldn't be telling you this, but be careful if any Buyer you're dealing with refers to subsequent negotiating as a **'GAME'**.

If a Buyer replies to your offer and refers to the eventual process of reaching a negotiated price as a *game*, you need to step back and think about your response. If the Buyer describes the aftereffects of playing the *game* and offers the benefits of reaching an agreement quickly in order to avoid playing *the game*, you need to stop and think before you offer a response that defuses that term. Because when a Buyer refers to negotiations as a *game*, it's designed to make the Sales Professional or Business Owner feel awkward and uncomfortable for even thinking of using negotiation strategies against him. Whether it actually works or not is up to you.

In using the word *'game'* the Buyer wants you to assume he is well suited and experienced in recognizing any potential strategies you plan to use against him; *that he's done his homework*. The Buyer wants you to assume he's been down that road before and has pre-described countermeasures to use against your strategies. The Buyer wants you to consider that in this specific *game of chess* he has a countermove ready for every possible move your board pieces can make; *that the Buyer has a pre-planned action ready to thwart your maneuvers*. The hope is that you'll surrender your Queen, throw in your cards, forsake your strategies and accelerate an agreement in the Buyer's favor.

In describing negotiations as a game, the Buyer may describe to you a well-rehearsed, step-by-step description of what will most likely take place on both sides of the table should negotiations continue. The Buyer may say:

"Your quote is simply not where it needs to be in order to receive the order. Now we can play the same old game where you tell me you've given me your best price, then I tell you I have lower quotes from other suppliers, then you'll contact me in a few days with a price reduction. We can play that game or we can forgo the rulebook and agree on a price right now that's fair and reasonable to both of us. So would you prefer to play the game and waste both of our times, or should I cut the order to you today with the price I need?"

At this point you have the advantage of saying one of two things, both of which will stall the Buyer and buy you time to regroup and rethink your strategies.

Response #1: *"I don't have the authority to agree to that price. I'll have to speak with my manager about it."*

Response #2: *"Let me go back and see if I can get my estimators to look at this again. Maybe we can squeeze some more money out of our own suppliers."*

Buyers are ready for both of those responses. The Buyer may reply:

"I'm under pressure to cut a deal today. If you can't agree on this price right now then you'll force me to contact the other suppliers to close the deal. I'd rather place business with your company but I can live with the other guy."

The beauty of this Buyer tactic is that it uses a *pre-planned negotiation strategy* to combat your own *pre-planned negotiation strategy*. The pressure is on you. Time is of the essence. I've personally sat through one too many sales seminars for vacation timeshares, real estate and other business offers in which I had to make up my mind on the spot or walk away, never knowing if I made a bad decision. *I hate that!* It's a time-pressured tactic Sales Professionals use on potential clients. *But now that same tactic is being used against the Sales Rep.* And here's how to react.

First, it's important for you to know approximately how many suppliers are out there that can offer the same product. Are there actual competitors currently working with your client? Do you compete against them often? Is the commodity you're selling easily available in the marketplace by other capable suppliers? Or is what you're offering so unique that not only is there limited competition, but those who can offer it are far below your quality, technology and capabilities? *The less proficient competition you have, the better your advantage will be in the Buyer's negotiation tactics.* The pressure of closing the deal on the spot will defuse the Buyer if you are the only game in town.

Second, if you are *not* the only game in town and you actually *are* supposed to receive permission from management, or if you really *do* need to have your estimators revisit the quote, make sure you do all of that *before* meeting with the Buyer so you know the answers ahead of time. *Never go into negotiations unprepared!* Let your manager know you're about to enter negotiations with the Buyer before you leave the office. Find out what bottom-line price he's willing to live with. Equally important, negotiate with your own sub-suppliers for the best possible price *before* you enter negotiations. *The key is to plan ahead and have your bottom-line answers ready before you sit to negotiate with the Buyer.* Do that just in case the Buyer *isn't* bluffing and he really *does* need an answer now!

Another way to defuse the Buyer's *game* tactic is to let them know that to you and your company, this is NOT a game; it's a business transaction. Don't play into their hand. Don't acknowledge that *you're* playing a game even if *they* are. You have quality products and services to offer. You have the best value that best fits the Buyer's needs. *And if your quote isn't where it needs to be, you look forward to finding a fair and reasonable solution.* Let the Buyer know that if time is of the essence, hopefully there's enough of it left for you to respond with a revised quote. You'd hate to have Purchasing procure inferior product from your competitor, thereby affecting the quality of what they're offering to their own clients.

Finally, remember this important bit of Advice from the Buyer's Desk: ***If the Buyer really does have other suppliers with equal product at lower costs, then why is he wasting his time with you?*** The reason is because the Buyer or End-User really does want to award you with the order but needs to get the best possible deal, *even if it isn't lower than your competitors.* Otherwise he wouldn't be pressuring you on the spot. So don't make it a game with winners and losers. Make it a serious business transaction that fulfills everyone's objectives.

FROM THE BUYER'S DESK: Play the offensive hand when negotiating with Buyer's. Anticipate what he might say or counter offer and be prepared with potential responses that are pre-approved by management. Despite what the Buyer may tell you, this *isn't* a game. ***It's your career!***

"Prevailing Over the Incumbent Supplier."

One of the most difficult Purchase Orders to be awarded is the one you take away from the *Incumbent Supplier*. Difficult, but not impossible. *And incredibly gratifying!* An *Incumbent Supplier* is a company who is currently providing specific products and services to the client. And in most cases, it's harder for the Incumbent to lose the order than it is for you to win it. In any industry, the Incumbent has obvious advantages over their competitors, especially if the Buyer and End-Users are satisfied with their performance. These advantages include:

- A reasonable price based on the quantity of product. Price may be within budget. Or the Buyer may be willing to live with the price based on the costs, time and effort associated with finding and sourcing a new supplier.
- A reduction or removal of non-recurring, one-time start-up expenses required with a new supplier.
- The Buyer's familiarity with the Incumbent's products.
- The End-User's desire to continue the use of the Incumbent's products and services.
- An existing business relationship between the Buyer and the Incumbent Sales Professional.
- Known issues that exist within the Incumbent's performance, but issues the Buyer and End-Users are willing to live with.
- The Incumbent's inside knowledge of the client's specifications and requirements.
- The Incumbent's proven track record of success and first-hand understanding of the Buyer's needs.

Some Incumbent Suppliers remain on top because they continue to provide what the Buyer needs at a reasonable price. Unfortunately, some Incumbents take advantage of the situation by nickel and diming the Buyer within a tolerated level. Others are making dangerous decisions that could ruin their future opportunities, including poor communication and a lack of action when issues arise.

The question is, why do Buyer's continue to source to Incumbent Suppliers if their products and business activities are creating problems? There are actually several reasons why Buyers won't necessarily be willing to switch to another supplier. *The number one reason is based on how much of a savings the Buyer can actually realize by switching.* Balancing a minimal amount of savings against the work and expense involved in finding and maintaining a new supplier will usually fall on the side of the Incumbent, depending on the dollars involved. Staying with the Incumbent Supplier, even a poor performing one, can keep investment and qualification costs at a minimum instead of taking on a new supplier. That's because new suppliers may require expensive one-time start-up costs and other non-recurring expenses. Staying with the Incumbent also greatly reduces the risk of sourcing to an unknown whose products are not yet tested and validated in the field. All of this being said, a new supplier may cause more issues and expense than the Incumbent, so why risk it?

From the Buyer's Desk, in order to prevail over the Incumbent Supplier, you will have to complete some deep-dive investigative homework on the Incumbent's products as well as the Buyer's wants and needs. **Every supplier has at least one weakness to exploit. It's up to you to find it.** For instance, the Incumbent may feel so confident they'll receive the order that they start charging more for the product beyond the Buyer's comfort zone. *At that point, their weakness becomes PRICE.* Another weak point could be the fact that the Buyer has had numerous problems with the Incumbent Supplier including late deliveries, product breakdown, incomplete documents, unresponsive sales representation and inadequate service. It's up to you to find out what, if any, problems are occurring and convince the Buyer that *your* product will not incur those same issues. But be careful not to put the Incumbent Supplier down in such a way that it turns off the Buyer. ***Buyers do not appreciate one supplier bad-mouthing another!***

Now let's look at overcoming the Incumbent Supplier from another perspective . . . YOURS! Let's say you have a friend who owns a lawn service that cuts your grass a couple times a week. You think the price is okay and you're not having any major issues with the lawn's appearance. Then another lawn service company knocks on your door and asks for your business. *What would it take for that new lawn service to make you want to tell your friend you no longer require his?* The number one reason would be *PRICE!* Not only will the other lawn service charge you less, but they will throw in a complimentary lawn cut every so often as appreciation for your business. Beyond price, maybe the other service has newer and better equipment that can leave a better looking yard. Maybe the other service can cut your lawn *faster* than your friend, thereby providing less disruption time. Maybe the other lawn service will show up when you *want* them to cut your grass, and *not* when your buddy has time for you. Maybe the other company offers free services that your friend doesn't; i.e. landscape trimming, weed and clippings removal, sidewalk and driveway blow-off, etc. In order for the new lawn service to take business away from your friend, they need to conduct homework to find out what weaknesses and pet peeves exist regarding your friend's services. So when it comes to your own company, do your homework. Prudently find out what weaknesses and pet peeves exist regarding the client's Incumbent Supplier and what it might take for you to be awarded the business. As stated earlier in this book, dissatisfied End-Users are usually a good source for this type of information.

Another way to take business from an incumbent is through the use of a Letter-of-Intent, or LOI. *(See the Section titled "Talk the Language of Purchasing" under the heading, "Letter-of-Intent", pg. 54).* Let the Buyer know during the initial sales meeting if your company is willing to accept a Letter-of-Intent to immediately move forward on a project. It could be an ideal opportunity to take business away from those who are not so willing.

Whatever weaknesses and pet peeves you find, it will be up to you to generate applicable documentation and convince the Buyer to forgo what advantages remain of giving the order to the Incumbent. It's up to you to make the Buyer *want to* forgo the Incumbent and feel comfortable in giving you the order. You're never going to be able to *force* the Buyer to hand you the business. Instead you're going to have to give the Buyer and/or End-User some compelling reasons to resource the order to you. *And* you'll have to provide them with enough ammunition to convince their own senior management to switch.

FROM THE BUYER'S DESK: Conduct research on your competitor's weaknesses. Prudently educate the Buyer on the differences between their capabilities and yours.

BUYERS WHO PREFER THIS: 83%
SALES REPS WHO DO THIS: 17%

"What To Do If You Win the Order."

Congratulations! *You won the order!* Your hard work, your persistence and determination, your dedicated time and your business strategies have finally paid off! You spent countless hours, generated innumerable documents, survived strenuous negotiations and even poured on your sales charm. And now you can sit back, relax and reap the financial and emotional benefits of receiving the order, right? *WRONG!* Don't even think about relaxing because your work has just begun. Based on the collective responses from the Buyers and End-Users I discussed this topic with, there are five things a Sales Rep should do *after* receiving the order to ensure future business:

1. Don't Disappear! The term 'closing the deal' seems to literally mean just that to some Sales Professionals. The deal has been made, the order has been received, *see ya later!* If any Sales Professional is interested in repeat business, they need to pay as much attention to the client *after* receiving the purchase order as they did during the quoting process. *A sufficient amount of post-order attention and responsiveness to issues will be noticed and will improve your opportunities to receive future orders.*

Nothing is more upsetting to a Buyer than a Sales Rep who hovers around his desk like a moth to a flame during the supplier selection process, then disappears once they're awarded the order. As stated earlier, the term 'closing the deal' seems to have a literal meaning to some suppliers. **The deal should never be closed.** When the purchase order has been placed and the handshake has been made, the deal should just be *opening*, not closing. Stand out from your competition by informing the Buyer that you will put as much time and energy on the actual job as you did in your attempt to win it! Hard to believe but I've rarely had *anyone* tell me that in my years in corporate purchasing.

Remember that sales representation is still required after the order has been placed because, in some cases, the Sales Rep is the *only* link between the Buyer and the supplier's company. *Making sure the Buyer is satisfied throughout the entire program is what helps to initiate repeat business.*

Have you ever dealt with a Sales Rep at a car dealership that was more than helpful before you signed on the dotted line, then after you bought the vehicle they never returned your calls? It's irritating in your private life and it's irritating in business.

2. Provide Contact Information. After receiving the order, provide sufficient company contact information to the Buyer as well as other applicable personnel within the client's company. The Sales Rep should make sure they provide a company organization document that specifies who to contact and for what. The document could include service, spare parts, training, accounts receivable, engineering, shipping, etc. That information is important to Purchasing and other client departments. It will also take some of the workload off the Sales Rep by reducing the amount of time spent as the middle-person between the Buyer and their own internal colleagues.

There are times when Buyers aren't sure who to contact when an issue or question arises so they tend to needlessly overwhelm the Sales Rep with telephone calls. If the Buyer prefers a single point of contact and if the Sales Rep can promptly handle every issue, that's fine. Otherwise, why become submerged in problems and questions that are either out of your control or are not your responsibility? Make sure the Buyer knows who to contact *directly* for faster results and make sure he knows you will always assist him if necessary. Another good tip is to actually ask the Buyer if he prefers a single point of contact. If so, be prepared to accommodate him and make sure every applicable person in your organization understands and complies with his preference.

3. Communicate Delivery Issues. Nothing frustrates the Buyer more than finding out a supplier is going to be late with their product, especially when the news came from everyone *but* the supplier. Sales Reps should be encouraged to immediately contact the Buyer when some action or inaction may cause the product or service to be late. Be honest, be up front and communicate the news, as well as a contingency plan.

Let's think again in terms of your own private life. Let's imagine you order a laptop computer from a local electronic retail store and they tell you it will be delivered in a week. That's good, because it's for your spouse's birthday which is three weeks away. A month goes by and still no laptop. Then you find out that the retail store *knew* it was going to be late but failed to let you know! *It's frustrating!*

Now I'm the first to admit that most Buyers need to remove the fear some suppliers have in reporting problems. But letting the Buyer know there's an issue after it's too late to do anything about it is going to make the Buyer even more upset than learning about it early on. This is especially true if the Buyer could have planned ahead if he had known the product was going to be late. In many cases, a Buyer not knowing the product is going to be delayed becomes embarrassing and upsetting, especially when his own manager finds out first! *And guess who's going to pay dearly for that one?*

4. Ask the Buyer for Help. One of the functions of a typical Buyer is to serve as the intermediary between the supplier and the End-User of the product, as well as other internal departments. If the End-User has an issue with a supplier they will usually contact the Buyer. At that point, the Buyer will contact the supplier and attempt to resolve the issue at hand. Conversely, the supplier should also be encouraged to contact the Buyer during any situation in which they have not received expected communication or documentation from the End-User that would jeopardize the project. This could include approved drawings, product qualification or other items that would impede the project's milestones. Understandably, some suppliers are afraid to contact the Buyer to let him know of any problems on the client's end. But it will become more of a problem if the Buyer finds out they could have made contingency plans on their end if they had known about it earlier. *It's easier to avert issues than it is to recover from them.* So after receiving the order, you should *always* discuss with the Buyer your ability to contact him when his help is needed.

5. Immediately Communicate Product and Service Issues. If your products are not performing according to the terms of the purchase order, don't let the Buyer hear it first from the End-User. *Let the Buyer hear it first from you!* Again, nothing is more embarrassing to a Buyer than to have his manager call him into the office and ask if he knew about a supplier's product causing problems. The Buyer is supposed to be on top of things. And if your product isn't living up to expectations you need to let him know immediately:

"Hello, Mr. Moore. I wanted to let you know as soon as possible that our product for the XL5 Program is down. We have a serviceman heading for the plant to work on it. He'll be there about 2:00 this afternoon and will stay until it's running to production levels."

It's hard for a Buyer to be mad at a supplier who's accepting responsibility and taking care of issues. However, it's extremely easy for the Buyer to get upset with a supplier who doesn't inform him of issues and doesn't take responsibility. Buyers would prefer to get the honest facts from the supplier *before* receiving an emotional phone call from the End-User. *When the End-User becomes emotional, so does the Buyer!*

FROM THE BUYER'S DESK: Give as much attention to the client after winning the order as you did in trying to win it in the first place.

BUYERS WHO PREFER THIS: 91%
SALES REPS WHO DO THIS: 42%

"What To Do If You Lose the Order."

We've already discussed what Sales Professionals should do if they end up winning the purchase order. That is, what steps should be taken immediately and subsequently after being awarded new business from the Buyer. As stated in the previous Section, winning the order doesn't mean the Sales Rep can sit back, relax and reap the financial benefits of new business. *Quite the contrary!* Receiving new business means your work has just begun.

So the question begs, what do you do if you *LOSE* the order? After all, in a competitive quoting environment *there will be more losers than winners.* And how you handle yourself as the loser will determine your future opportunities as a winner. For the rest of the suppliers who weren't fortunate enough to receive the order, their hard work and strategies didn't pay off this time. And I want to stress that it doesn't matter if the successful supplier deserved to win the order or not. The fact is, the countless hours and negotiations didn't end up in your favor. And just as winning the order doesn't give you time to sit back and relax, *neither does losing it!*

Even if you don't end up with the prize, your work has just begun in developing and following through with contingency plans. *In fact, from the Buyer's perspective there are several things a Sales Professional should do after losing the order.* The following recommendations are based on the experiences and advice from hundreds of Buyers and End-Users across the Nation who have been on the receiving end of *supplier reactions* due to losing the order. This feedback is based on what Sales Reps have consequently done or failed to do that have ruined their future opportunities for business.

First and foremost, if your company lost an order to a competitor, whatever the reason behind that loss, *do not bad-mouth the competition nor the Buyer's supplier-selection process.* Put yourself in the Buyer's shoes for a moment. If you were a Buyer, why would it upset you to listen to a Sales Rep who lost the order complain about your own *flawed* supplier-selection process? A Sales Rep should *never* discuss in a pessimistic way their negative experiences during the quoting process. Because the fact is, there's no perfect way to select the right supplier on any given project. Buyers can define processes and guidelines and hope they make the right decision. *Unfortunately there are times when today's right decision ends up being tomorrows headache!* (See the Section titled, *"The Supplier Selection Process"*, pg. 42.)

As stated before, Buyers are human. They are not perfect. They can make mistakes during supplier-selection despite what they sincerely believe is the right decision. In a perfect business world there are processes that define the right supplier for the right job. But we don't live in a perfect world. Unfortunately, some Sales Professionals attempt to conduct business in the vacuum of a perfect world. They become incensed when they don't get the order despite the fact they may have been the best supplier for the job. *So if that's what really happened, don't put Buyers in a difficult position to discuss in a negative way what they already know and can't do anything about.* Stay positive. Complaining about it won't get you the order and it may in fact affect your chances of receiving future business. Instead of complaining in a negative way, accept the decision especially if you know it's final.

The second bit of advice from the Buyer's Desk: **If you lose the order, try to be *proactive* about it.** Prudently and positively find out why you didn't receive the order and how your company can do a better job next time. Maybe it wasn't anything you did or failed to do. Maybe it was a total mistake on the client's side that you didn't receive the order. Maybe the client clearly gave the order to the wrong supplier but it's too late to do anything about it. It never hurts to ask for constructive feedback. Say to the Buyer with a positive approach, *"I believe my company would be a great asset to your firm. Can you offer any constructive feedback as to what we could do better with our next opportunity?"*

Third, it's important to know that a small portion of orders lost to competitors may take place due to business politics. Under this scenario the Buyer's hands may have been tied when it came to trying to place the order to the deserving supplier. It's certainly a dishonor when clients place orders to the wrong company for more money than what you were offering. Maybe it was because someone with more authority than the

Buyer, possibly from another department, wanted the job to go to their favorite supplier. It does happen and I'm sure you've witnessed it from time to time. *So what can you do about it?* First, it may be reassuring to know that it doesn't happen as often as you may think. It was much more prevalent in prior decades. Companies have much more stringent processes and ethical guidelines in place than there were in prior years to prevent this type of situation from happening. And the Business Practices Office of many major corporations have made it easier for biased decisions to be reported anonymously by both the corporate employee and the supplier. Therefore, you may want to visit the client's corporate website and find out what steps to take should it ever happen on a project you're quoting.

Not reporting this type of unfair business practice only encourages more of it. In our private lives we may have witnessed a shoplifter in a retail store and not said a word to store management. In the end it hurts all of us because shoplifting creates a large percentage of the price we pay for retail products. When we don't report unfair business practices, it encourages the corporate employees to continue its process of unjustly selecting suppliers. And just like in shoplifting, if a more expensive supplier was picked because of dirty politics, it's consumers like you and I that end up paying for the extra cost.

A WORD OF CAUTION: If you decide to take this course of action in reporting illicit business practices, you must be absolutely positive that this is what *actually* took place and make sure you have all your facts correct. Don't make assumptions based on unproven rumors or sour-grape comments from other people, no matter what their position is in your company or the client's, and no matter how close they were to the issue. If you decide to go the Business Practices route and you're unable to substantiate your claims, or if key personnel within the client's companies are brought into it unjustifiably, you can expect to never be asked to quote anything for that company again.

During my time in Purchasing I've spent quite a bit of time and effort putting together documentation proving that the right supplier *was* selected. This was due to losing suppliers who had a case of sour grapes and didn't have their facts straight. I recall one supplier who claimed *they* were the low bid, and that the winning supplier didn't even quote to our specifications. It was the losing supplier's perception that, in many cases, they were rated both technically and commercially number one, yet failed to receive the order. However there was absolutely no way the complaining supplier could have known that unless he had access to the other supplier's quotes. Here was the last paragraph in my comprehensive report to the supplier and Purchasing Management:

"I have no issues with reviewing project outcomes with suppliers. In fact I highly encourage it. But it would be appreciated if the supplier had their facts straight before I invest hours of my time in reviewing technical and commercial concerns. In the four projects investigated, not one claim by the supplier was found to be accurate.

It's also important to know that sometimes, Buyers are kept out of the loop in corporate sourcing decisions and the reasons to give the order to a seemingly non-compliant supplier may be perfectly legitimate. So unless you're absolutely positive and have concrete proof that the decision was against corporate policy, don't turn to drastic means.

If somehow you have found a way to have the order pulled from the winning supplier and resourced to you, step back a moment and think twice about following through with it. *Because it may be in your best interest not to!* If your company's product gets jammed down the throat of an End-User who clearly does not want it, what are the odds your product will sincerely get qualified or will genuinely work in the field? Odds are the End-User will look for any reason, any excuse as to why they shouldn't use you again. You'll be under their microscope during the entire process and life use of the product.

Of course, there have been cases in which an order placed to the wrong supplier was eventually cancelled and placed to the deserving company. But this does not occur very often. A number of things must be in place in order for it to happen. First, you must have a Buyer, Senior Purchasing Manager and a percentage of End-Users willing to fight for you. Second, you must have your information organized and factual to show that the decision to give the order to the wrong supplier was unwarranted. Third, you must be willing to accept the backlash of whoever wanted the wrong supplier in the first place. *Again, changing suppliers after the order has been placed does not happen very often.* You may want to have a private discussion with the Buyer to see if he has ever experienced it and, if so, how the decision got reversed.

FROM THE BUYER'S DESK: Find out why the order was lost in order to improve future opportunities. Be prudent in your questions and reaction to the Buyer.

BUYERS WHO PREFER THIS: 84%
SALES REPS WHO DO THIS: 23%

"Don't Bad-Mouth the Competition."

While working as a Senior Buyer at a previous employer, I had an introductory sales meeting with a local Representative. Among the topics discussed was the current business environment. We talked in general terms about how some companies managed to survive the recent downturn while others were forced to close shop.

The Sales Rep then turned the conversation to how he's surprised that some of his own competitors (which he mentioned by name) are still in business due to their poor financial outlook and their substandard products. He said, *"The last thing I want to do is bad-mouth my competitors."* Then he proceeded to bad-mouth his competitors! He discussed the poor financial status of his rival suppliers and how their products were failing in the field. He went so far as to warn me about placing future orders with them. The entire time, he acted as if he was *doing me a favor* by providing 'beneficial' information about his competition. After his comments I abruptly ended the meeting with an explanation that I had an assignment to complete before lunch.

The truth is, I ended it on purpose because I was completely turned off by his negative comments regarding his competitors! Being a Buyer by trade, I take everything I hear with a grain of salt. In my line of business it's in my own best interest to be suspicious of every supplier and skeptical of everything they tell me. And even if I wasn't skeptical, *why in the world would I take the advice of a supplier regarding his own competitors?*

Think of an instance in your private life in which you dealt with someone in retail who downgraded the competition in front of you in order to get the sale. Did you believe him? Did it make you feel you could trust that person? Or would you rather make up your own mind about competitive products based on your own research?

Some Sales Professionals have a tendency to bad-mouth their competition during the quoting process. And they make it sound like they're doing me a favor. *But from the Buyer's perspective, a Sales Rep should never discuss their competitors in a negative manner.* They should never bring up rumors they've heard about their competitor's products, financial situation, or problems the End-User is having with them. I've discussed this very topic with numerous Buyers and most feel it's unprofessional. It's certainly not welcomed. No one likes a gossip and Buyers do not want to hear about a supplier's inadequacies from the subjective competition.

As a Buyer, I rely on my *own* End-Users, engineers, financial and quality groups to determine product and service capabilities. I rely on my own company's knowledge and experience to determine commercial aptitudes. Researching suppliers' financial status and requesting feedback from the End-Users is part of the Buyer's yearly goals. And while some Buyers may seem interested when you talk about your competitors, in reality they would prefer you remain positive and constructive, leaving the analysis process to them. From the Buyer's perspective, you need to concentrate and improve on your own failures as a supplier rather than someone else's in an attempt to win the job.

In addition, nothing is more of a turn-off than to listen to a Sales Professional bad-mouth a supplier they were previously employed at. *Think about that!* One week you're working for Company A and telling me all the **good** things about Company A. The next week you're working for Company B telling me of all the **bad** things about Company A. *This immediately destroys any credibility you have and I can no longer trust you. Period.*

If you had internal issues with your previous employer, never discuss them with the Buyer. It's none of the Buyer's business and he probably doesn't care to be involved in any bad blood that may have occurred. If asked, all you need to say is that there were irreconcilable differences with your previous employer and you wish them all the best.

Another lesson to learn here is that the business world is a small one and you never know who you may be working for next. Bad mouthing Company C one week and working for them the next destroys your credibility with the Buyer. Again, too many Sales Professionals have said to me *"I don't like to bad-mouth my competitors . . ."*, then they proceed in doing exactly that! From the Buyer's perspective it's a major turn off. Don't do it. Use positive comparisons instead, like *"This is how my competitor does it, and this is how we do it."*

FROM THE BUYER'S DESK: Never speak in a negative way about your competition to the Buyer. Negative rumors and accusations aren't something they want to hear from you. Remain positive and leave the gossip to the newsstand tabloids.

BUYERS WHO PREFER THIS: 87%
SALES REPS WHO BAD-MOUTH COMPETITORS: 43%

SECTION 6

Follow Up and Communication

- Maintaining Commitments
- Unresponsive Suppliers
- How Sales Makes it Difficult for Buyers to Respond
- Hello? Hello? Anyone There?
- Communication Between Buyers and Sellers
- I'll Take the Next Person In Line
- Do Unto Others . . .

"Maintaining Commitments."

A few years ago my wife and I ordered new carpeting from a local retailer for the second floor level of our house. The retailer had contracted installers who scheduled a day and time of 1:00p.m. to show up and install the new carpet. My wife then made plans to be home on that day and time by taking a half-day vacation from work. *(Does this sound familiar?)*

On the day of the installation the installers called about 12 noon and said they would need to move the start time to 2:00. This was due to the fact that the earlier jobs were taking longer than had been planned. At 2:30 and with no sign of the installers my wife called and was informed they would be there by 4:00 and could still finish the job that day. At 4:15 another call from the installer moved the time to 5:00. At 5:30 the installer called and asked my wife to reschedule to a new day and time.

For obvious reasons my wife was livid! Not only had she taken a half day vacation for nothing, she would now need to reschedule the installation and take additional time off from work. We later found out that the installer never really planned to show up at all. They had overbooked the entire day but were too afraid to let us know the afternoon before. Of course if we had been told a day earlier, my wife could have gone into work and simply rescheduled the vacation time. *But now it was too late.*

This story isn't a new one. It's happened to nearly everyone reading this book. A retailer makes a commitment. You make plans based on that commitment. The retailer then breaks their commitment without ample time for you to develop a contingency plan. Sometimes the retailer calls too late to make other plans. Sometimes they don't call at all. And with both scenarios you probably won't be buying anything from them again. *Welcome to the World of Corporate Purchasing!*

Let's put this in a business perspective. A supplier makes a commitment for a product to be delivered on a specific day. I then communicate that commitment to other departments in my company, i.e. planning, manufacturing and management. The commitment isn't met by the supplier and I end up with egg on my face. Had I known ahead of time that the product would not be arriving as promised I could have made contingency plans by working around it and focusing on other project tasks. But now it's too late.

I understand there are times when Sales Professionals are blind-sighted by their own suppliers or even by the people within their own company. Information wasn't reported to them in a timely manner if at all and the Sales Rep is just as surprised as I am that the commitment wasn't met. But there are other times when Sales Reps know the commitment won't be met at all and don't say anything because they're afraid of the immediate repercussion from the Buyer. *And let's face it, a large percentage of Buyers can make your sales life miserable.* But not informing the Buyer as soon as possible about a time delay, even a potential one, will never help. This is especially true if the Buyer finds out you actually knew about it ahead of time but said nothing.

Inform the Buyer as quickly as possible about any delay or potential delay that would prevent him and his company from meeting their own deadlines. Yes, the Buyer will initially be upset. Nothing can prevent that. But it will be much worse if there had been time for the Buyer to make a contingency plan, and now that time is gone. This is true not only for large commitments related to documentation, product delivery and service repairs, but even smaller things like committing to a phone call or an e-mail. You tell a Buyer you'll send him an e-mail by 3:00 with information he's asked for, but it never happens. Like any promise, the Buyer most likely made plans on his end based on the information he was expecting in your e-mail. And in most cases the Buyer made his own commitment to management or internal departments based on yours. So if you don't come through on your promise, neither can he. *And there's nothing that upsets a Buyer more than having to take the heat from management when the fault was the supplier's!*

The minute you realize you can't follow through with a commitment you need to immediately contact the Buyer and let him know about it so he can make other plans. *And from The Buyer's Desk, here's the best way to handle a delay in commitments:*

1. Apologize for the delay and take responsibility for it. Don't try to blame it on others when you're the one who made the commitment.

2. Let the Buyer know what you're doing to ensure the new commitment will be met as soon as possible. Give the Buyer some detail and offer to provide a step-by-step corrective action plan, including when each step will take place. Communicate periodically, even if it's to only say there's nothing new to communicate at that time.

3. Offer a 'consolation prize'; a price reduction, free options, or something of value that will help to offset what was lost. Ask if there's anything your company can do in the meantime to minimize the issue you've created for the client.

4. Provide whatever product, service or information you can for now with a follow-up of the full commitment at a new specified time. If you can't delivery 100% of the products you committed, maybe 65% is enough for the Buyer to get by for now.

5. And finally, absolutely ensure that the new commitment is met as quickly as possible and is completed on or before the revised promised time.

Not meeting a commitment when you were unaware of the cause is *understandable*. But not making sure the Buyer is aware of it as soon as possible is *inexcusable*. Will the Buyer be upset? Of course. But initial irritation and negative consequences will be short lived if the Buyer is informed ASAP.

FROM THE BUYER'S DESK: Don't over-promise and under-deliver. Commit to agreements and schedules you can comply with. If they can't be met, inform the Buyer immediately with a contingency plan.

BUYERS WHO PREFER THIS: 93%
SALES REPS WHO DO THIS: 32%

"Unresponsive Suppliers."

During a project meeting between myself and a Production Planner, it became quite evident that a specific supplier had been continuously *unresponsive* in replying to our numerous e-mails and voicemails requesting information. Incoming product expected within the next few weeks still did not have an estimated-time-of-arrival (ETA) and the responsible Sales Rep had not responded to our requests for lead times. We were obviously becoming concerned.

But the reality is that most professionals in the business environment are bombarded with e-mails and phone calls without enough time in the day to respond to everyone. Because of that, overlooked e-mails that should have been responded to days or even weeks ago is a daily occurrence no matter how good your time management skills are. But this section of the book is not about missing one or two e-mails from the client. ***It's about not responding at all!***

I have to believe there are several reasonable explanations as to why Sales Professionals are unable to respond to a deluge of requests regarding the same issue from the same Buyer. And I'm certain that spending time *behind the Sales desk* would prove beneficial in my understanding. But until then, it appears that some Sales Professionals are anything *but* professional. *When a Sales Rep is consistently unresponsive, it leaves an obvious negative impression with the Buyer, especially if the Buyer doesn't have a clue why the Sales Rep isn't responding.* From the Buyer's perspective, the Rep is simply not interested in future business.

Again, I understand the amount of e-mails and phone calls we all receive on any given day. And it's not that I expect to receive a response within a matter of minutes, within the hour, or even within the same day (unless it's an emergency). But when days and weeks go by without a response, especially after numerous communications from me, I find it difficult to understand why some Sales Professionals can't reply at all – *even if it's simply to acknowledge that my communications were received.* I also wonder if their management is even aware of it. In this instance, Sales Management is either condoning this lack of action or is completely unaware of what their sales people are doing. And I'm not sure which is worse. So if you're a Sales Manager thinking, *"Not my people"*, I suggest you contact your clients and find out for yourself. Personally, if I find a Sales Rep negligently unresponsive, *I will call their manager to find out what the problem is!*

There are a few companies I've dealt with who could be counted on to *NOT* respond to my requests within a reasonable amount of time, if at all. And it didn't matter what global division or area they were located in, it was nearly impossible to get *any* of their Reps to respond to any Buyers in our department. I don't know if ignoring clients is part of their mandatory training or if they have so much business that they don't need to be responsive. Whatever the root cause is, it's important to know that Buyers try very hard *not* to place business with unresponsive companies no matter how good their products are.

Some Sales Professionals don't call back simply because they haven't yet received the information the Buyer is asking for. *Big mistake.* Just because you currently don't have the information doesn't mean you can't reply to the Buyer and say, *"Just wanted to let you know I received your communication. I don't have what you need at this moment but I am working on it and I'll have it to you as soon as possible."* If I send a request out and don't get *any* kind of reply back, I have no idea if my request even made it to Sales Rep. Acknowledging the Buyer's request at least lets them know the communication was received, was understood, and is being worked on.

Sometimes the reason a Sales Professional doesn't call or e-mail back is because they're out of town or on vacation. When it comes to electronic communication, e-mails and voicemails (both office and mobile) are critical tools in conducting business with the client. That's why it's essential for the Sales Reps to leave a message on their e-mail and voicemail if they're traveling, on vacation, or if they're simply out of the office for an extended period of time. The message should clearly state when they'll be gone, when they'll be returning and who to contact in their absence. This is common sense. *But from my side of the desk, a large percentage of Sales Reps do not do this.*

At a previous employer, I attempted to contact a Sales Rep to invite him to a supplier line-up meeting and quote on a major project. I left voicemail after voicemail trying to get a hold of him to make sure he would attend the meeting. *(Trust me, very few Buyers would do that!)* I later found out that the Rep was on vacation all week but never left a voicemail message to say he'd be out or who to contact in his place. Unfortunately I found out too late and his company never had the opportunity to quote. ***Can your company afford to make that kind of oversight?*** If you're a Sales Manager, are you ensuring your team consistently uses out-of-office tools when applicable?

Here is the type of message you should leave on your voicemail and e-mail if you're out of the office even for a day:

"This is Barbara Evans, Sales Engineer for The ABC Company. I am currently out of the office and will be returning to work the morning of June 24. If this is an emergency please contact Jeff Wayne at 555-123-7654. Otherwise, please leave a message and I'll respond when I return."

From the Buyer's perspective, unresponsive Sales Professionals will lose business for their company due to these kinds of simple oversights. Improving your time management skills and ensuring a call back or e-mail reply will greatly improve your opportunities, even if it's a short one giving acknowledgement and even if you don't quite have all the answers yet.

FROM THE BUYER'S DESK: Respond to the Buyer or End-User within a reasonable amount of time, even if it's to say you have nothing yet to respond with. Use out-of-office tools when applicable.

BUYERS WHO PREFER THIS: 79%
SALES REPS WHO DO THIS: 47%

"How Sales Makes it Difficult for Buyers to Respond."

During my years in Corporate Purchasing I've asked various Sales Professionals what their biggest pet peeve is regarding Buyers. **By far the number one complaint is a lack of responsive communication from the Buyer!** For instance, the Sales Rep sends an e-mail or leaves a voicemail asking for a reply from the Buyer that never comes. Quotes are submitted without a rejoinder from the Buyer. Business cards and company brochures are mailed to Purchasing without feedback. This leads to the conclusion that the Buyer is rude, callous and insensitive to Sales communications. And in some instances the Sales Rep is probably right. *But it might surprise you that in other cases, the individual to blame for the Buyer's lack of responsive may very well be the Sales Professional himself or herself!*

One of the most important responsibilities of any Sales Professional is to ensure that the lines of communication between themselves and the Buyer are open and easily accessible. That is, making sure the Buyer has your updated contact information and that you are ready and able to receive their communications. As a Sales Professional you should make certain you are readily available to receive an invitation to quote, or able to respond to any questions and requests the Buyer might have. **Unfortunately, many Sales Reps unknowingly make it difficult for Buyers to easily get a hold of them!** So from the Buyer's Desk, here is a *Top Ten* list of the things Sales Professionals do, or fail to do, that make it difficult for Buyers to contact them:

1. The Buyer can't read the Sales Rep's telephone number or e-mail address on their business card. In most cases, this is because the text on the card is too small or the text ink is way too light against the background. Make sure the text and font on your card is large enough and clear enough to read without having to use a magnifying glass. In addition, I've come across many business cards that don't have the most updated contact information on it . . . old phone numbers, out-of-date email addresses, even the wrong location for the main corporate office.

2. More times than not I've come across business cards that only had the Sales Rep's main office number on it, *but not the Rep's actual phone extension!* That forces me to use the telephone name directory which is frustrating and time consuming. Even if you have to write your extension on the card, do it before handing it out. In your private life I'm certain you hate playing with phone directories. Well, we Buyer's hate it more in our business life because we constantly have to do it. I've known Buyers who have not asked suppliers to quote on projects simply because it became difficult to contact the Sales Rep. (See the Section titled, *"The Hidden Power of Business Cards"*, pg. 129.)

3. It's been my experience that 70% of the time Sales Reps do not leave an out-of-office message on their voicemail or e-mail. The Rep is out of the office on vacation, in training or traveling, and cannot be contacted by the Buyer. But the Buyer doesn't know they're out because the Rep failed to create an out-of-office message. As stated earlier in this book, every out-of-office voicemail and e-mail should inform the caller when you will be returning and who to contact in case of an emergency. *"Hi, this is Susan Smith. I am out of the office on vacation, returning the morning of June 24. In my absence please contact Tim Jones at 555-987-1234 or leave a message and I'll get back to you when I return."* Common sense, right? But it's *not* done as often as you'd think.

4. The Sales Professional's contact information is not stated at the beginning or at the end of the quote package. Many Sales Rep's include their name and job title at the end of the quote along with the statement, *"Please contact me if you have any questions."* But they fail to leave their contact information after that very statement on the quote.

5. The Sales Rep leaves a voicemail on the Buyer's phone asking for a call back, but fails to provide their full name, company name or even their phone number. And even if the phone number *is* left on the voicemail, *it's either too unclear or it's given too fast to write it down.*

If you want a call back don't leave a message that says, *"Hi Dave, this is Jessica. Give me a call back."* No matter how well you know the Buyer, do this: *"Hi Dave. This is Jessica Silver with Acme Company. My number is 123-456-5555. Appreciate a call back to discuss the widget quote. Again my number is 123-456-5555."*

6. The Sales Rep doesn't check their e-mail or voicemail on a *regular* basis for potential business opportunities from the Buyer. On several occasions I've tried to contact Sales Reps to invite them to a supplier line-up meeting. Their e-mails and voicemails never indicated they were out of the office and they missed out on a great opportunity to quote because they never checked their messages. *Unbelievable.*

7. The Sales Rep doesn't respond to the Buyer's request within a reasonable amount of time. I've e-mailed RFQs to expedite a quote that took a week for suppliers to get back with me. By then it was too late.

8. The Sales Rep's voicemail has reached its limited amount of calls it can receive so the Buyer can't even leave a message. Hopefully your voicemail can take an unlimited amount of calls. Otherwise you'll never know what opportunities you missed out on.

9. The Sales Rep's voicemail *recording time* is limited. The Buyer attempts to leave a message but the recording time runs out before the message is completed. The Buyer must now call back and leave yet another message to finish up his communication. And guess what, sometimes we call back . . . and sometimes we don't. Even worse in this day and age, *some Sales Reps do not even have voicemail set up on their desk phone or cell phone!*

10. The Sales Rep does not leave their contact information at the bottom of their e-mail signature. A Sales Professional should *always* leave their full name, job title, telephone number (be it a number with an extension, a direct number or a cell number), e-mail address and website address at the bottom of every e-mail they send or reply to.

FROM THE BUYER'S DESK: Make certain you're easily accessible to the Buyer in every communication format. Don't unknowingly make it difficult for them to contact you regarding sales opportunities.

BUYERS WHO PREFER THIS: 82%
SALES REPS WHO MAKE IT DIFFICULT: 53%

"Hello? Hello? Anyone There?"

Every day in our business and personal life we experience less-than-perfect communication from others; communication to keep us updated, to reply to something we've asked about, or to inform us of a future event. And when communication is less-than-perfect it affects our ability to make decisions and move forward. John Powell once said, *"Communication works for those who work at it."* And while I admit I am communication-challenged at times, I make a concerted effort to reply in a timely manner to those who are in need of information.

I can understand a Sales Rep missing a voicemail, accidently skipping an e-mail and simply forgetting to respond to an individual's request. After all, there isn't enough time in the day to complete tasks and get back to those who have connected with us. But when numerous e-mails and voicemails from the Buyer are ignored or when promises aren't kept, it leaves those in need of information and action in a distressed position. Not only is the Buyer unable to move forward or make decisive decisions, they're also unable to complete their own tasks mandated by their senior management. *That obviously frustrates Buyers.* Frustration turns into anger. Anger turns into retaliation. And retaliation turns into the Buyer's-own silence when it comes to sourcing business to suppliers. *Let me put it another way:* If I can consistently count on a Sales Rep NOT replying to my communications, then that Sales Rep can consistently count on me NOT including them on future projects. So from the Buyer's Desk, here are some of the major areas where Sales Professionals and Business Owners can enhance communication, thereby improving future opportunities:

235

1. Don't over promise and under deliver. A number of suppliers on every project I've worked on made promises to ship specific quantities of product by specific dates. Then the day before they were scheduled to ship, I was informed by the Sales Rep that not only will they be days or weeks late, the quantity to ship had been reduced. *Really??? When did they know this? And why wasn't I informed the moment they knew?* Too many times, suppliers will tell me what they *think* they want me to hear instead of the truth because they're afraid of potential repercussions. *That's the wrong road to take.* Not meeting a commitment when you were unaware of the cause is understandable. Not making sure the Buyer is aware of it as soon as possible is inexcusable. Inform the Buyer as quickly as possible about any delay or potential delay, whether it's a prior commitment on your end or something that would prevent the Buyer and his company from meeting their own deadlines. Yes, the Buyer will initially be upset. Nothing can prevent that. *But it will be much worse if the Buyer found out they missed a chance to create a contingency plan simply because they were informed too late.* This is true not only for commitments related to deliveries, but even committing to a phone call or an e-mail to provide requested information.

2. Re-review e-mails requesting information to make sure everything was answered. So many times I'll send an e-mail to a supplier with several questions, only to have one or more of them go unanswered in their reply. Before you hit that *send* button, go over the Buyer's e-mail again to make sure you've answered everything they've requested. Even if you don't immediately have the answer, acknowledge the request and let them know when you'll be able to reply with the proper information. *Don't be unresponsive just because you don't have the answer now.*

3. Check e-mails you may have missed. At the end of every day, go back to the first e-mail sent to you and ensure they've all been responded to. Many times I've made mental notes of e-mails sent to me with the intent to respond that same day. Then I get busy or pulled away to handle an emergency and I forget to respond to that specific e-mail. So before I leave work to go home I'll go back and read any e-mails I may have missed. If I plan to respond the next day I'll mark it accordingly. With the amount of e-mails we can receive on a single day it's impossible to stay caught up on every one of them. Going through them again at the end of the day or even at the end of the week will help improve response time.

4. Report back, *even if it's to say you have nothing to report.* Not responding to an urgent request simply because you don't have the information in front of you is as bad as not responding at all. With several suppliers I've sent e-mail after e-mail and left voicemail after voicemail asking for the same information. *When no one responds after a few days I don't even know if my messages are getting through.* At the very least, reply to the person requesting action or information so they know you're aware of the request. Then let them know when you'll be able to provide what they're asking for.

5. Communicate potential issues with a contingency plan. We don't live in a perfect world. That's why I'm always leery of suppliers who provide seemingly impossible delivery schedules when there are so many things that could go wrong. Suppliers who count on their own vendors for components, material or information need to ensure they are held to timelines that support their own production and delivery schedules. With so many products and services on any given project, suppliers need to take into consideration the potential things that could go wrong with their own vendors that could affect their promised delivery dates. I once had a supplier provide a *Letter of Commitment* for the delivery of their parts. They even had it signed by their Vice President of Sales. That date of commitment on the letter came and went without product in house. *So much for a Letter of Commitment! What was the point of that?* The reason the product was late wasn't based on their own parts. It was with one of their own vendors who never told them they would be late with a sub-component. When you provide a Buyer or End-User with a planned ship date, let them know of potential things that could go wrong. And if they happen, let them know what your contingency plan will be to correct it.

FROM THE BUYER'S DESK: Direct, open and responsive lines of communication is one of the best ways to increase sales.

BUYERS WHO PREFER THIS: 88%
SALES REPS WHO DO THIS: 29%

"Communication Between Buyers and Sellers."

I've had the good fortune of being employed in the business environment for going on 40 years. One-third of that time has been in Corporate Purchasing . . . years of project budgets, request-for-quotes, quote comparisons, negotiations, supplier selection, purchase order awards and the resolution of project issues. And in all that time, the hardest thing I've found we Buying and Selling Professionals do is to properly and clearly **COMMUNICATE.**

In fact I've always found that the *easiest* thing to do in the business environment is **MIS-communication** . . . with our colleagues, with upper management, and with each other. *Trust me, I do it on a daily basis.* When considering communication, what we Buyers and Sellers really need to agree on is *HOW* we are going to communicate with each other. What are the guidelines? Who are the players? What are the expectations? What are the resources? For instance:

"Can we agree that if the specifications change, Christine Beddow will contact all of the people on this list via e-mail."

"If you are going to be late with your product, can we agree that you will contact all of the people on this sheet via telephone."

"If you ever have an issue, I would appreciate it if you didn't go over my head to get what you need. Communicate with me first. Then, if I don't respond within 24 hours, I won't be able to complain if you contact my senior manager."

It is impossible to ensure perfect communication for the simple fact that there *IS* no such thing. That's because everyone has their own definition of *perfect* communication. At some point in time during the progression of a project, a number of things will be missed, a number of people will be ill-informed, and a number of communication tools will not be utilized to their best capacity.

- *"Why didn't you tell me the product was going to be late?"*
- *"Why didn't you let me know your service crew was going to show up this morning?"*
- *"I can't comprehend the document you sent. I don't know what you're trying to tell me?"*
- *"Why didn't you inform me the repair was more complicated than previously thought? I'm not a mind reader."*

The best way to ensure good communication, especially between Buyers and Sellers, is to be **'APT'**. Although **APT** is an acronym we'll use in this book, the definition of the actual word 'apt' means "to be appropriate". So as far as we're concerned, **APT** is also an acronym for Action, People, and Tools.

ACTION: What am I doing right now? What do I plan to do later?
PEOPLE: Who does this directly or indirectly affect?
TOOLS: What's the best communication tool to use to inform each affected peoson about it?

In other words, in order for communication to be **'apt',** to be **appropriate,** you must constantly think, *"What am I doing or going to do, who does it affect, and what's the best way to let them know about it?"* The best way to accomplish this is to create a list of all the internal and external people on any given project. Include their responsibilities, telephone numbers, e-mail addresses, cell phones and mailing address. You could set up a number of e-mail group addresses so that every time there's a change in plans regarding a specific item, you can e-mail it to the appropriate group to make sure everyone knows about it. Every time take action or make plans, *"Who does this affect either directly or indirectly, what's the best way to let them know, and what's the best way to get feedback?"* If Buyers and Sellers were more **APT**, projects would run a lot smoother.

The main problem with communication in the business world is that it's become too bureaucratic, too complicated, and too impersonal. Effective communication is relatively rare in the business world. Until recent, **trickle-down** and **one-way communication** was the widely accepted form of business interaction. The problem is that it does not provide for **feedback**. It does not provide the sender the assurance that the communication was received and understood.

A good way to ensure that communication is understood is to keep it **'two-way'** and, most importantly, keep it **simple**. As an example, if two people lived next door to each other in a subdivision and one of them wanted to borrow a hammer, he would either call the neighbor on the telephone or simply walk across the lawn and ask to borrow it.

However if these two neighbors were in a corporation using typical corporate communication processes, the first neighbor would give his son the message who would tell his sister, who would tell her mother, who would go next door and tell the second neighbor's wife, who would finally tell her husband. By that time, the request would be so diluted that the second man would ask himself, *"What is my neighbor is trying to tell me?"*

There is no secret recipe for learning to communicate well. But there are some basic concepts that can be mastered with relative ease. In fact, there are **three basic steps** to improve communication.

The First Step is to allow your communication to accept **feedback** in order to ensure that the receiver obtained and understood the communication. Many times, communication is sent with the assumption that the message was received and the task will be carried out to the sender's expectations and timing. Sometimes the receiver never even gets the communication. And sometimes the receiver either does not have time to fulfill the expectation, or is too embarrassed to admit they really didn't understand what was expected. Feedback will ensure that the sender's message has been received, understood, and (hopefully) the content of the communication will be followed through with and completed on time.

The Second Step is to ensure that documented communication is not *overcomplicated.* In today's world of overburdened responsibilities, the average worker does not have the time to sift through pages and pages of information, retain the contents, then be expected to adhere to the criteria and goals. The same is true when you're forwarded a long string of e-mails and somehow must decipher what needs to be done. The document or e-mail owner should review the content and remove any repetitive and overcomplicated themes, directions or explanations.

Many times Buyers we will receive a document that is either too overwhelming to read and comprehend, or the basic task and required outcome is diluted. Make sense of what can be excluded from the document and don't overwhelm the receiver with unnecessary and recurring content. Make sure the content criteria and goals stand out and are easily understood. The use of condensed, comprehensive bullet-points in place of long winded paragraphs can help.

The Third Step is to make sure you don't get trapped in the bureaucratic process of **trickle-down** and **one-way communication.** If you need to let someone know something important, *walk over to their desk and tell them!* Don't expect a voicemail, e-mail or a second party to do it for you. I've had people who literally sat across from me at work send me an e-mail asking for information. *Dude, I'm sitting right next to you!* Employee workload and lack of time doesn't guarantee the receivership and follow through of electronic or secondhand communication. Face-to-face communication may be the most basic form, but it's still the most effective and genuine type to use.

FROM THE BUYER'S DESK: Buyers and Sellers can both ensure the best possible communication by allowing for feedback. Don't attempt to overburden others with non-essential information.

BUYERS WHO PREFER THIS: 92%

"I'll Take the Next Person In Line."

A few years ago I went to pick up my dog from the pet groomer after work. It was 5:00 in the afternoon and I had dropped her off in the morning for a 10AM appointment. When I arrived at the groomer I was informed my dog was not yet ready and would need another ten minutes. I was stunned to hear the news so I asked how that was possible when I had dropped her off for a 10AM appointment? It wasn't the first time this had happened and, in fact, had become more the norm than the exception.

The person behind the counter (who ended up being the business owner) repeated that my dog would be ready in just a few more minutes. So I again asked why my dog wasn't ready *seven hours after her appointment?* I also inquired about the dogs who had scheduled appointments *after* 10AM and yet were obviously done before mine? The owner snapped back, *"If you don't like how we do things you can take your dog to another shop."* Just then the groomer brought my dog out and handed me the lead. I said to the owner and groomer, *"I'm not dissatisfied with the service. Your staff does a great job. What I don't understand is why other dogs with appointments **later** than mine, get done hours **before** mine."* With that the owner stood up, pointed her finger at the front door and yelled, *"GET THE HELL OUT OF MY SHOP!"* Obviously the situation had quickly gotten out of hand so I left with my poor frightened dog promptly leading the way!

Clearly this shop owner was out of her mind. Under normal circumstances there would have been an apology and explanation as to why they were behind and why appointments had been rearranged. But too often in our private life we experience schedules that are not met and not completed in a chronological or *common sense* approach. You stand in line at a retail store waiting to purchase your selection. You finally make it to the counter and the store telephone rings. In that situation who usually gets serviced first, you who have been standing in line for several minutes or the caller? *Usually the caller!* You sit at a restaurant waiting for your meal when people who were seated after you are already eating. You stand in line at the grocery store with two items, behind another customer with a full cart. Does the cashier ask the person in front of you if they mind if you went first? Of course not. These scenarios take place in our private lives and in our business lives. It upsets you in your private life as a consumer, *and it upsets Buyers like me in our business life.*

I've placed orders with suppliers for long lead, complicated products that I knew would take some time to manufacture. So when issues arose and delays occurred I didn't have a major problem because I still had time to meet our own production schedules. But as I got closer to meeting our own timing and the product *still* wasn't at my facility, I became agitated. The order was placed with a quoted nine month lead time. *It's now been over a year and the supplier is still scrambling to push product out.* In the meantime, other clients who placed orders well after mine have received their products.

Yes, I know the other client products are less complicated and less time consuming to make than mine. Yes, I know specification requirements are less stringent and technical issues less likely with the other client. But why isn't the supplier working on my order with a sense of urgency when they're clearly late? Remember your own experience sitting in that restaurant starving to death while everyone around you is getting their meals that were ordered long after yours? Did you care if your meal was more complicated to make? Did you care if your specific prep directions was beyond the norm? Or did you sit there waiting for your meal thinking, *"I'll never come back here again!"* Well, Corporate Buyers are thinking the same thing.

The truth is, most Buyers don't really care if you have other clients to provide product to. They don't care if their product is more complicated to make than other clients. Just like in your own private life, *Buyers are mainly concerned about their own wants and needs and not those of other customers.* And when they find out that scheduled shipments to their clients are being met while their own product is late, they become infuriated.

Now, if the parts are considered *off-the-shelf* there may be an easy remedy. If one client's order was placed before another's, that first client should obviously receive their order first. But if the second client has a greater need for immediate product than the first client, the supplier should consider sending what's on hand to the second client now, especially if it won't affect the first client's schedule. Several times I've worked with suppliers who used sub-components of another customer to build my product first because my need was more urgent than the other client. It was greatly appreciated, and I certainly remembered it when it came time to source other projects.

But if the product is custom built to the Buyer's specifications and replacements aren't an option, the best thing to do is inform the Buyer as quickly as possible about delays in shipping. We all appreciate restaurant wait-staff apologizing and informing us of a meal taking longer than it should, along with a reward for our patience (free drink, dessert, etc.). So the minute you realize you can't follow through with quoted deliveries, you need to immediately inform the Buyer so they can make contingency plans on their end.

FROM THE BUYER'S DESK: Don't let the things that upset you in your own private life as a consumer happen to those who buy from you in your Sales life.

BUYERS WHO PREFER THIS: 76%
SALES REPS WHO DO THIS: 23%

"Do Unto Others . . ."

The last recommendation in the previous Section stated:

"Don't let the things that upset you in your own private life as a consumer happen to those who buy from you in your Sales life."

In other words, there are unpleasant scenarios you experience in your private life as a consumer that compel you to never buy products and services from certain companies again. So as a Sales Professional, *make sure you are not creating those same upsetting scenarios for the Buyers of your own products and services.*

Suppliers spend thousands of dollars trying to understand the Buyers and clients they want to sell to: What motivates them to buy? What are they willing to spend? How do they select suppliers to place orders to? What upsets them that would reduce supplier opportunities? What excites them that would improve those opportunities? The answers to those questions are simple enough if you're willing to look within your own desires as a private consumer.

Many times in this book I've offered the advice to **THINK LIKE A BUYER . . .** *think like the person you're attempting to sell to.* Try to understand what the Buyer is responsible for. Try to understand the Buyer's own goals. Mentally put yourself behind the Buyer's desk and consider what might motivate them to buy from you. Consider what they might be willing to spend. Contemplate how they might select suppliers to place orders to. Think about what might upset them that would reduce your opportunities. And consider what might entice them that would improve your chances in securing the order.

We've covered this a few times already but it deserves mentioning again. It shouldn't be difficult to put yourself in the shoes of a Buyer . . . *because YOU are a Buyer!* Think about experiences in your own private life as a consumer that annoyed you going through the sales process. How about salespeople who tried to sell you something you didn't want. Tried to sell you options you didn't want. Acted in an unprofessional manner. Did not pay enough attention to you. Were unprepared and not sure what to do. Over-promised and under-delivered. Were insincere and concealed information. Were too persistent or too aggressive. Did too much talking and not enough listening. Failed to provide any post-sales follow up.

Now consider the experiences in your private life as a consumer in which the sales experience was positive. What enticed you to want to go back to that business? Maybe they looked out for your best interest. Didn't try to sell you on options you didn't want. Acted in a professional manner. Paid attention to you and your needs. Were prepared to work with you. Delivered what they promised. Were honest and trusting. Followed up after the sale. *Don't let the things that upset you in your private life as a consumer happen to those who buy from you in your Sales life.*

FROM THE BUYER'S DESK: Make sure the unpleasant scenarios you experience in your own private life as a consumer don't become a reality for those looking to buy product from you.

SECTION 7

The End-Users

- The End-Users
- Resolving On-Site Service Issues
- Resolving Invoice Issues

"The End-Users."

When conducting business with Corporate Buyers it always helps to know what they're really thinking but, for business and political reasons, may not be telling you. The same is true with the **'End-Users'** of your products and services. *In fact, knowing what an End-User is really thinking becomes especially important if your access to the Buyer is limited or non-existent.*

As stated in the Section, *"Gaining Access to the Buyer"* (pg. 21), depending on what type of industry you sell to, an **End-User** could include engineering, manufacturing, management, retail specialists, administration, quality and production personnel. In other words, this group of individuals within the client company who are the eventual *'end-users'* or *'end-receivers'* of your products and services. The term *End-User* encompasses all of the groups, other than Purchasing, who are directly or indirectly affected by how your products and services perform, and those who can influence your future business opportunities. Just like Buyers, most End-Users do not want Sales Professionals to know what they're really thinking. In fact they may go so far as to mislead the Sales Rep into believing everything is fine in regards to your company, product or capabilities. *WHAT???* Can that be true? Say it's not so! *Ladies and gentlemen, welcome to the real world!*

Most End-Users do not want to become directly involved in issues concerning a Sales Rep's inability to properly quote, nor their company's inability to conduct business and provide product according to their preferences. In terms of candid feedback, most End-Users would rather complain about the Sales Rep to the Buyer instead of directly to the Rep. *Why?* Because most End-Users would rather not get involved in the efforts and politics of straightening out a Sales Representative or his company, nor spend the time correcting their oversights.

Generally speaking, it's the End-User's conviction that Purchasing is the responsible organization to handle Supplier issues, not theirs. They believe that Buyers have more leverage and influence on the supply base than an End-User. *And in most cases, they're right!* Buyers usually do have more influence when it comes to supplier issues than an End-User because, as stated earlier, Purchasing usually holds the ***financial hammer*** over the supplier's head. Therefore, some End-Users will use the threat of Purchasing against a supplier like my Mom used to use on me when I was a kid, *"You wait until your Father gets home!"* Obviously there are exceptions to the rule. There are some End-Users that will become *quite blunt* with suppliers without Purchasing's assistance. But for the most part, and depending on the company, End-Users rely on the Buyer to deal with supplier issues in order to avoid any potential dilemma.

In case you've ever had a suspicion, I can personally confirm that there are times when a Sales Professional asks an End-User if their quote is acceptable, and the End-User replies that everything is fine, *when in fact it may not be.* Quite candidly, the End-User may be misleading, may put off a reply or may simply perjure themselves about a supplier's chances of receiving the order. Go ahead and ask any End-User. ***They'll deny it!*** They'll tell you they're not intentionally misleading you, *but that's not what they're telling me!* What the End-User is *really* hoping for is that the supplier's quote will be *commercially* disqualified due to price or some other justification. That way they won't have to take the time and effort to meet with the Sales Rep and discuss why it wasn't *technically* acceptable. Of course this doesn't happen with every End-User on every project, but it does happen *and more often than you think.*

Here's a real-world scenario that takes place more often than not: A Sales Rep meets with an End-User to discuss the technical portion of their quote. The End-User tells the Sales Rep they have no major concerns or questions. The Sales Rep then informs the Buyer of their *perceived* successful meeting with the End-User. Afterwards, the Buyer speaks with the End-User and finds out that in fact the quote was *NOT* acceptable. Specific product information was missing. The product did not meet specifications. Or the End-User simply doesn't want to use the supplier based on previous experiences, things they heard in the field or the fear of the unknown. The Buyer then asks the End-User why they didn't give an honest response to the Sales Rep. The End-User replies that they don't have the time, patience or desire to sit with every supplier and inform them of their deficiencies, *especially if they have no interest of placing the order to them.*

Can we blame the End-User for not necessarily being as straight forward as they should be with Sales Professionals? **Not really, because we do the same thing in our private lives!** We would rather not have to explain to a retailer why we didn't choose to buy their products or services. We will not always be honest or forthright when telling someone why we don't want to buy from them. Have you ever have a bad experience in a restaurant (i.e. poor service, lousy food) and when the manager asks you if everything is okay you keep your negative thoughts to yourself? You smile, shake your head and mislead the restaurant manager, thinking all the while to yourself that you won't be back. Most consumers do not want to become involved in issues or get into confrontational situations. That's human nature. Most people would rather avoid those scenarios knowing they won't be returning anyway. *Well, End-Users are no exception, though there are exceptions to the rule.* Just as some us of DO complain to companies about poor service and faulty products, some End-Users absolutely LOVE confrontation with suppliers. Unfortunately those types of scenarios are usually *counter-productive* and don't tend to improve the situation or create future opportunities for the supplier.

So what are the End-Users really sharing with the Buyer's they work with, but may not be sharing with you? Throughout my career in Corporate Purchasing I've asked hundreds of End-Users that exact same question. And surprisingly enough, based on their collective responses, there are really only a handful of things that Sales Professionals do, or fail to do, that inhibit their opportunities for future business with End-Users. But keep in mind these are MAJOR issues as far as the End-Users are concerned. And they are not easily correctable by the supply base. It will take time, energy, understanding, training and acceptance before a supplier changes the way they conduct business and provides the End-Users with what they want and need.

1. LACK OF COMMUNICATION. The number one concern from End-Users regarding the supply base is *a lack of proper and sufficient communication.* Now when we say *communication* we don't necessarily mean the Sales Rep can't carry on a conversation or that they're difficult to understand. Remember that good communication means proactively informing the *right people* at the *right time* about the *right topics* with the *right facts.* Equally important from the supply side is follow up, feedback, responsiveness to issues and the successful completion of promises. *The bottom line question is, do you do the* *things you say you're going to do when you say you're going to do them?*

The main area of concern from the End-Users when it comes to communication is the Sales Professional's failure to inform them of late deliveries. *(Sound familiar from previous Sections?)* Late deliveries include deliveries of **product or service**, deliveries of **documentation**, and a delivery of **information**. End-Users become upset when suppliers promise a delivery date they know they can't meet or didn't strive to meet. The reason they become upset is because End-Users rely on products and services being delivered by specific dates in order to meet their own schedules. And when their schedules are not met, the result is a loss of planned income by the client, *not to mention a poor evaluation from the End-User's manager.* Here are some of the things the End-Users I spoke with said about supplier communication:

"Quote me a delivery date you can achieve, and then do it!"

"I hate it when a supplier promises to meet a delivery date just to get the job. That's the last job they'll get if I can help it."

"I prefer to be kept up-to-date on deliveries; keep me in the loop."

"What I can't tolerate is a lack of communication on key issues that affect timing. If you're going to be late on your end, let me know so I can make adjustments on my end."

"A promised date or commitment made to my company that is not kept is my biggest pet peeve!"

2. DISAPPEARING AFTER THE ORDER IS PLACED. The number two concern from the End-Users is a lack of communication and follow up from the Sales Professional *after* the order has been awarded. One corporate engineer summed it up perfectly when he said,

"It seems that after the program contract has been awarded, the Sales Rep disappears, only to return again as my best friend during the next program. I have no desire to discuss future programs with any Sales Rep who has not suffered through their past problems with me."

Just like with Buyers, it is the perception by many End-Users that Sales Reps love to hover around their desk during the quoting process. But once the order is received they fail to return e-mails and voicemails in a timely manner, *if at all.* To many Sales Reps, the term *'closing the deal'* seems to literally mean just that! The order has been received . . . SEE YA LATER! If they're interested in repeat business, Sales Professionals should pay as much attention to the End-Users *after* the order has been issued as they do *during* the quoting process. After receiving the order, Sales Reps need to return e-mails, return telephone calls, and initiate a call on their own to see if there's anything they can do for the End-User. *That type of post-order attention will be noticed and will improve your chances of receiving future orders.*

3. NICKEL AND DIMING THE ORDER. Concern number three from the End-Users is the supplier practice of low-balling the quote to win the purchase order, then nickel and diming the order afterwards to make up for the losses. Obviously not all suppliers do this. But some suppliers have an advantage because they know their own products better than the End-User. For instance, some Sales Professionals will quote a job by removing necessary but unidentified product options in order to ensure their quote is priced below their competitors. Then once they receive the order, they *educate* the End-User of the importance of including those necessary options; options that should have been part of their original quote but are now *added expenses.*

Unfortunately the End-User may accept these options because of their unawareness of the product. And these additional options may be marked-up due to their particular function, which will eventually make up for the low-ball bid. Some End-Users may seem like putty in the hands of the supplier because of their perceived ignorance of product requirements.

But based on the End-User responses I received, most are aware of what the supplier is doing, though they may not mention it to the Sales Rep. Instead they mention it to the Buyer who collectively agrees to either not allow that supplier to quote again, or to make it difficult for the supplier to receive future orders. Here are some of the comments from the End-Users regarding this topic:

"Nickel and diming a low-ball bid really irritates me. The supplier expects to make up their costs on additional but necessary items to make up for it. I may not be an expert on what I need, but I know when I'm getting ripped off."

"I'm sometimes forced to pay additionally for things that I know should have been part of the original quotation. I may not like it and I may end up paying for it, but I'll think twice about inviting that supplier to quote again."

"I understand when suppliers legitimately overlook required items and I have no problem paying for a legitimate mistake. But when suppliers get greedy and either nickel and dime or over charge specific items, I get really irritated."

"I think it's unprofessional for a supplier to come back to me and say, 'Oh, we forgot to include this item.' If it's your mistake you should eat the cost. An oversight on your part should not automatically mean another dollar out of my pocket."

"Suppliers continuously 'buy' jobs without reading and understanding the specifications. Then they attempt to either delay the job or add extra cost after the fact when the specifications are finally understood."

4. ON-SITE SERVICE. The subject of on-site service is one of the most frustrating topics to discuss for both the End-User and the supplier. End-Users expect immediate service. Suppliers expect to be fairly paid for their time. Sometimes neither situation happens which tends to drive a wedge between the two groups.

The main problem is that the End-User and the supplier *rarely* sit down in the early stages of a program to agree to the rules and define responsibilities for on-site service. Too many assumptions are made on both sides and it ends up affecting both parties.

A supplier who can go above and beyond the call of duty in providing adequate service in a timely manner, without financial or personal issues to appease the End-User's concerns, will stand out from the competition. It will also encourage the End-User to recommend the supplier to the Buyer for future business. Most End-Users will admit they expect problems with products; *that there is no perfect mousetrap.* What gets their attention is the supplier who does everything in their power to ensure that product is working again as soon as possible, and without being prompted to do so by the Buyer or End-User. More insight and advice regarding on-site service is described in the next Section titled, *"Resolving On-Site Service Issues."*

5. THE QUOTING PROCESS. It's important to understand where the mindset of the End-User is regarding the quoting process. The collective responses from the End-Users confirm it's important to read, comprehend and quote to the specifications in the Request-for-Quote package. Quotes that are not properly addressed, not thoroughly covered and not itemized will *NOT* be well received by the End-Users. As with the Buyer, ask the End-User what their *preferred* quotation format looks like. Let's remember the strategy in the previous Section titled, *"How to Submit the Perfect Quote"* (pg. 179). This same strategy can be used on End-Users as they're used on the Buyer. Ask them how *they* prefer the quotes they receive should be organized and detailed. Here are some of the comments from the End-Users regarding supplier quotes:

"Not enough information. I have no idea how the components of the product are going to work."

"I prefer an operation-by-operation description in detail so that I can 'mentally' see what the product is going to do."

"I can't stand it when a supplier's quote is too vague. What that says to me is that the supplier really doesn't know what's going on or what I'm asking for."

"First, give me exactly what I ask for. Then offer a best solution. If I don't seem to know what I'm talking about or what I need, politely educate me."

"You need to convince me that your product will work. Don't just hand me a quote and tell me to call if I have any questions. I may not always have the time to sit and discuss your quote, but I need to know upfront if your product can do the job."

"Don't just hand me a quote, sell me on a solution!"

FROM THE BUYER'S DESK: Maintaining sufficient on-site service after the sale will lead to more orders. Taking care of the End-Users will get back to the Buyers in way of positive feedback.

"Resolving On-Site Service Issues."

Does this conversation sound familiar?

END-USER: "I need someone at my plant within the hour to work on this product per its warranty."

SUPPLIER: "The serviceman you want is at another client's facility. Besides, that's not a warranty item so I'll have to charge you for it."

END-USER: "You didn't send someone who knows the product the first time. Now it's going to cost me twice as much to get it fixed."

SUPPLIER: "I sent someone to your facility for three days last week but you only paid me for two."

END-USER: "You didn't get anyone to approve your work order so I can't pay you."

SUPPLIER: "I showed up to qualify the product but your installation crew didn't complete the job."

END-USER: "Your products don't work. I'm tired of having to call for service."

SUPPLIER: "Your people are not maintaining the products per our recommendations and warranty statements. It's not our fault the unit isn't working."

In my years in Purchasing I can say unequivocally that the subject of on-site service is one of the most frustrating topics to discuss for both the End-User and the supplier. End-Users expect immediate service. Suppliers expect to be fairly paid for their time. Sometimes neither situation happens which tends to drive a wedge between the two groups.

The main problem is that the End-User and supplier rarely sit down after the order has been awarded and/or in the early stages of a program to agree to the rules and define responsibilities for on-site service. Too many assumptions are made on both sides and it ends up affecting both parties. At the very least, the End-User and supplier needs to meet before service is ever required to review the following items.

1. Define and detail exactly what a service warranty covers. How long does it cover the product and exactly when does it start? Where will the Service Rep be coming from to support the warranty and what is the lead time between the service call and the Rep showing up? How will both parties resolve issues on whether it was a warranty service call or not? What is not covered under warranty? Exactly what client actions, or lack thereof, will void the warranty? How much is an extended warranty?

2. Clarify the differences, in both definition and price, between a 'standard' service call and 'emergency service'.

3. Define the entire process of service: Which facility entrance should the Service Rep show up at? Who should the Service Rep contact if any issues arise during the on-site visit? What, if any, safety equipment and procedures is required by service? What type of work order needs to be approved before service can be called or work can start? Who has the authority to sign and approve the work order? What are the rules when it comes to providing service in a Union environment?

4. When the call is made to the Supplier for service, find out exactly what the problem is and what type of service is expected. If the issue is not known, try to get a feel as to who should service the product. An electrician? A mechanic? Someone from IT? Nothing is worse than to have an expert Service Rep show up for the wrong problem; something that's out of their service capabilities.

5. Determine what each party expects from the other. Buyers should expect a competent and professional service crew, while the Supplier should expect the products to be ready and available for service when they arrive.

6. Finally, maintain an updated contact information sheet, including who to contact for emergencies and during off-hours (weekends and Holidays).

Products never seem to fail at an opportune time. When a product fails, loss of time and money are inevitable. The quicker the service and repair, the less time and money is lost. But when a Buyer's corporate process dictates that a simple telephone call to a supplier is not an accepted practice to allow them to work, it becomes a mad rush to either convince the supplier to show up with a firm order, or the Buyer has to push through a work order as soon as possible.

So what does the Buyer do in an emergency when the product is down and it takes several days to get a work order through to the supplier? These are the types of questions that the Buyer and the Sale Rep needs to discuss before the contract has been awarded. After all, is the Buyer's company willing to lose production simply because they can't get a work order to the Supplier in a reasonable amount of time?

It's understandable that suppliers become irritated when they show up without a work order then never get paid as they were promised. The Buyer should follow through in ensuring the supplier gets paid within a reasonable amount of time. In fact, that lead time between service completed and invoice paid should also be discussed and agreed on ahead of time. *If the Buyer doesn't initiate these types of conversations then it's in the best interest of the Sales Professional to do so!*

Suppliers need to know where they stand with the Buyer regarding service calls. Are they allowed to be a proactive supplier and show up when their product is not working, or must they officially receive an order before showing up at the Buyer's facility? If the latter is the case, then the supplier has every right to refuse to send service without a work order and without feeling the indignation from the Buyer or End-User. In fact, if your service is not allowed to start until an order has been received, you need to inform the End-Users of their own company's rules. *Regardless, it's imperative that the supplier find out what their obligations are in regards to servicing the client.*

One last thought about service. Maintaining good local support is incredibly important to the End-User at their facility. Some End-Users actually get evaluated on production outcomes based on the products they bought. Keeping products running properly, maintaining uptime and meeting (if not exceeding) production requirements are major concerns for the End-User. A Supplier who can go above and beyond the call of duty in providing adequate service in a timely manner, without financial issues to appease the End-User's concerns, will stand out from the competition. It will also encourage the End-User to recommend future business with that supplier. What gets their attention is a supplier who does everything in their power to ensure that their product is working again as soon as possible and without being prompted to do so by the Buyer.

Some of the End-User's I've talked with about on-site service also recommended that if a Service Rep is at the client's facility and has successfully completed the scope-of-work, they should find out if anything else in the facility requires their assistance before leaving. At the very least, talk to someone in charge on the way out and ask how their other products are working. **Not only will it show both the End-User and the Buyer that you're proactive, it may very well increase the value of your service call!**

FROM THE BUYER'S DESK: Sufficient and agreed-to on-site support can improve both relationships and opportunities.

"Resolving Invoice Issues."

In some purchasing organizations, Buyers are responsible for approving, tracking and/or resolving issues pertaining to supplier invoices. Other companies utilize other departments or personnel to process the invoices, including accounts payable, engineering, planners or the End-Users of products and services. But whether or not the Buyer is directly responsible for supplier invoices, it's a given that they will ultimately become involved if an issue requires their attention.

So what does this have to do with improving sales opportunities? Quite simply, if the Buyer gets dragged into an invoice issue and it ends up being the supplier's fault, it will leave a sour taste in the Buyer's mouth. I've also known suppliers who were in financial distress due to unpaid invoices by *other* clients. And no matter whose fault it is, Corporate Buyer's don't like to place business with financially distressed companies!

Here's a typical invoice scenario I'm sure you're familiar with: A purchase order is placed to a supplier for goods. The supplier successfully provides the goods associated with the order. The supplier invoices against the order for the goods provided. But the invoice payment is not received by the supplier in a timely manner, if at all. The supplier refuses to send additional goods until the invoice is paid. The client's Buyer is then pulled into the middle of it and all hell breaks loose. The ending of the story depends on how much time, information and cooperation takes place between all parties involved.

There are numerous reasons why an invoice is paid late, if at all. Sometimes it's the fault of the client. Sometimes it's the fault of the supplier. In the case of the client, an understaffed accounts payable department may be the culprit. Or invoice approvers, whomever they may be, will at times intentionally *not* authorize an invoice. This may be based on an unresolved supplier issue. Or it may be based on the fact the approver is being difficult. Of course they are a vast number of reasons why invoices don't get paid, some justified and some not. Whatever the reason, the payments of invoices is an essential and sometimes explosive issue. After all, it's directly tied to the lifeblood of the supplier's and client's cash flow.

When I first started in Purchasing, I found that a good portion of the Buyer's time was spent chasing invoice issues; invoices that, for whatever reason, just weren't getting paid. And even though the Buyers did not directly approve invoices, it was still their responsibility to resolve any commercial issues they created. Some issues were directly related to the End-Users not being happy with the performance of the products and services, and were therefore holding back payment.

But for now let's focus on another reason why invoices aren't being paid; reasons that you, the Sales Professional or Business Owner can quickly resolve. After spending some time in Purchasing, I noticed that 75% of the invoice issues I was pulled into were due to the information on the invoice not matching the information on the purchase order. And if there's one rule in accounts payable it's this: *Invoices that don't match Orders, don't get paid.*

After comparing notes with other Buyers from across the Nation, most of us agree that a good portion of invoice payment issues could be easily resolved at the supplier's end. This is good news because it's something you have direct control over. So here's some Buyer feedback regarding the resolution of invoice issues:

1. Before your company submits an invoice, especially for a significant sum of money, you should always first contact the individual(s) who will be actually approving the invoice. If you have no direct contact to the individual(s), especially those in accounts payable, then contact the Buyer or End-User. Inform them that an invoice for a specific amount of money is being sent that covers specific products and/or services. *Then ask if they are aware of anything that would inhibit the payment of the invoice per the terms of the contract.* In other words, make sure the invoice will be willingly approved **BEFORE** sending it in! Make sure there aren't any unforeseen issues regarding the payment of your goods or services. You should never assume that everything is okay and that the invoice will be promptly approved. *This is because you never know what others are thinking and not necessarily telling you.* It's always in your best interest to spend a few minutes to find out if the client is in agreement that the invoice will be paid *before* you submit it.

2. Find out who actually receives and approves the invoices. What is the step-by-step process? What departments and/or specific individuals are responsible? What is the expected lead time between each step? Make certain you have the proper contact information instead of bothering people who may not be involved. I'd be more than happy to share that process and contact information with my suppliers, *but I've rarely had anyone ask for it!* Most important, if the Buyer does not receive or approve invoices and doesn't wish to be involved in the resolution process, you need to know that ahead of time.

3. Find out the preferred way to submit your invoice to the client - be it e-mail, regular mail, fax or some other means. I knew several companies who submitted invoices through regular U.S. Postal Service mail. But they were never getting paid because our accounts payable department preferred to receive invoices via e-mal. Unfortunately the supplier never bothered to ask about the client's preferred method.

4. If an invoice is rejected, do you know who the preferred person is to contact about it? Is it accounts payable? Is it the Buyer? This is another good question to ask and know the answer to. For instance, if the reason is due to a technical issue, should you call an End-User or the Buyer? Find out ahead of time how the client prefers to handle it.

5. As a Sales Rep it's important for you to know that a large percentage of rejected invoices are due to supplier error. So it's imperative that your accounts receivable department has an updated copy of the purchase order to compare against the invoice for any potential variances. Anytime you receive a purchase order update from the Buyer, make sure it immediately makes its way to your accounts receivable department.

6. In order to reduce oversights, the supplier's accounts receivable group should verify the following invoice information and compare it with the actual purchase order: The correct purchase order number. The correct Line Item Number as it appears on the purchase order. Any special numbers, letters or characters that should be included on the invoice per the client's request. The correct price associated with the Line Item Number per the order. The correct Unit of Measure (U/M) or Quantity associated with the Line Item Number exactly as it appears on the order. The U/M could be LOT, or EA (each), or HR (hour), or some other unit of measure. Finally, your supplier vendor code as indicated on the purchase order.

Non-matching information between an invoice and a purchase order is the biggest reason why invoices don't get paid; especially the price on the invoice. I found out that some suppliers do not even look at the purchase order while creating the invoice. They simply charge what items actually cost without verifying the contractual cost. They also manage to do what I'm notorious of doing: fat fingering while typing. They will input an incorrect order number, price or part number on an invoice without double checking it. Not taking a few extra seconds to double check data on the order vs. the invoice may cost the supplier days if not weeks of non-payment. *Supplier invoices that don't match client orders don't get paid.*

7. Finally, find out if the client has a supplier information document with directions as to how to prepare and submit invoices. I created such a document at one of my former companies and it closely resembled the actual Section of the book. I'd hand it out to my suppliers so they had a better understanding of how to submit invoices and what to do, or avoid doing, that would inhibit payment. *It drastically reduced the amount of invoice issues on both my side and the supply side.*

You need to know that the vast majority of Buyers, End-Users and Accounts Payable personnel really do want to get the supplier paid per the terms of the order. I've sat in numerous purchasing department meetings that covered this very topic. Most of us are smart enough to know that non-payments will most likely result in the non-receivership of goods and services, which means having to answer to senior managers. And yes there are a percentage of clients who make suppliers jump through hoops to get paid for things they successfully and contractually completed, while others refuse to pay at all. Unfortunately there are countless suppliers who have gone out of business for that very reason.

Remember to ask the Buyer *ahead of time*, before any order is received, who you should contact in the chance that an invoice isn't paid during the agreements of the contract. If it's not them, most will be happy to point you in the right direction.

FROM THE BUYER'S DESK: Make certain invoices are created per the client's requirements and contractual terms. Don't let the reason for not getting paid be due to your own company's oversight.

About the Author

CHRISTOPHER LOCKE is a Certified Professional in Supply Management and has over 35 years of diverse experience in the global business environment. His background includes plant engineering, project management and global purchasing. He received a Master of Science Degree in Industrial Management from Central Michigan University, and has taught various business and manufacturing classes at the University level. As a Senior Purchasing Manager, Chris is a proven and motivated cross-functional team leader in the planning, organizing, direction and control of global sourcing strategies, supply-chain management, and *cradle-to-grave* procurement responsibilities.

During his career, Chris has purchased billions of dollars-worth of diverse products and services; everything from office supplies worth a few dollars, to complex automotive powertrain assembly systems worth tens of millions. His purchasing experience includes capital equipment, construction design and installation, production materials, industrial assembly systems, office supplies, on-site services, equipment installation, maintenance, chemicals, and military components.

Starting in 1977, the first 21 years of Chris' career were spent working for various architectural/engineering companies in the Metro-Detroit area as a plant and project engineer. It was also during this time that he came into full contact with Sales Professionals and Business Owners, gaining a valuable understanding of how Sales and End-Users interact and conduct business.

In 1998 Chris was hired by Chrysler Corporation as a Plant Engineer in Advanced Manufacturing, coordinating the installation and qualification of powertrain manufacturing and assembly systems. A few months later 'Chrysler' became 'DaimlerChrysler' during the historic merger with Mercedes Benz. In 2000, Chris was promoted to the position of Senior Buyer in the International Procurement Group. For the next seven years, Chris managed the procurement of capital equipment, powertrain assembly systems, construction, corporate services and industrial materials for DaimlerChrysler's global manufacturing facilities.

Chris' first assignment as Senior Buyer was the procurement of 75% of the capital equipment and assembly systems for the W5A580 Transmission; a 600-million dollar powertrain program in Kokomo, Indiana. During this project he facilitated the very first on-line auctions for DaimlerChrysler powertrain purchasing. Chris was also honored with the distinction of being one of only two designated Global Lead Buyers in the U.S. for the Powertrain Group. He was also selected as a Communications Officer between the American and German procurement departments. His time at DaimlerChrysler required numerous trips overseas to Europe and Japan, meeting with procurement counterparts and touring supplier facilities. Chris also spent time in Mexico where he was commercially responsible for the Hemi Engine upgrade programs, as well as the Viper V-10 projects in Detroit.

After spending a few years *behind the Buyer's desk* it became apparent to Chris that the relationship between Buyers and Sellers could be greatly improved. It was his belief that Sales Professionals could greatly enhance their opportunities if they could only experience the sales process *from the Buyer's perspective.* So in 2003, Chris started including *buyer-endorsed* recommendations in his Request-for-Quotes, thereby educating suppliers how they could improve their opportunities. Eventually, through the direct approval of DaimlerChrysler, those recommendations turned into a full-fledged sales workshop called *"Buyer-Endorsed Sales Training"* or *"B.E.S.T."*

Buyer-Endorsed Sales Training was a 4-hour, open-forum workshop written, developed and facilitated by Chris and another Senior Buyer from DaimlerChrysler. Held in an amphitheater at a local conference center, B.E.S.T. was the *only* sales seminar in the Nation developed and run by Corporate Buyers. This unique workshop provided candid feedback, real-world sales advice and 'Buyer-Endorsed' strategies based on the responses of hundreds of diverse Corporate Buyers and End-Users from across the country.

B.E.S.T. ran for four successful years and was attended by hundreds of the top Tier 1 automotive and industrial suppliers in the country. One anonymous attendee summed up his seminar experience when he wrote, *"Without question, the most informative, real-world sales training I've attended."* Chris and his seminar colleague also took B.E.S.T. on the road, holding workshops for various corporate sales teams and International business events. Eventually, Chris and his co-facilitator ended B.E.S.T. to spend more time focusing on their careers.

In 2007 Chris was hired by American Axle & Manufacturing in Detroit as a Senior Buyer of Direct and Indirect Procurement. During his time at AAM, Chris managed the procurement of capital equipment, axle assembly lines, construction, corporate services and industrial materials for American Axle's global manufacturing facilities. In 2010 Chris was hired as a Senior Buyer by MTU America, a division of Rolls Royce Power Systems, to procure off-highway diesel engine components for military and commercial projects. Today, Chris is a Senior Manager of Purchasing responsible for the procurement of capital equipment and MRO for a global company in Charlotte, North Carolina.

In addition to his years in the industry, Chris was an Adjunct Instructor at the university level for several years, teaching technical and administrative courses for Central Michigan University's Off-Campus engineering programs in the Metro-Detroit area. Chris is an active member of the Institute for Supply Management and is recognized by the ISM as a Certified Professional in Supply Management (C.P.S.M.).

In his spare time, Chris is committed to improving the business relationship between Buyers and Sellers. He has been the Key Speaker at various industry and organizational events, providing an insight into the world of Corporate Purchasing, and informing companies how to improve their business opportunities with Corporate Buyers. Prior organizations who invited Chris to speak include the Association for Manufacturing Technology (AMT), the Original Equipment Supplier's Association (OESA), the Michigan Minority Supplier Development Council (MMSDC), the National Association of Women Business Owners (MAWBO), the Michigan Hispanic Chamber of Commerce, and the Asian Pacific American Agenda Coalition (APAAC).

If you would like to contact Chris regarding speaking engagements, you can e-mail him at: TheBuyersDesk@aol.com

Made in the USA
Charleston, SC
07 August 2015